Appraisal and repair of timber structures

Peter Ross

Thomas Telford

Published by Thomas Telford Publishing, Thomas Telford Ltd,
1 Heron Quay, London E14 4JD.
www.thomastelford.com

Distributors for Thomas Telford books are
USA: ASCE Press, 1801 Alexander Bell Drive, Reston, VA 20191-4400, USA
Japan: Maruzen Co. Ltd, Book Department, 3–10 Nihonbashi 2-chome, Chuo-ku, Tokyo 103
Australia: DA Books and Journals, 648 Whitehorse Road, Mitcham 3132, Victoria

First published 2002

Photographs by the author, unless otherwise credited.

A catalogue record for this book is available from the British Library

ISBN: 0 7277 2051 1

Typeset by Academic & Technical Typesetting, Bristol
Printed and bound in Great Britain by MPG Books, Bodmin

Contents

1. Introduction 2

2. A history of building form 6
   2.1. Introduction 6
   2.2. The medieval period 6
   2.3. The seventeenth and eighteenth centuries 14
   2.4. The nineteenth century 18
   2.5. The twentieth century 25

3. The characteristics of timber 32
   3.1. The living tree 32
   3.2. Softwoods and hardwoods 33
   3.3. Moisture content and movement 35
   3.4. Durability 38
   3.5. Material properties 39
   3.6. The behaviour of timber in fire 46
   3.7. Commercial supply 47

4. Timber in the building environment 52
   4.1. Hazard classes 52
   4.2. Natural durability 56
   4.3. Preservative treatments 56
   4.4. Protective coatings 57
   4.5. The performance of timber in relation to environmental conditions 57

5. Building legislation 60
   5.1. The Building Regulations 60
   5.2. Loading 63
   5.3. Fire 64
   5.4. Listed buildings 65

6. The commission 68
   6.1. The client's concern 68
   6.2. The brief 69
   6.3. Conditions of engagement and fees 69

Contents

7.	The general diagnostic sequence	72
	7.1. The survey	72
	7.2. The appraisal	72
	7.3. Remedial work	73
	7.4. The repair contract	73
	7.5. Phasing survey work	73
8.	Initial visual inspection	76
	8.1. Existing information	76
	8.2. The inspection	76
	8.3. Recording techniques	77
	8.4. Concealed elements of structure	78
	8.5. Level of inspection	78
9.	The range of possible defects	80
	9.1. Fungal attack	80
	9.2. Wood-boring insect attack	81
	9.3. Instability	82
	9.4. Deterioration of joints	83
	9.5. Deformation	84
	9.6. Noise transmission and vibration of floors	84
	9.7. Accidental damage	85
10.	Investigative techniques	90
	10.1. The Borescope	90
	10.2. Moisture content	90
	10.3. Auger drilling	91
	10.4. The Sibert drill	92
	10.5. Non-destructive testing	92
	10.6. Dendrochronology	94
	10.7. Radiocarbon dating	94
11.	The appraisal	98
	11.1. Strength	98
	11.2. Stability	100
	11.3. Deformation	101
	11.4. Durability	103
	11.5. Accidental damage	104
12.	Timber repairs	108
	12.1. Repairs to exposed members	108
	12.2. Metal reinforcement	117
	12.3. Adhesives	119
13.	Historic buildings	126
	13.1. Cultural significance	126
	13.2. Remedial work	129
	13.3. Upgrading historic structures	130
14.	The report	138
	14.1. Report layout	138

14.2. Drawings and photographs 140
14.3. Report style 141

15. The repair contract 144
15.1. Precontract work 144
15.2. Tendering 145
15.3. Contract documentation 145
15.4. The specification 145

16. The specification of timber for repair 148
16.1. Softwood 148
16.2. Temperate hardwood 150

17. Moving timber frames 154
17.1. The survey 154
17.2. Dismantling and re-erection 155
17.3. The lift and slide method 155

18. Case histories 160
18.1. The Belfast truss and the Duxford airfield hangars 160
18.2. 26–28 Charlotte Square, Edinburgh 165
18.3. The Royal Festival Hall: strength assessment of the acoustic canopy 173
18.4. The church of St. Mary the Virgin, Sandwich, Kent; the repair of the seventeenth century roof 176
18.5. The dismantling and re-erection of Alderham Farmhouse 183
18.6. The Tyne Theatre 191
18.7. York Minster: the south transept fire 198

Appendix
1. Codes and Standards 211
2. Analysis and load testing procedures 215
3. The CP 112 grading rules 221

BSI codes 232

Bibliography 233

Index 237

Acknowledgements

The author would like to thank the many colleagues who have so willingly given comment and advice, including present and former members of Arup staff Poul Beckmann, Michael Bussell, Alan Coday, Andrew Gardiner, Anthony Lawrence, Clare Perkins and Eddie van de Straeten, together with Christopher Holland, of BRE and Christopher Mettem of TRADA.

Thanks are also due to Ove Arup and Partners for permission to include the case histories described in Chapter 18.

I

The Church of St. Andrew, Greensted-juxta-Ongar, Essex. Perhaps the oldest standing timber building in the UK, dating from around 1000 AD, and the only surviving example of vertical oak staves.

1

Introduction

Timber is probably the oldest of man's building materials. It has an unmatched variety of historic form, reaching in an unbroken line from the split oak logs of Greensted Church to the modern glulam spaceframe. Up to the fifteenth century it was also the most used building material, until it then gave ground to brick, and later to iron. Nevertheless, it has continued to be used both in domestic construction, and for exposed frames and medium-span roofs, where its visual and tactile qualities give it a unique appeal.

Today, the building scene is dominated by concrete and steel, and designers are less familiar with the properties of timber and its structural vocabulary. Thus timber, which makes up some proportion of most of our existing structures, is perhaps the least understood of the materials which are the subject of this series. For this reason, the next four chapters of this book form an extended introduction to timber as a building material: its various forms and properties, its response to environmental conditions, and the Building Regulations relating to its use. Later chapters follow the general sequence of work, starting with the commission, and then dealing with the survey, the investigation and then the appraisal. The appraisal is the pivotal point of the sequence, when the most appropriate form of remedial work is selected, and it is followed by chapters on repair options, report and specification writing, and the additional factors which have to be taken into account when dealing with historic buildings.

The case studies also illustrate the simplification, albeit inevitable, of the book's title—structures built entirely of timber are very rare. Even the medieval barn has a tiled roof, and has generally had some form of masonry strip footing built under its walls. In post-medieval structures timber is generally a secondary, if still important, element. Most appraisals of timber structures therefore require some account to be taken of the condition of other structural materials, from the pitched or flat roof above to the walls and foundations below.

The subject of timber in building is a very broad field, and some chapters, such as the one which deals with the characteristics of material, rely primarily on the expertise of other authors. Principal sources are given at the end of each chapter, and referenced fully in the Bibliography. Subjects which are dealt with in several existing publications, such as rot and beetle attack, receive a relatively brief treatment, leaving more space for topics such as the strength assessment of timber elements, and non-destructive load testing.

This book is written principally for engineers, and therefore concentrates more on the structural aspects of repair, and less on matters such as surface finish. Nevertheless, I hope it will be of interest to architects and surveyors who carry out much work in this field, and who on occasion request an engineer's assistance.

Further reading

There are relatively few books which deal solely with the whole process of the repair of timber structures. Charles' (1984) classic work, now reprinted, relates entirely to timber framing, predominantly of the medieval period. Fielden (1982) and Melville and Gordon (1973) deal with timber among other materials, the former for historic buildings, and the latter for domestic construction.

2

Great Coxwell Barn, Oxfordshire. One of the finest surviving medieval barns in England. In oak, built early in the thirteenth century.

2

A history of building form

2.1. Introduction

We cannot see the beginning of the carpentry tradition. Archaeologists have shown that the Romans bought expertise with them, and the earliest frames which still stand where they were originally erected show an assured technique despite the fact that they were built nearly 1000 years ago. Any attempt, therefore, to outline a history of this whole period within a single chapter will obviously be a gross simplification. Nevertheless, I have thought it useful to try, both as a basis for the survey and appraisal process, and because the more detailed sources given at the end of the chapter generally focus on a particular period.

Throughout the history, I have tried to identify the factors which have influenced change and development, and to concentrate on the frame as structure, in terms of members and joints. We should always seek to understand a structure before we repair it—it may, in some instances, then become apparent that no repairs are necessary.

The history can be divided into four main periods. The medieval period, timber's golden age, with mainly exposed hardwood frames in an all-timber vocabulary. The seventeenth and eighteenth centuries saw the rise of brick, with timber (now mainly softwood) infilling masonry walls as floors and roofs. The nineteenth century, in turn, saw the rise of iron and steel, while bringing new applications for timber in the industrial field. In the twentieth century, the use of metal connectors, and adhesives to make compound elements, such as plywood and glued laminated beams, became general.

2.2. The medieval period

During the medieval period timber was the dominant building material. Stone was used only for prestigious buildings, or where it was particularly plentiful, and cob, or unbaked earth, reserved for the humblest dwellings. Timber was used for framing generally, and almost universally for roofs. There are today in England some 9000 parish churches built before the first quarter of the sixteenth century, and all (excepting some half a dozen which are vaulted) with open roofs of timber. The general form is that of a doubly pitched

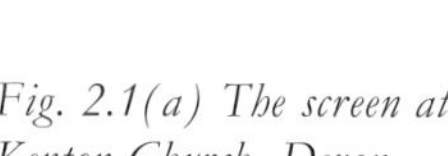

Fig. 2.1(a) The screen at Kenton Church, Devon

Fig. 2.1(b) The nave of Saffron Walden Church

Fig. 2.1(c) Avoncroft cruck barn

roof over the nave, spanning between 8 and 12 m, with lean-to or pitched aisle roofs on each side, of approximately half the nave span.

Earlier roofs are steeply pitched, covered in slates (or, perhaps, originally thatch), oversail the walls at the eaves, and are a significant part of the building elevation. Later roofs often have a shallower pitch, achieved by the use of lead, and are virtually hidden behind an ornate stone parapet. While the arrangement is architecturally effective, an increased risk of water penetration from the parapet gutter has plagued parish councils ever since.

No two churches are identical—indeed, their glory is in their diversity—but strong regional styles emerged, from the low barrel vaults of the West Country to the taller hammer-beamed naves of East Anglia (Fig. 2.1(a)–(b)).

And so to framed structures generally, beginning with the cruck; not necessarily the oldest, but the most elemental form. Two halves of a tree, perhaps a trunk and its principal branch, split and turned to prop one another, and demonstrating most graphically the principle of triangulation for stability. But a triangle is a rather inconvenient shape to live in, and eventually the aisled frame became dominant. Originally an omni-purpose form—church, dwelling, storage—the surviving examples are almost entirely houses or barns. The structural form is clearly seen, with the member sizes determined by the available timber stock; loads are passed from member to member primarily through end compression, and the whole assembly is held together by interlocking joints.

Medieval life under the feudal system was hierarchial, but communal, and the early interior was often a single hall, with minor rooms at each end. Later buildings developed the concept of separate rooms, and then a second storey. This, in turn, led sometimes to the construction of a forward projection, or jetty, at the first floor level. It has been argued that the purpose of the jetty was to increase the floor area for a given plot size, or to protect the framed walls below. However jetties can be found in the country, where land value were surely not an issue, and on one side of a building only, leaving the back unprotected. So it may also be true that jetties were desirable because they were more difficult to build and, hence, prestigious.

There are two major stylistic forms of the timber frame: the Lowland style, with close verticals, used mainly in the South and East, and the Highland style with square panels, infilled, for important buildings, with non-structural decorative members. Paycocke's house of 1401, in Essex, is in the lowland style. The frame can be seen from both inside and out, together with its diagonal bracing and the floors show clearly their primary/secondary/tertiary construction. It would be difficult to find a building with a more honest structure (Fig. 2.2(a)–(b)).

Speke Hall, near Liverpool, in the northern style, is later. The form of the floor structure can still be seen, but it is now plastered over and decorated with a vine leaf pattern. The walls are panelled, both for appearance and for insulation. Fireplaces are now installed in most principal rooms, and the windows are larger, as glass becomes more generally available.

All these frames need some form of infill. For the simplest buildings, only a rainscreen is necessary—perhaps woven panels, or lapped boards. For dwellings, the earliest infill in general use was wattle and daub, where the wattles are woven, basket-fashion, around vertical staves before being daubed with a mixture of clay, dung and chopped straw. Alternatives were mortared stone and, later, brick, but these materials introduce extra weight, and tend to hold moisture against the return faces. In later life, many frames were disguised with an overlay of battens and plaster or tiles which, as the tide

Fig. 2.2(a) Exterior, Paycocke's house

Fig. 2.2(b) Interior, first floor, Paycocke's house

Fig. 2.2(c) Exterior, Speke Hall

Fig. 2.2(d) Interior, The Great Parlour, Speke Hall

of fashion turned, were often stripped away again, leaving only the nail-holes as evidence.

Surviving frames from this period are almost entirely in oak, with a few in chestnut or elm. Members are adzed or sawn, and cut on the principle of maximising the use of the log—hence, many members are approximately square or half-square (Fig. 2.3(a)). Sapwood, or even bark, may appear on the corners, or may have been cut off, resulting in wane, or missing timber. The inclusion of the pith of the tree within the section (boxed heart) generally produces one major and several minor fissures. The straightness of members has generally been determined by eye. Sometimes the line of the grain is deliberately followed to produce a decorative curved member.

All the members of a frame are in a common plane, with end loads transmitted primarily in compression from one member to another. Frame stability is obtained by triangulation, which is either direct (as in the cruck frame), (b), or combined with portal action. This applies for both gravity and wind loads. Thus, wind loads acting on a barn structure from either direction will bring one of the knee braces into compression, stiffening the main portal (c). The same arrangement is used along, as well as across, the building. The barn is thus a 'perfect' structure in the sense that, within an all-timber vocabulary, it cannot be improved.

Jetty beams (d), are generally anchored against up-thrust at their inner ends, for the weight of the floor alone may not be a sufficient counterweight.

All roofs, including those on masonry walls, are in timber, employing an endless variety of form and decorative treatment. The simplest are triangular, with principal rafters and a bottom tie. For steep roofs, the span of the rafters can be broken by a simple cross-strut, perhaps with wind-bracing. An elegant elaboration of this form is the crown-post roof (e), where the post itself is in compression, transferring part of the load to the main tie in bending, but reducing the out-thrust of the rafters.

Most of the more elaborate forms, with raised collars, rely more or less directly on arch action (g). The hammer beam roof uses the propped cantilever of the beam to reduce the central span of the arch and, thus, in turn, the out-thrust on the walls (f). Rare attempts to build a true A-frame (with a raised tie in tension) requires multi-dowelled arch braces.

In all framed structures, the joints (Fig. 2.4) are generally the most critical elements. Only the basic joints have been illustrated.

- *Mortice and tenon*: primarily transmits compression through bearing on the shoulder, and shear by the interlock of the tenon and mortice. It is pegged primarily for location during assembly and general integrity. Since the end distances beyond the peg are necessarily limited, the joint is not relied upon to transmit significant tensile forces (Fig. 2.4(a)).
- *Notched lap*: used more on early structures, and has small tensile strength. It was most often employed on diagonal wind braces (b–c).
- *Scarf joint*: used to extend long members within their profile. Since it can never be as strong as the unjointed section, the joint is placed at a less critical position in the member length. There are an amazing number of variations on the basic form, using blades which are either tapered

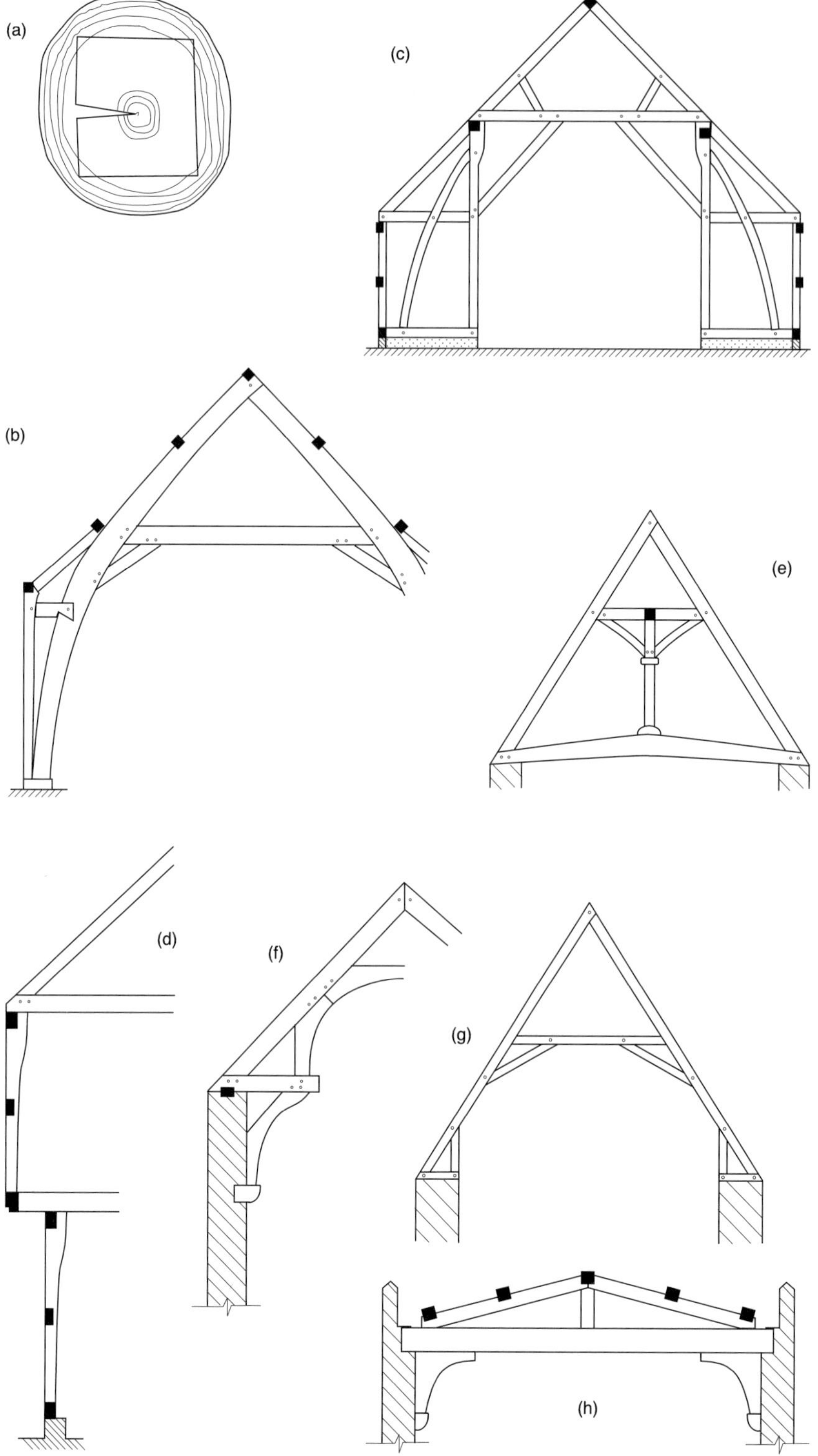

Fig. 2.3 Medieval framing

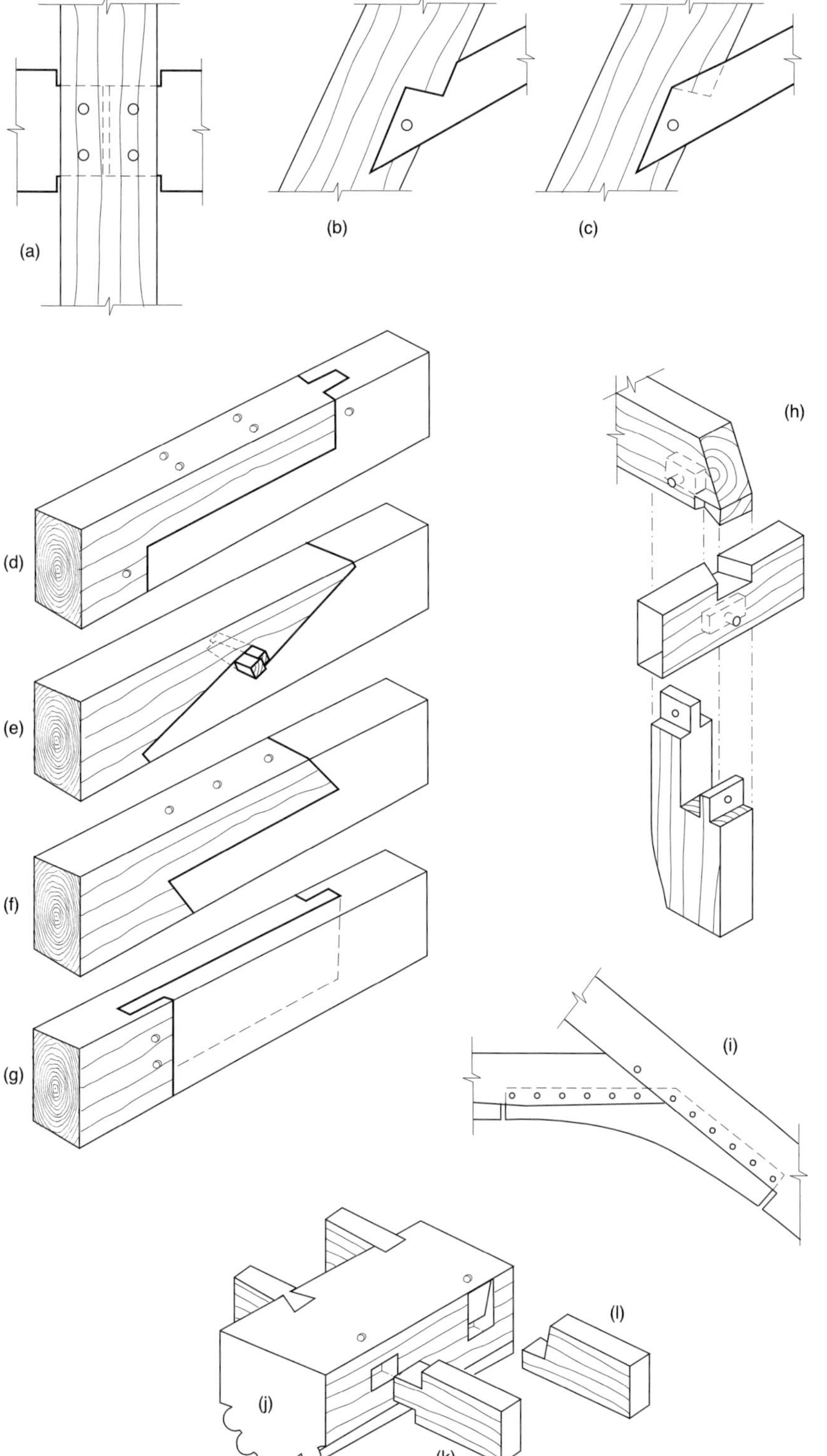

Fig. 2.4 Medieval joints

or simply halved, and set either vertically or horizontally, together with different methods of locking the two halves together with dowels or more elaborate mechanical interlock (Fig. 2.4(d–g)).

- *Post head and tie beam joint*: a joint used to deal with the critical point at which a roof truss sits on a post. It is basically two tenons at right angles, and the post section is sometimes enlarged to give the necessary breadth. This joint has to take the complementary tension to the compression in the knee brace. Variations include the use of a dovetail for the outer tenon (h).
- *Floor*: structures are built up from a hierarchy of primary and secondary beams, generally connected by mortice and tenon. Since for most of the period the floors were open, i.e., with no ceiling below, many of the beams were moulded for decorative effect (j). Early tenons, with a large bottom notch, tended to induce splitting in the secondary beam (k). The later haunched tenon corrected this, while increasing the tenon strength, and reducing the effective loss of section in the primary beam (l).

2.3. The seventeenth and eighteenth centuries

The history of timber is inextricably linked to that of the other building materials. Before going forward we must retrace our steps and look at the development of brick. Originally introduced into Britain by the Romans, the technique of brickmaking was lost on their departure, and only reintroduced at a much later date, from the Continent. Small buildings in brick can be found from the thirteenth century on, mainly in areas with little natural stone, leading to the first major use of brick for the West front of Hampton Court (Fig. 2.5(a)) in 1525, although this could be seen as embracing innovation, rather than as strict economics.

Brick, moreover, was incombustible. Even engineers can remember the date of the Great Fire of London, but many towns with closely packed timber framed houses had experienced large conflagrations before then. The London Rebuilding Act of 1667 laid down requirements for party walls and front walls to be of brick, and, as methods of constructing large kilns developed, brick was amenable to volume production in a way that could never be achieved with the timber frame.

The other significant factor in the rise of brick was the change in architectural style. Originating in Italy in the middle of the fourteenth century, the Renaissance finally reached England with Inigo Jones' Banqueting House of 1622, the first fully classical building in London. The style was based on the architecture of Greece and Rome, and the timber frame, quintessentially medieval, had no place in the new order of things. Frames can be found for another 100 years or so, more particularly in rural areas, with timber barns still being built in the nineteenth century, but by the end of the seventeenth century the carpenter's role was, in the main, confined to the construction of floors and roofs within masonry walls. Neither element was now exposed, but concealed behind plaster ceilings.

The new style brought significant changes in form. The king post truss came into widespread use, although now concealed from general view by

Fig. 2.5(a) West front of Hampton Court

Fig. 2.5(b) Square Chapel, Halifax. Roof truss tie beam strap

the ceiling below. Iron straps were introduced to reinforce the central tension joint between the post and tie beam (Fig. 2.5(b)). Floor construction was radically changed in order to present a flat ceiling for plaster; the principal beams carried a 'double' floor, i.e., floor joists above and ceiling joists below, sometimes with a pugging layer to contribute to sound reduction.

Since the principal beams determined the overall thickness of the floor, the depths were often kept to a minimum, resulting in ambitious span/depth ratios. For the larger spans, attempts were sometimes made to improve their stiffness by the addition of iron catenary rods, or shallow arches, but rarely with any degree of effectiveness.

As longer spans were attempted, some use was made of interlocked compound members, particularly for the long bottom tie. Other roof shapes appear, such as the mansard, and produced alternative truss layouts, such as the queen post and multiple-bay trusses. The quality and efficiency of all these roof structures depended very much upon the individual carpenter's understanding of the principles, and knowledge of standing examples.

These principles of the truss were also applied to some internal house walls, allowing the construction of framed partitions. These had great advantages, allowing the room layout to vary from floor to floor (an almost universal requirement of house planning) and, perhaps, even supporting floor loads on the bottom flanges. The principal difficulty came in relation to the possible clash between the triangulating members and the door openings, especially where the door was close to the support.

Since all the timber in the building was now protected from the direct effects of rain and sun, there was less need for the durability of oak. Softwood was used increasingly (Fig. 2.6), and much was imported, as the native supply of coniferous wood was quite inadequate for the demand.

Fig. 2.6 Cromford Mill, Derbyshire

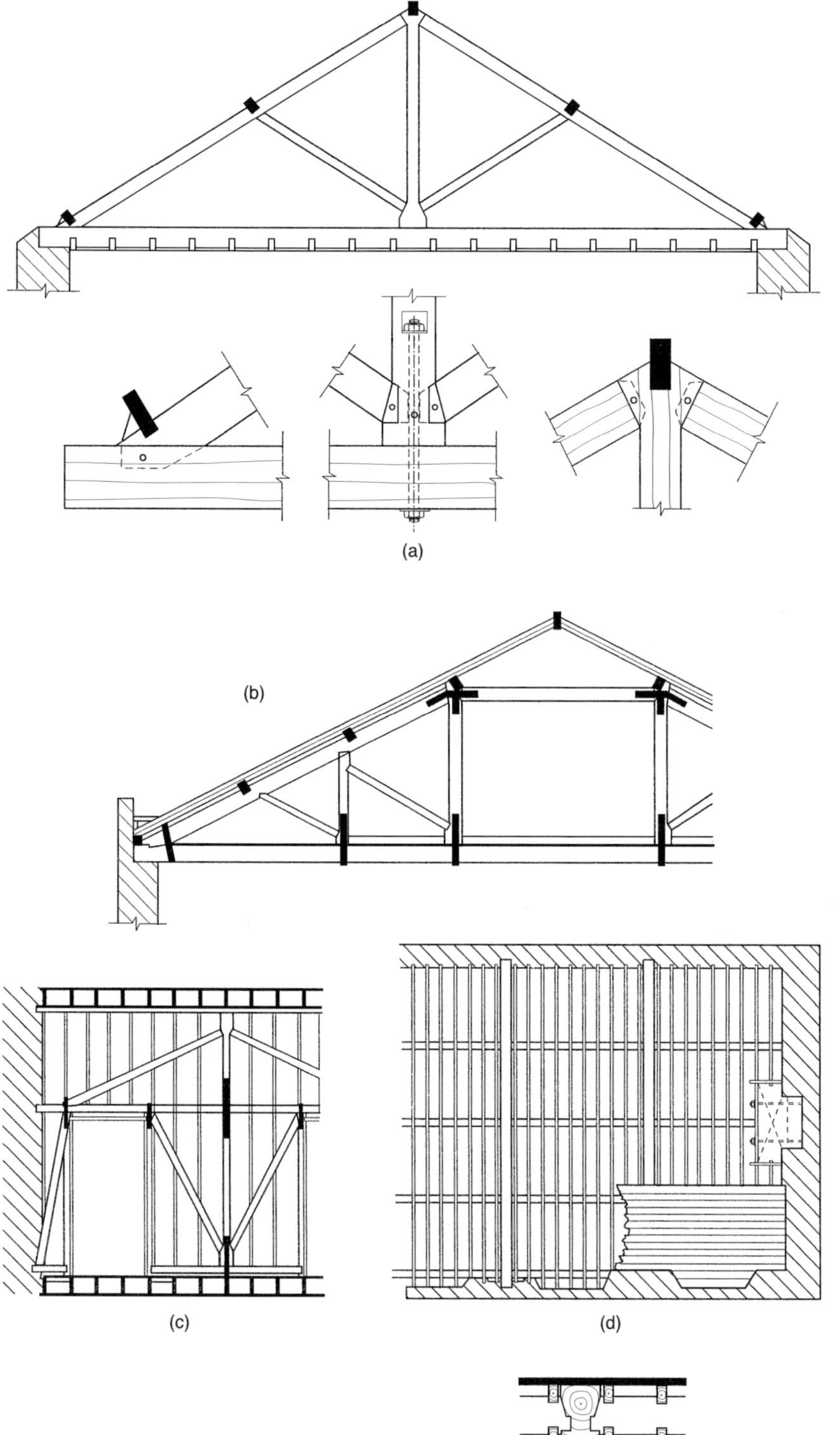

Fig. 2.7 Eighteenth century framing

Intercontinental trade also introduced the tropical hardwoods, although most of them were used either in joinery work (for their surface figure), or in external and marine applications (for their durability).

The king post truss was a response to a need to provide rigid support for roofs of larger span, and shallower pitch, which at the same time were carrying the additional load of a ceiling on the tie member (Fig. 2.7(a)). The span of the rafters was broken ingeniously by raking struts, springing from splayed haunches at the base of the king post, which transferred its load to the rafters by similar haunches at its top. Thus, while the post itself was in tension, the associated timber joints were still in compression. The only point where a tension connection was needed was at the bottom of the king post to pick up the tie member. In smaller trusses this was achieved by a pegged long tenon, but this was soon replaced by an iron strap, held in position by a forelock bolt which was tightened by driving a wedge into a slot.

The truss was now effectively triangulated and, hence, rigid. Larger trusses could be made by extending this basic system, leading to the queen post truss (b). In this case the lack of triangulation in the centre bay was accepted, since here the out-of-balance loads were least, and could be accommodated by the continuity of the rafters and tie. The open bay, thus created in the area of maximum headroom, was of great advantage for additional accommodation. It was also possible to extend the range of the truss further with multiple side bays. The out-of-balance lateral force at the foot of the smaller posts was taken on the base tenon in shear or, for larger spans, through blocking pieces planted on the bottom tie.

Although most of the timber in the building was now protected, truss tie members and floor joists were still at risk of decay where they were built into solid external walls. In addition, binding timbers were sometimes built into the inner face of the wall around mid-storey height, in a misguided attempt to strengthen it.

Load-bearing partitions were built as trusses, with triangulated or arched members bringing the loads to tie members heeled into the masonry walls (Fig. 2.7(c)).

Floors of medium span might be based on a two-tier system of principal beams with common joists notched into them (d). For larger spans, a three-tier system of primary and secondary beams with haunched end tenons support floor and ceiling joists. Pugging, or sound insulation, was introduced as a layer of sand or shells supported by boards on runners nailed between the floor joists.

2.4. The nineteenth century

The nineteenth century was marked principally by the radical changes in society and technology brought about by the Industrial Revolution. Machine power was harnessed to facilitate the conversion of timber from the log, and there was a general expansion in all fields, with a need for new classes of industrial building, principally the mills and warehouses (Fig. 2.8). These began basically in the late eighteenth century as an enlargement

Fig. 2.8 Warehouse at Gloucester Docks

of domestic construction—brick walls with timber floors and a roof, stabilised by 'box' action. The floors, needing to support heavier loads, reverted to open construction, with large square primary beams supported at intervals by columns. These beams are often of impressive length, and so it must be presumed that the economics of obtaining and lifting them outweighed the costs of extra joints.

Roofs were also required for progressively larger spans, on both industrial and commercial buildings. Iron was increasingly used for strap connections and, as the principles of statics became more clearly understood, substituted as rods in place of timber tension members. It is, in fact, time to look back again, this time at iron.

The technique of cast iron manufacture was first developed abroad in the medieval period. Cast iron is a material which is strong in compression, but brittle and weak in tension, due largely to its high carbon content. Reheating the cast iron in a charcoal furnace, with air blown over the molten metal, extracts much of the carbon to produce wrought iron, a ductile material, with an improved tensile capacity. The charcoal (produced by slowly burning off the other constituents of timber to leave almost pure carbon) was necessary to obtain the high temperatures required, and its supply limited the amount of iron which could be made.

The breakthrough in volume production was made by Abraham Derby who, in 1709, used coke (again, largely carbon, produced by burning off the impurities in coal) as a substitute for charcoal. This technique dramatically increased production capacity, with a consequent reduction in cost.

The first half of the nineteenth century saw the gradual application to mill construction of iron technology; initially to the columns, which as a simple compression element could be made easily in cast iron. The timber floors were a major fire risk, since lighting was by oil lamp, flickering above boards soaked with lubricating oil which had dripped from the machinery.

Early attempts at a fireproof construction produced a small number of composite floors—timber principals with cast iron wedges bolted to their sides, which carried brick jack arches. By the middle of the nineteenth century, however, cast iron beams had replaced the timber principals, leaving the roof as the only timber element in the building.

Warehouses were of broadly similar construction. They were designed simply for the storage of man-handled sacks, and so the storey heights were lower and the columns more closely spaced. Since they were largely unoccupied and unlit, the fire risks were less and the internal frames were built in timber into the second half of the nineteenth century.

The railway companies were perhaps the organisations most wedded to iron, but Brunel chose timber for the shed at Temple Meads, Bristol, in 1841 (Fig. 2.9(a)) (albeit with concealed iron rods to anchor the cantilevers). The first major London train shed, Euston (in iron), was followed by Kings Cross in 1852, originally built with a timber roof formed from a series of bolted laminated arches, built up from thin planks. However they performed badly, due apparently to the steam from the locomotives, and so they were taken down and replaced by iron. A more successful application of the 'boltlam' can still be seen nearby, in the former German Gymnasium of 1860.

By the middle of the nineteenth century, the techniques of rolling wrought iron angles and plates, and connecting them together with rivets, had been developed commercially, and became a cheaper alternative to timber for the large-span industrial roof. This change can be seen clearly at Chatham Dockyard, for instance, where covered slip No. 3, of cathedral-like proportions, was built as a timber frame in 1837. The adjacent slip, barely eight years later, is in iron, as are its successors up to slip No. 7 (Fig. 2.9(b) and (c)).

These industrial buildings were in the main designed and built by engineers. From the seventeenth century on, however, the field of domestic, commercial and public building had been increasingly the preserve of the

Fig. 2.9(a) Temple Meads, Bristol

Fig. 2.9(b) Chatham Historic Dockyard: No. 3 Slip

Fig. 2.9(c) Chatham Historic Dockyard: No. 4 Slip

architect, a profession which rose on the new wave of classicism. Up to the end of the eighteenth century, an architect had been clear as to the current style, and why it was to be preferred to previous styles. In the nineteenth century, however, style became something that was consciously chosen from the pattern book of history. By and large, banks, public houses, theatres and other heathenish activities lined up behind the pediments and porticos of the classical style. Educationalists, building museums and libraries, wavered, but the church, predictably, returned to the true styles of the medieval period, with a marked preference for thirteenth century early English. Thus, while the classicists continued to employ king post trusses concealed by plaster ceilings, the considerable number of new churches needed for the growing population largely sported open timber roofs, in inimitably Victorian versions of medieval forms (Fig. 2.10(a)).

From the inventiveness of the Industrial Revolution emerged the first patents for the mass production of nails and bolts, which up to now had been individually made by a blacksmith. These resulted in a dramatic reduction in cost which, in turn, led to a fundamental change in construction technique for industrial carpentry. For the whole period of this history, frame members had been assembled in a single plane, with their ends shaped to fit one another. If, instead, they were simply lapped, they could be nailed or bolted together. The joint would now rely entirely on the fasteners acting in shear, but would be equally strong in compression *and tension*, the weakness of the traditional joint. This technique could be extended to fasten three or four layers of timber together.

One particular form—known as the Belfast truss, from the city of its origin—was made up in this manner, using a bowstring form with an orthogonal lattice of diagonals. With a system of purlins and boards, it was created for the then new wonder material, bituminous felt, the first waterproofing material which could be laid on a flat, or nearly flat, surface, at a fraction of the weight (and price) of lead sheet. With spans up to 100 feet, many still exist at various locations (Fig. 2.10(b)).

Roofs were built for even larger spans. There was an increasing use of metal, sometimes as castings to house member ends (Fig. 2.11(a)), or as wrought iron rods for tension members, using nuts and large washers to distribute the load in the perpendicular-to-grain direction. Side straps, sometimes decoratively shaped, trimmed joints, and the jib and cotter fastening was developed for the bottom strap, which could be tightened to accommodate any residual shrinkage in the tie. Eventually the tie member itself was sometimes formed from rod, making a true composite truss (c).

The advent of machine-powered saws significantly reduced the costs of processing timber, which could now be cut economically to proportions of 3:1 and 4:1 (d). Floors were increasingly constructed of simple common joists, with boards above and ceilings below, often with one or two lines of herringbone strutting as an attempt (not always successful) to dampen vibration.

Floors for mills and warehouses continued to utilise square or near-square primary beams, spanning over columns at around 3–4 m centre, and often three or four bays in length (e). Common joists spanned between the primaries, sometimes notched, or sometimes cogged into them, with boarding over.

The nineteenth century also saw the development of engineering principles in structural design, and their application to timber. Tredgold's book, first published in 1820 and subsequent editions, outlined a design method with worked examples, and from this time on there was a gradual dissemination of technical information, although most design was still done on the basis of experience and rules of thumb. Thus, member sizes of structures from this period and later can generally be justified by present-day calculations, while eighteenth century elements, such as the principal beams of floors, routinely

Fig. 2.10(a) All Saints Church, Lyndhurst, the New Forest

Fig. 2.10(b) Hanger at Duxford Airfield, Cambridge

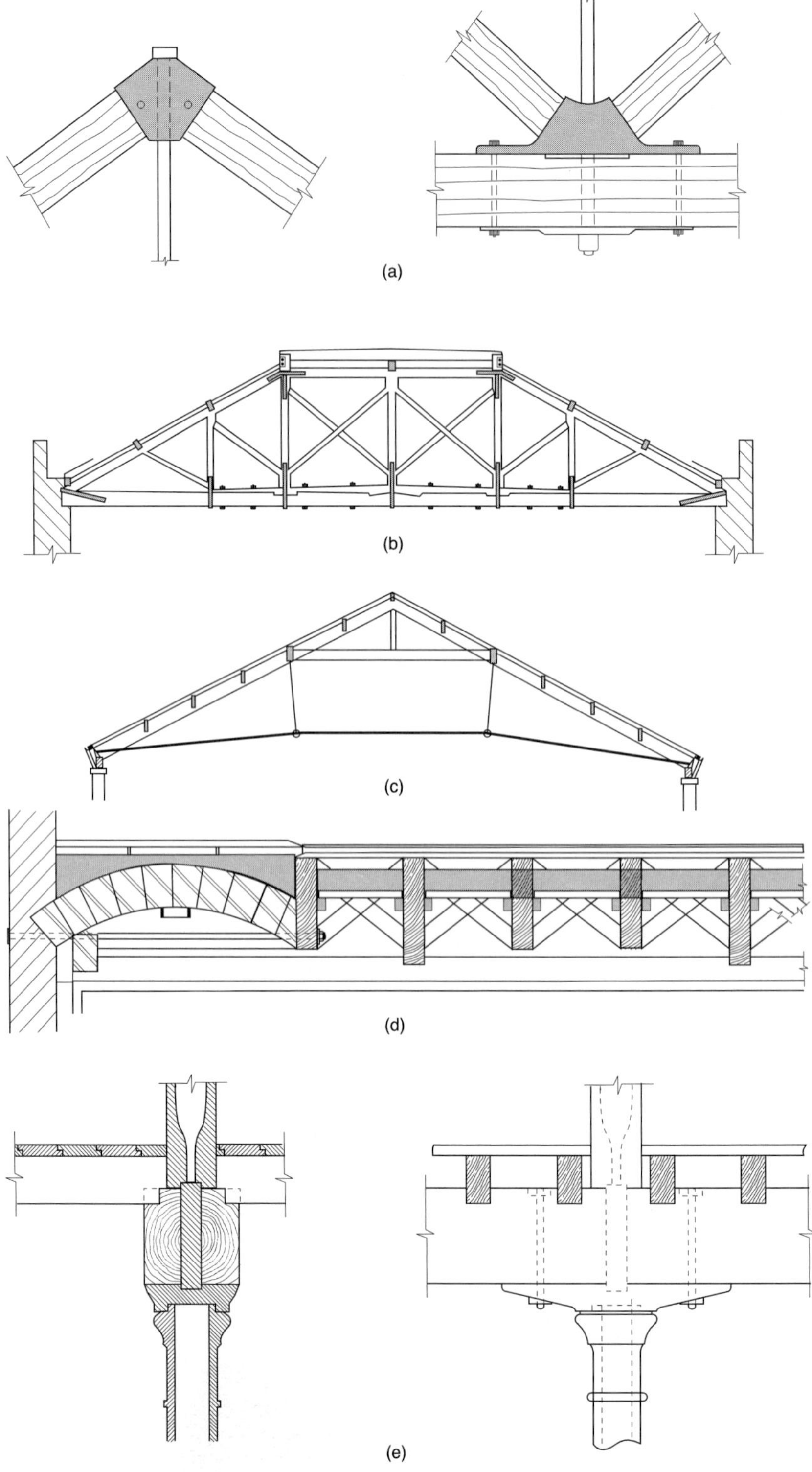

Fig. 2.11 Nineteenth century framing

show 'over-stress', despite the fact that most have performed satisfactorily for some 200 years.

2.5. The twentieth century

With the use of mass-produced bolts and, in the early twentieth century, a range of connectors designed to improve their shear resistance, even larger spans were fabricated. Trusses of the Howe, Warren and Pratt types were borrowed from the vocabulary of steel and used predominantly for industrial structures, although few now remain in existence (Fig. 2.14(a) and (b)).

The timber frame of modern times had its origins in America. As long ago as 1830 a Chicagoan named George Snow discovered that small softwood sections could be rapidly fixed together using a large bag of the new mass-produced nails, without all the labour of the traditional mortice and tenon joints. 'It's as easy as blowing up a balloon', he said. The analogy was questionable, but the name stuck, and the balloon frame (always clad externally, most often with horizontal weather boarding) became a standard form of construction throughout America. Examples can be found over here from the mid-nineteenth century onwards, sometimes for upper storeys only, and clad mainly with tiles.

From the 1960s, as part of the housing drive, many timber framed houses were built across the UK, although the full-height studs of the transatlantic model were modified to storey height, in a system known as the platform frame. The cladding was almost always brick, set away from the timber, and preserving the principles of the cavity wall (c).

The roofs were made with trussed rafters, again a construction form with its origins in America (d). Embedded in the timber by hydraulic presses, pressed metal plate fasteners enabled pitched trusses of domestic span to be made cheaply and easily (Fig. 2.12).

Fig. 2.12 Trussed rafters. Church, Walderslade, Kent

In America they were stabilised by an over-sheathing of ply, but when the principle was taken up in the UK, it was decided (except in Scotland) that the ply was expensive and unnecessary, and stability was achieved by a combination of the tiling battens and triangulating members. Their success was immediate, and it is estimated that from the 1960s on, they were used for 95% of new-build low-rise housing, and that upwards of 50 million have been installed. With the domestic market conquered, the fabricators then extended the use of truss rafters into the field of larger-span institutional and commercial buildings.

The great shock of the twentieth century, in the fields of art and architecture generally, was the advent of Modernism. From earlier origins, it was embraced enthusiastically in the post-war period but, regrettably, in timber as in other materials, the image sometimes outran the technology. Some lightweight flat roofs were constructed with waterproofing membranes of low tensile strength, laid with no fall on moisture-susceptible chipboard, over cold unventilated cavities. Not surprisingly, their useful life was brief. Now that the technology has caught up, there is a neo-vernacular return to the pitched roof. On the other hand, the post-war period has seen the building of many fine modern timber structures, using glued laminated members to span distances which were greater than anything which had gone before.

The relative ease with which wood can be glued had been known to most civilisations from the Egyptians onwards. In the eighteenth century, adhesives were used extensively in joinery, both for the joints, and for fixing thin veneers of decorative woods to the frame. These were animal glues, extracted from fish, and later casein, obtained from skimmed milk.

In America the idea of veneering was taken a step further with the first patents for plywood in the 1860s; peeled veneers were glued together with successive plies at right angles, producing boards of unprecedented width and stability. At the turn of the century, glued laminated construction, that is, the building up of a large member by gluing together thin planks, had begun in Germany (Fig. 2.14(e)).

Organic glues performed well in dry conditions, but they were moisture-susceptible. The formaldehyde glues, developed in the 1930s, were more resistant, but phenol–formaldehyde, the first to be produced, needed heat while curing. While this was possible in plywood manufacture, it was difficult to heat large structural components. The urea–formaldehyde glues, which cured at normal interior temperatures, were developed commercially during the second World War, and used on the later models of the Mosquito aeroplane. From the 1950s onward, glued laminated beams with moisture resistant adhesives came into general use for structural work, and allowed the fabrication of timber elements which were limited in size only by considerations of transport (Fig. 2.13).

Most of the buildings constructed during the 1950s and 1960s had low thermal insulation values, in response to the very modest demands of the Regulations. In this respect, timber framed houses which could conveniently include insulation in the frame cavities often exceeded the minimum requirements.

Fig. 2.13 Dome, 70 m span, of glued laminated timber, at Center Parcs, Sherwood Forest

The principle of lapped timbers connected by nails in shear was extended to large trusses, using multiple members interlapped at joints. The shear capacity of the bolts was further increased by the inclusion of toothed plate, split ring or shear plate connectors.

The timber frames of the 1960s were made quite simply, with a succession of vertical studs trimmed by a sole plate and a head plate, and additional cripple studs to support lintels over openings. Stability was obtained by the diaphragm action of applied panels, generally plywood. Floor joists of constant depth formed a platform, and the wall construction was then repeated for the second storey, with internal partition walls largely supported on the first floor.

In most cases the roof was formed with trussed rafters spanning directly between the external walls, and allowing the interior to be made waterproof as quickly as possible. The trusses were made by placing precut members into a table jig, locating the plate fasteners in position and then embedding them with hydraulic presses.

Further reading

Histories of western architecture abound, such as those by Pevsner (1943) and Watkin (1992), but since they deal with polite, rather than vernacular architecture, timber is hardly mentioned. Quiney (1995) and Brunskill (1971) cover vernacular English building, including timber, but best value is undoubtedly Harris (1978). Hewett (1980, 1982, 1985) in his three books, makes a detailed study of timber roofs and framing.

All these references relate predominantly to the medieval period. Roofs of the eighteenth century are dealt with in detail by Yeomans (1992), which also includes an excellent bibliography. Construction of the nineteenth century is

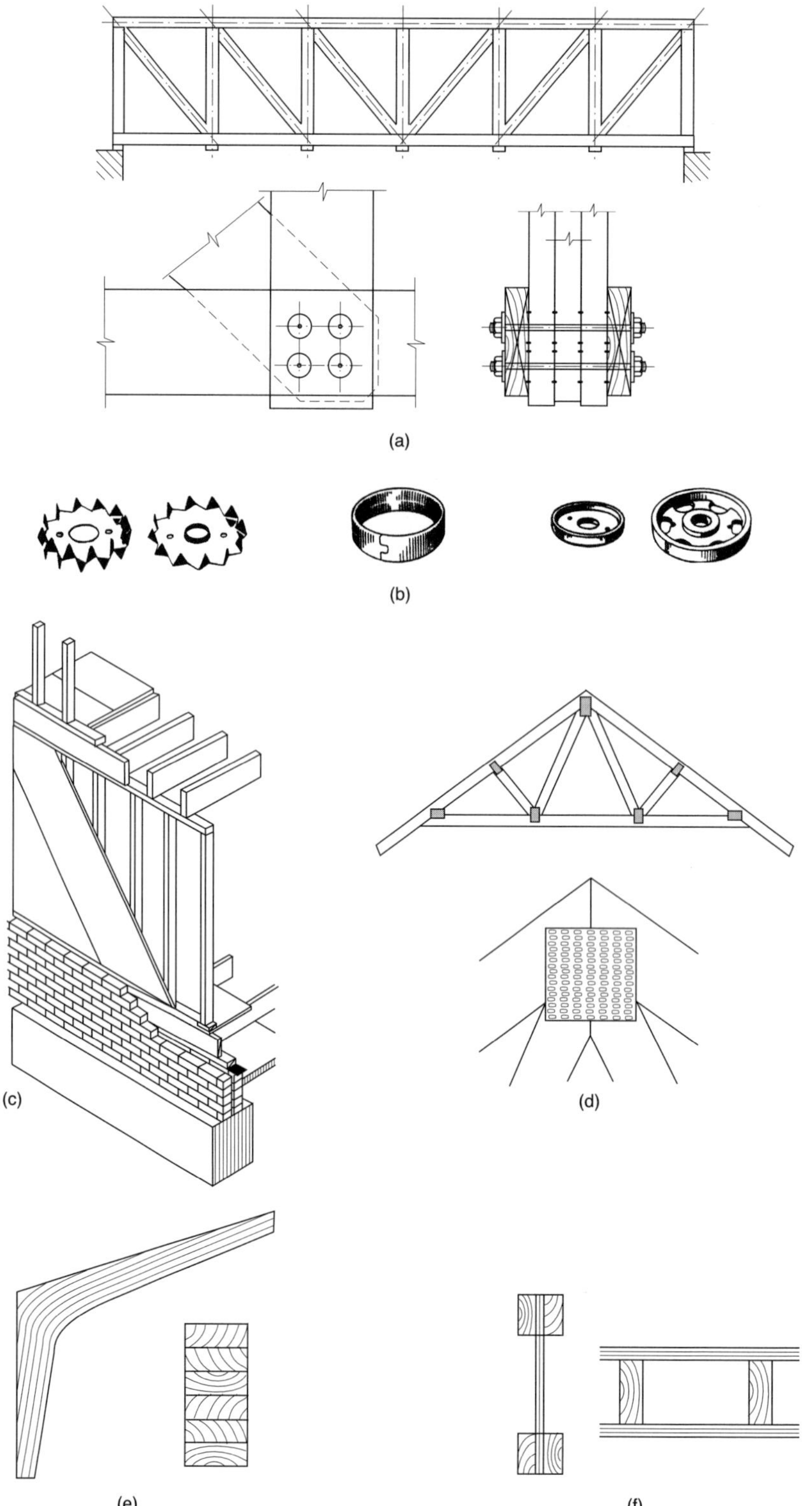

Fig. 2.14 Twentieth century timber framing

described by authors of the time, such as Newlands (1857) and Tredgold (1840). Construction of the twentieth century (with other materials) is given in textbooks such as McKay (1944) and Mitchell Building Series (Bromwell, 1976). Wainwright and Keyworth (1988) describe the modern timber frame in detail. Beckmann (1995) addresses the structural aspects of building conservation.

3

Penhurst Place, Kent. The roof to the Great Hall, which remains almost precisely as it was when originally built by Sir John de Pulteney in 1340.

3

The characteristics of timber

No intelligent appraisal of any structure can be made unless the characteristics of the construction material are understood. While this is true generally, it is especially so for timber which, as an organic material, has a particularly complex structure. In order to understand the characteristics of cut timber, therefore, it is necessary to first look at the way in which the tree from which the material was cut was able to grow to maturity.

3.1. The living tree

All trees are perennial plants capable of secondary thickening, that is, they are capable of adding yearly growth to the previous year's wood. The main part of the tree is the trunk, which supports the branches and leaves (or needles) forming the crown. The bark (Fig. 3.1) protects the cambium layer, where growth takes place. The trunk itself is made of cells, which are generally elongated in shape. Water from the soil, containing nutrients, moves upwards through the sapwood cells to the leaves. There the process of photosynthesis takes place—water combines with carbon dioxide from the atmosphere, (catalysed by chlorophyll using energy from sunlight) and produces a basic sugar. The sap carries this sugar back down through the inner bark to build new cells in the cambial layer.

The majority of cells are orientated parallel to the direction of the trunk. The dimensions vary between species, but they are typically 100 times as long as they are wide and some 4 000 000 of them may be contained within a 25 mm cube of wood. Scattered throughout the wood are groups of cells (5–10% by volume) aligned radially, called rays, which are comprised mainly of parenchyma cells storing the carbohydrates manufactured in the leaves. No cells run tangentially. The structure of wood is thus markedly anisotropic.

Most of the twigs and branches of the crown are sapwood. In the trunk of the tree, however, the older cells nearer the pith at the centre cease to conduct sap, and accumulate extractives because of their distance from the living, actively dividing cambium. They are then referred to as heartwood, which in many species is darker in colour than sapwood. The toxicity of the extractives makes the heartwood more durable than the sapwood.

Growth takes place while environmental conditions are suitable. In temperate climates, following the dormant winter season, the earlywood is

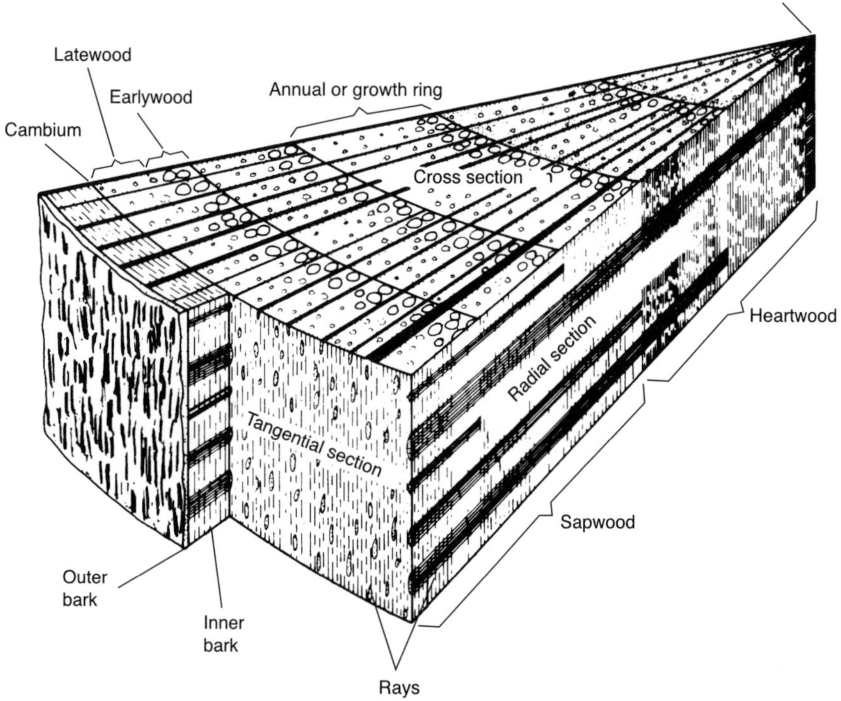

Fig. 3.1 Diagram of a segment cut from a five-year-old stem of a hardwood

characterised by relatively rapid growth, of a different texture to the latewood. This annual cycle produces a distinctive pattern of growth rings which can be seen most clearly in the transverse section. In tropical areas growth is more or less continuous, but seasonal variations in rainfall may produce a similar, although less pronounced, effect.

Thus, the trunk of the tree has three basic functions

- support for the crown of the tree
- storage of food materials for the spring growth
- conduction of water and dissolved mineral salts from the roots to the leaves.

The cellular structure of the wood has developed to perform these functions, although the two basic divisions of trees, the softwoods and the hardwoods, have developed different ways of meeting these demands.

3.2. Softwoods and hardwoods

The two broad divisions into which trees are classified are the softwoods, confined mainly to the northern temperate zones, and the hardwoods, which occur both in temperate and tropical regions. Before looking at their characteristics, however, it will be useful to understand the way in which trees are classified. Like other plants, they are grouped according to the characteristics of their flower. The broadest grouping is that of the family,

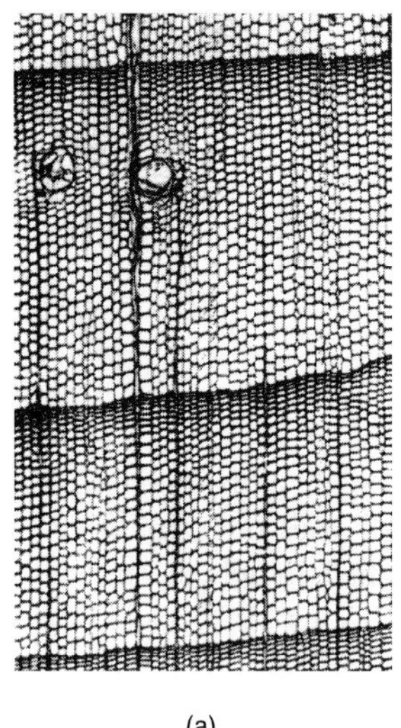

(a)

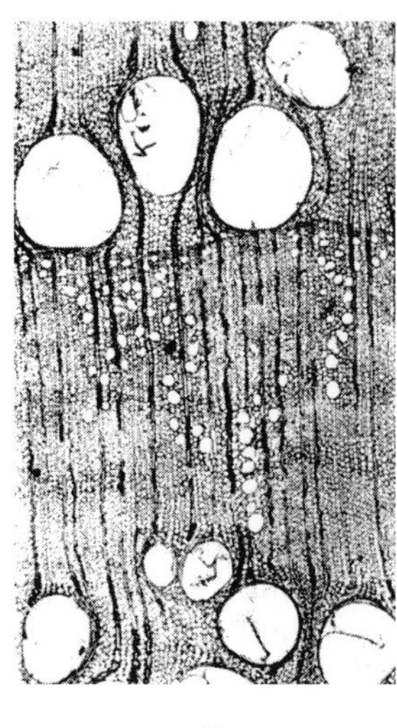

(b)

Fig. 3.2 Cross-sections to approximately the same scale of (a) a softwood (Pinus sylvestris) with growth rings around 1 mm apart and (b) a hardwood (European Oak) showing vessels in growth rings around 2 mm apart

which consists of a number of different trees, more or less closely related to one another. Each kind of tree has a Latin botanical name, indicating the genus (plural genera) to which it belongs, and the specific name, indicating the particular species of the genus.

Thus within *Pinaceae*, the pine family, there is *Pinus palustris*, the American pitch pine and *Pinus sylvestris*, the Scots pine. Since this latter species can also be referred to as redwood, or even deal, the advantage of the Latin name, agreed internationally and unique, becomes clear.

Consider first the softwoods, which are a relatively small number of cone-bearing, or coniferous species, mostly with evergreen needles or scale-like leaves. They are relatively fast-growing, generally as a single stem to the top of the tree, and currently supply the bulk of the world's commercial timber. If a cross-section is examined under a microscope the earlywood is seen to be made up of square or hexagonal cells, called tracheids, with thin walls and comparatively large open cavities which enable them to conduct sap (Fig. 3.2). The latewood cells are similar in form, but have thicker walls and correspondingly smaller cavities, and function primarily as structural support.

The hardwoods, in evolutionary terms, are more developed than the softwoods, and have two distinct types of cell for water conduction and structural support. The water-conducting elements, or vessels, are a series of open-ended cells set one above the other and are generally large enough to be seen with a 10× hand lens. Support is provided by the fibres, thick-walled cells which are broadly similar to the latewood tracheids of the softwoods.

The growth pattern of the cells is unique to each species, and the standard method of identifying a timber sample is to examine a cleanly-cut cross-section of the grain. In most cases, a piece as small as 12 mm square will be sufficient.

3.3. Moisture content and movement

While the tree is living, the trunk will have a relatively high moisture content (MC). The moisture content of a timber sample is defined as the ratio of the weight of contained water to the weight of dry wood, and is generally expressed as a percentage. The heartwood of a freshly cut trunk could well have an 80% MC, with even higher values in the sapwood. This, of course, is due primarily to the presence of the sap, which is mainly water with dissolved nutrients and carbohydrates.

If a piece of cut timber is kept in air, it will, as a hygroscopic material, gradually lose moisture by evaporation from the surface. Immediately after cutting, the cell walls are still fully saturated, with the remaining moisture occupying the cell cavities. As the timber dries out, this 'free' water in the cavities is lost first, until a state is reached in which the cell cavities are empty, but the cell walls are still saturated. This MC is called the fibre saturation point (FSP). The FSP for redwood is about 30%, but the value varies slightly between different species. Since there is no change in the moisture content of the cell walls, there is not generally, at this stage, any dimensional change in the timber.

As the moisture content continues to fall, the cell walls now begin to lose moisture, which results in shrinkage across the width of the cell structure at a rate, from FSP to zero MC, which is roughly linear. At the same time, the properties of the timber change; both the strength and the stiffness (the modulus of elasticity or E value) increase as the MC reduces. Eventually (for a given relative humidity (RH) of the surrounding air) the MC will stabilise at a value known as the equilibrium moisture content (EMC). The relationship between air RH and timber EMC is shown in Fig. 3.3. It can be seen that the difference between the graph for 30°C and 10°C is only

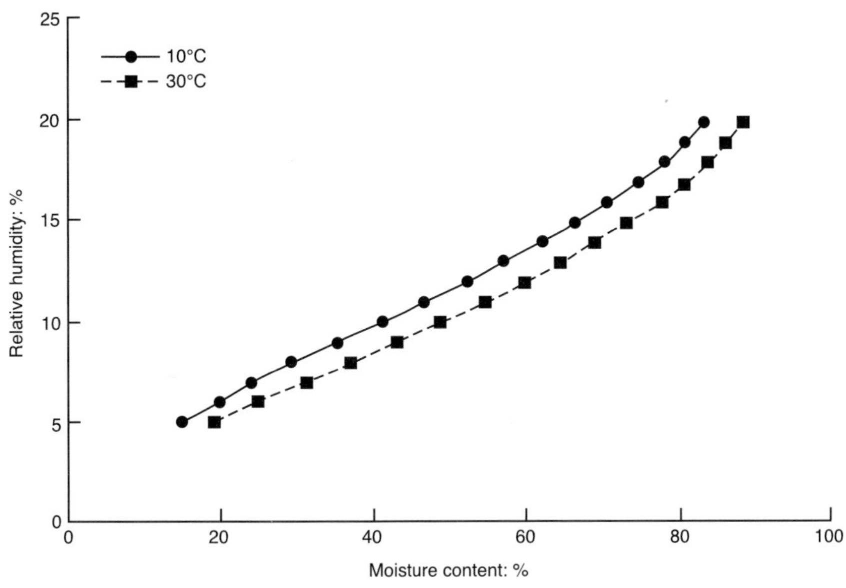

Fig. 3.3 Relationship between RH and EMC

10%. Thus the MC of timber depends almost entirely upon the RH of the surrounding air, and very little upon the ambient temperature alone.

It is at first difficult to accept this statement, for we are used to timber inside a building being warmer, and drier, than timber outside. Timber is also oven-dried to obtain its weight at 0% MC. What must be remembered is that, in general, the RH of air falls as its temperature rises, and the timber is responding primarily to this, and not to the rise in temperature. If timber is put into a steam box (i.e., a RH of 100%) both temperature and MC rise.

The rate and extent of shrinkage varies according to species. Remember that significant shrinkage only occurs perpendicular to the grain—the reduction of length along the grain for all species is approximately 0·15% from green to oven-dry, which, for all practical purposes, can be ignored. In general, radial shrinkage (the direction which is partly stabilised by rays) is about half the value of tangential shrinkage (the direction with no stabilising cells).

Looking at the effect of this shrinkage on the timber profile, let us consider first some short pieces of oak cut from a large log (Fig. 3.4). The distortion of the square piece (a) into a diamond demonstrates the different rate of radial and tangential shrinkage. Floor boards which are quarter- or rift-sawn (b) will stay flatter than boards which are plain-sawn (c). As an aid to predicting the distortion, imagine that as a piece dries the growth rings tend to straighten out.

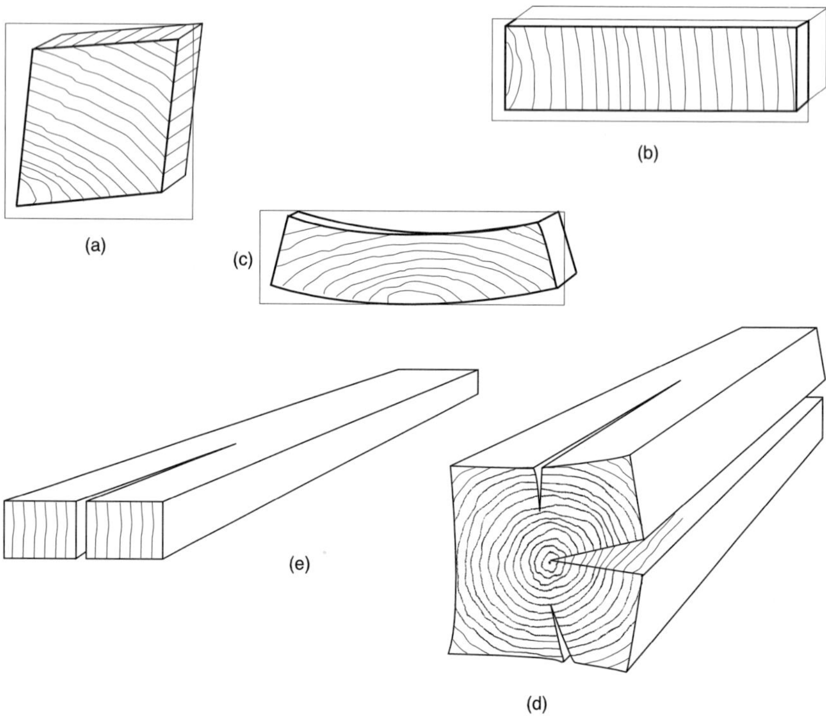

Fig. 3.4 Drying distortion of timber sections

These pieces were deliberately cut as short sections, and as a consequence dried out rapidly, because timber is some 20 times more permeable along the grain than across the grain.

For a larger, longer section, perhaps including the pith (a section known as boxed heart), the situation is more complex. There will now be a significant moisture content gradient across the section, as the moisture can only leave from the surface. As the MC of the outer layers fall below the FSP, they will start to shrink, producing tangential tensile stresses which may overcome the very modest strength of the timber in this direction, causing several small fissures to develop. As drying progresses, it is likely that one of the fissures will gradually extend to the pith (Fig. 3.4(d)). This fissure will tend to occur along the weakest line, i.e., the shortest distance from the pith to the surface, and so it is almost always found that the depth of the fissure is not more than one half the width of the piece.

In general, the only case when drying fissures will occur through the full depth of the piece (when they are known as splits) is at each end. Due to the more rapid loss of moisture from the end grain, the whole cross-section will try to shrink against the restraint provided by the body of the piece (e).

Not surprisingly, the movement of timber in relation to RH is reversible. If the ambient humidity of the air increases for a period of time, or the piece gets wet, the MC of the outer layers will increase, with some consequent radial and tangential swelling—but for this, and any subsequent movements, the rates of swelling and shrinking are roughly half the initial values. Thus, drying fissures may get narrower if the timber is re-wetted, but will never re-close

Table 3.1. Some properties of common building timbers

Species	*Movement class*[(1)]	*Durability*	*Permeability*[(2)]	*Average modulus of rupture*[(3)] *N/mm²*	*Nominal specific gravity*[(3)]
Softwoods					
Redwood	medium	ND	MR	89	0·46
Douglas fir	small	MD	R	91	0·44
Pitch pine	medium	D	MR	107	0·62
Western Red Cedar	small	D	R	65	0·33
Whitewood	small	ND	R	66	0·35
Temperate hardwoods					
Oak	medium	D	ER	97	0·61
Elm	medium	ND	MR	68	0·46
Tropical hardwoods					
Ekki	large	VD	ER	178	0·95
Greenheart	medium	VD	ER	181	0·88
Iroko	small	VD	ER	90	0·58
Keruing	medium	MD	R	110	0·58
Teak	small	VD	ER	106	0·58

(1) Movement classification in accordance with Farmer (1972).
(2) Durability classifications (ND—non-durable, MD—moderately durable, D—durable and VD—very durable) and permeability classifications (MR—moderately resistant, R—resistant and ER—extremely resistant) in accordance with BS 5268: Part 5.
(3) Modulus of rupture and specific gravity for small clear specimens taken from Lavers (1969).

completely. Table 3.1 gives movement coefficients for common timber species.

3.4. Durability

All plants have some position within the food chain. Celery, for instance, can be broken down into starches and sugars by the relatively feeble human digestive system, and herbivores such as cattle are able to eat grasses and leaves within grazing height. If a tree is to run its allotted span of, say, 200 years or more, it will need to protect the vulnerable sapwood with bark, which contains tannin, and to offer fruits as a distraction to other animals.

Nevertheless, the substances of the trunk—cellulose, hemicellulose and lignins—are combined in such a way that only a relative handful of fungi and insects have discovered a method of using timber as a food source, and then only under certain conditions.

Timber in a building has existed in three very different states

- the growing tree
- the felled log, or timber undergoing seasoning
- in service as a building element.

The prevention of fungal or insect attack in the first two states will primarily have been the responsibility of the forester or the merchant. We are concerned mainly with the possibility of attack after the timber has been installed although, of course, not every piece may have been attack-free at the time of construction.

Fungi

The spores, or seeds, of fungi are microscopic and widely distributed by air currents. To germinate they need

- a food source
- oxygen
- a suitable ambient temperature range
- adequate moisture.

Within a building, the chances of germination of a spore landing on timber will therefore depend primarily on the moisture content of the timber. If this is below 20%, growth of fungi will not occur. Above this level, and up to an optimum of about 35–45% MC there is a chance that some spores will eventually germinate. Growth will then take place of the mycelium, made up of exceedingly fine tubes call hyphae. These grow at their tip, and pass through the cells of the host timber, feeding on it, and causing decay.

It was noted in section 3.1 that the heartwood of timber contained extractives. The toxicity of these extractives for each species determines its durability. In the UK a classification system of durability has been established and is described in section 4.2. Since sapwood contains no extractives, and is rich in starches, sapwoods of all species are either perishable or non-durable. The principal species of fungi which can grow in the building environment are described in section 9.1.

An alternative method of making perishable timber durable might be to try to fill it with some form of poison. The techniques of timber preservation by chemical impregnation are summarised in section 4.3.

Insects

The most voracious devourer of timber, the termite is, thankfully, largely confined to tropical and subtropical regions. In the UK there are a few species of beetle which, although preferring damp timber, can attack it when it is dry. Larvae hatch from eggs laid on the surface of the wood. They then bore into it, creating extensive tunnels as they feed and develop, before leaving holes on the surface when they finally emerge as adult insects. The principal species are described in section 9.2.

3.5. Material properties

We have seen that timber has a very directional structure, with a principal axis lying along the member in the direction of the grain. In a very simplistic way, this structure may be represented by a bundle of drinking straws held together with elastic bands (Gordon (1976)). The straws represent the tracheids or fibres, overlapping at their tips, strong and continuous in one direction, but held together only by the relatively weak bands which represent the rays.

The strength of timber

In order to get some quantitative understanding of the strength of timber, look at the results of standardised tests in accordance with BS 373 (1957):

Fig. 3.5 Static bending test using 300 × 20 × 20 *mm specimen (Princes Risborough Laboratory, © Crown Copyright)*

Methods of testing small clear specimens of timber. Clear specimens are straight-grained pieces, with no strength-reducing defects such as knots or fissures. The bending test, for example, is carried out by loading 300 × 20 × 20 mm samples to failure over a period of a few minutes (Fig. 3.5). Typical results for the modulus of rupture (assuming simple bending theory) of redwood at 12% MC are shown in Fig. 3.6(a); the relatively large deviation reflecting the variability in the strength properties of timber. If, however, the strength results were to be related to sample density, the scatter would be considerably reduced.

Redwood is a medium strength softwood, with an average density at test of around 460 kg/m^3. The same tests on greenheart, which has a density of approximately 880 kg/m^3, show a proportionate increase in strength (b). In general, the correlation between density and bending strength is independent of species. This relationship is also true of compression parallel to the grain, which averages a value of about half the bending strength. Figure 3.7 shows the relationship between maximum compression strength and density (actually plotted as nominal specific gravity) for all species, for the green condition (>30% MC) and air-dried (12% MC). The difference between the two lines shows that the strength of timber is also dependent upon moisture content. The relationship between these two factors for redwood (corrected for density) is shown in Fig. 3.8. The increase in strength below FSP to 0% MC is almost linear. Remember, however, that this is for small clear samples. The effect is less pronounced for structural sizes with defects in them. Knots, for instance, remain the same size as the timber dries, and fissures may get a little deeper.

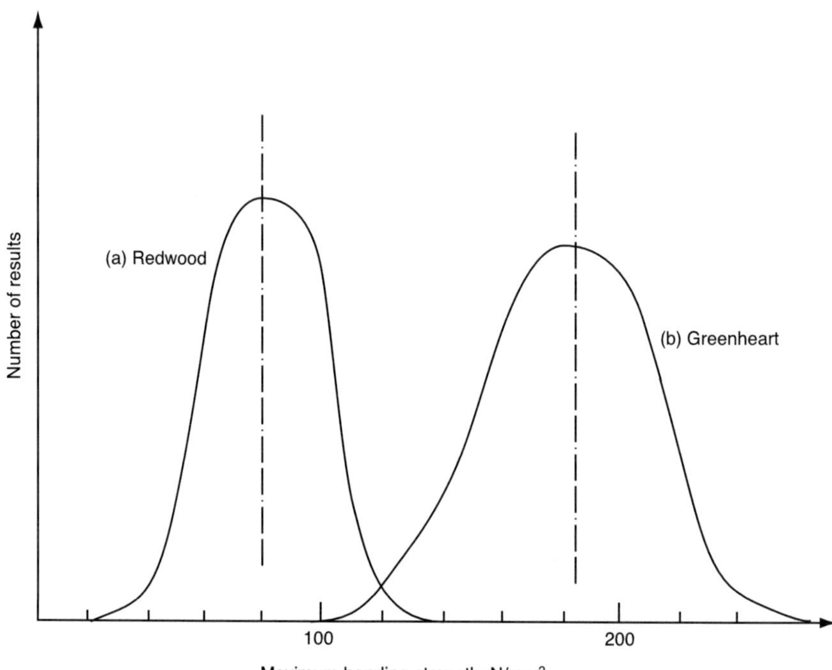

Fig. 3.6 Results of small clear bending tests on (a) Redwood and (b) Greenheart

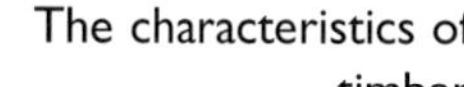

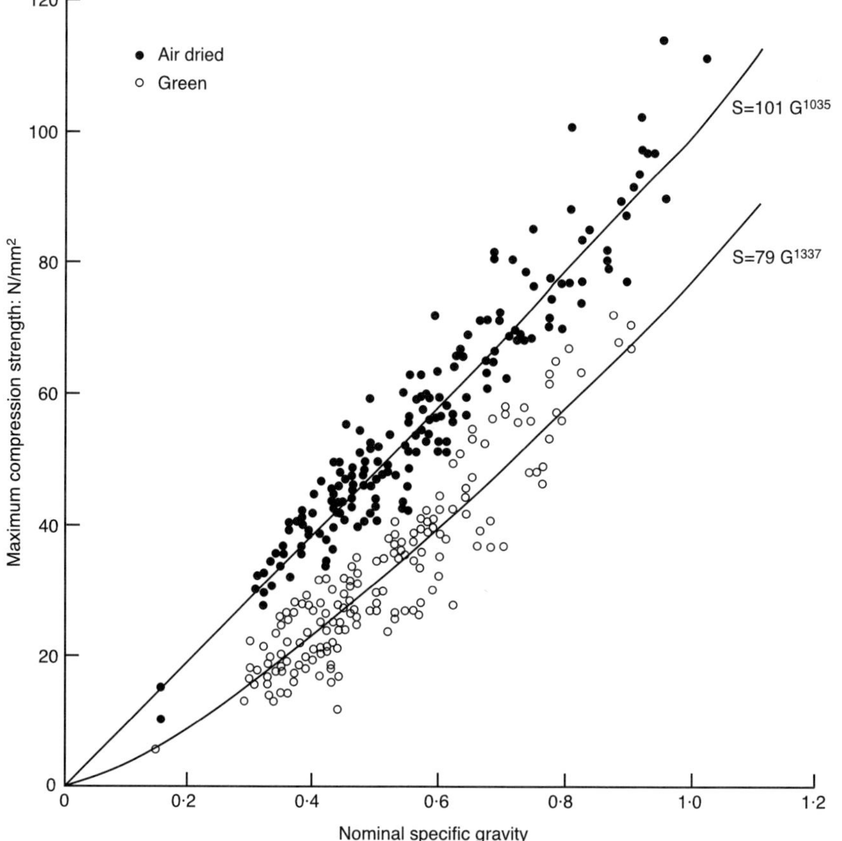

Fig. 3.7 The relation of maximum compression strength to nominal specific gravity for all species tested, green and air dried (Princes Risborough Laboratory, © Crown Copyright)

Also note that timber is stronger in the short term than in the long term. The load which could be carried indefinitely by a piece of timber will only be about half the load which would cause short-term failure (Fig. 3.9).

The strength properties which have been looked at so far—bending and compression—have given quite high results. In fact, if a comparison is made on a strength/weight basis, the specimens out-perform mild steel. However, these are the 'with-grain' properties of 'clear' timber. Tests for shear strength and compression perpendicular to the grain, give markedly lower results. Going back to the bundle of straws analogy, shear strength is related to the rubber bands, modelling the relatively weak bonding effect of the cells in the radial direction, and a compression force perpendicular to the grain crushes the straws, which represent the cell walls. Results from shear strength tests average only 10–15% of the bending strength. In compression perpendicular to the grain there is no failure as such, and the tests usually performed are based on the surface penetration of the timber by a steel dye with a rounded point. These give strengths which are in the order of 10% of the compression strength parallel to the grain. It is also obvious by now that timber has relatively little strength in tension

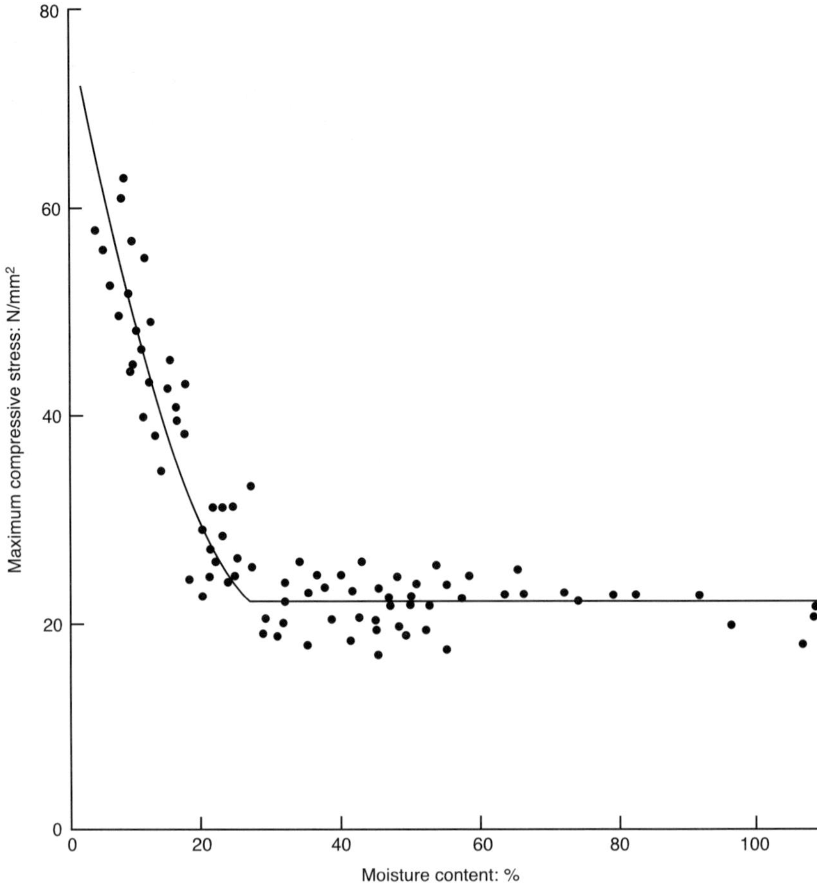

Fig. 3.8 The relation of maximum compressive strength to moisture content. Timber species—Douglas fir

perpendicular to the grain, and is sometimes subject to local failure as a result of drying shrinkage.

In summary, we find that the material properties of clear timber are related to the direction of grain. It is very strong for its weight in

- bending
- compression
- tension

but significantly weaker in

- shear
- compression perpendicular to the grain
- tension perpendicular to the grain.

Strength is also dependent upon

- density (increasing as density increases)
- moisture content (increasing as the MC decreases)
- duration of load (increasing as load duration shortens).

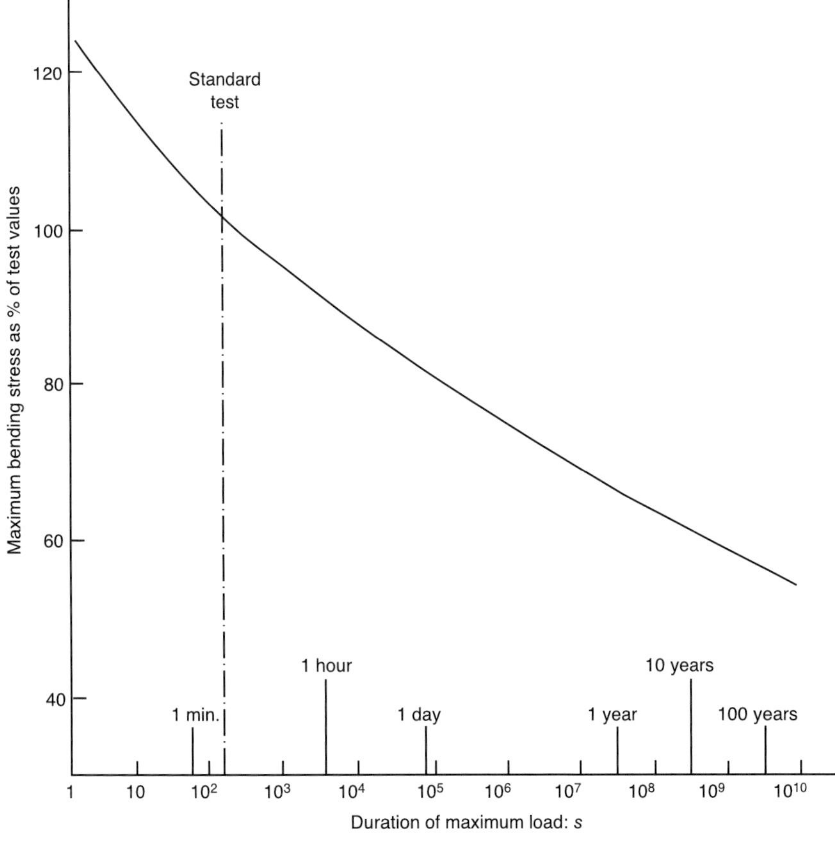

Fig. 3.9 The relation between maximum bending stress and duration of load (the Madison Curve)

Strength-reducing defects

All these tests have been based upon small clear specimens, which are convenient for laboratory work. Structural timbers are much larger, and because of their size inevitably include some of the characteristics of growth which will reduce the member strength, and which are generally known as defects. Principal defects are noted below.

- *Knots* The effect of a knot is locally to produce a marked disturbance in the line of the grain. Going back to the model of the drinking straws, it is obvious that this weakens the piece as a whole, more particularly in tension, since lateral compressive and tensile forces are needed to divert axial forces along the grain lines (Fig. 3.10(a)). If the knot is near the centre of the piece there is more chance of mobilising these forces than if the knot is nearer the edges, or margins. In addition, the grain line of an edge knot is generally 'cut' by the edge of the piece, which further reduces the strength.
- *Wane* A term for missing timber, generally at an arris (the edge of the member), stemming from an over-ambitious attempt to cut a rectangle from a circle (Fig. 3.10(b)). Wane is seen more on older timbers, and often relates to the removal of sapwood.

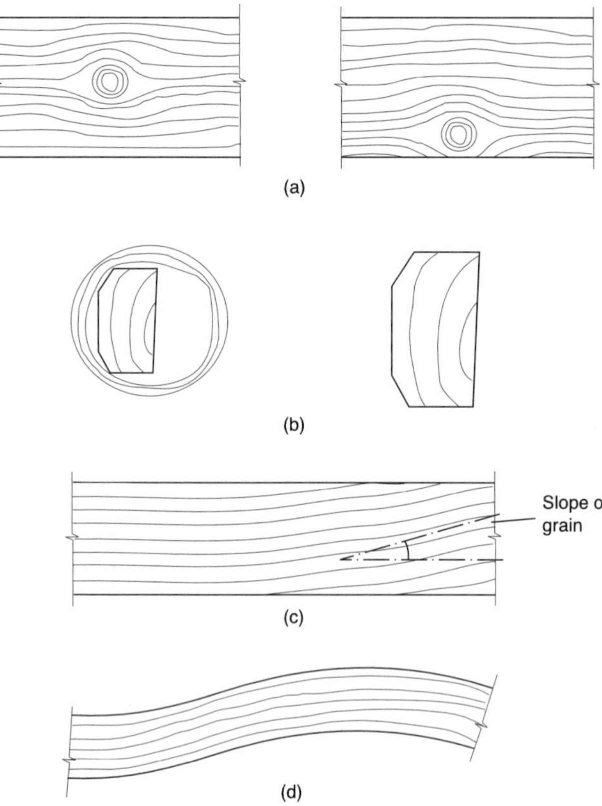

Fig. 3.10 Defects in timber

- *Slope of grain* Since the test specimens were small, it was possible to align their faces with the grain. When sawing a structural piece from a trunk which may be slightly curved or bowed, the grain will lie at an angle to the face for some part of its length (Fig. 3.10(c)). Cutting across the fibres again reduces the strength of the piece. It should be noted, however, that much medieval timber was split, rather than sawn. Examples can be seen of decorative braces where the line of the grain has determined the line of the piece, giving a slope of grain which is effectively zero, and optimising its strength (Fig. 3.10(d)). Hanging knees for timber ships were cut from the trunk and a principal branch in order to turn the angle while giving the piece strength, and the technique of cleaving, or following the grain, is still employed today for some fencing work. The technique should also improve durability as the surface contains less cut cells and, hence, is less likely to absorb water.
- *Rate of growth* The rate of growth of a tree, and the proportion of early to late wood, influence the density of the timber which, as we have seen, determines its basic strength. For softwoods a high growth rate, shown by wide growth rings, produces lower density timber. For hardwoods, however, the reverse is true.
- *Fissures and splits* As has been seen in section 3.3 the tendency for timber, especially the larger sections which include the heart of the tree, is to

develop fissures as the timber dries, and they result primarily, as would be expected, in loss of shear strength. Where the fissure is parallel to the lines of principal stresses, such as compression or bending, and the shear stress is not particularly high, there is generally no significant loss of strength.

- *Distortion* Again, a result of drying shrinkage. The distortion of the cross-section has already been described, but if the slope of grain changes along the piece, then drying distortion can also take place in its length. However, this longitudinal distortion can largely be controlled by keeping the piece to line while seasoning.

Timber grades

Since timber is a naturally variable material, some form of grading system is necessary in order that the material can be bought and sold. The problem is that timber comes from different parts of the world and is required for a great variety of end uses.

The bulk of our softwood is supplied by the Scandinavian countries, Russia, America and Canada. For some time each has had its own grading rules, of a rather general character, supplemented by the mark of the mill on the end of each piece. While of passing interest, these rules are of no particular use to the engineer. In the 1952 edition of CP 112, the UK pioneered a grading system designed specifically for structural work, allocating permissible stresses to a series of grades, each of which was defined specifically in terms of allowable values for the defects described above.

Although CP 112 is now a superseded document, the rules have been mentioned because they can still be of use in the strength evaluation of existing timber (see appendix 3). However, they were never generally accepted by the trade for the sale of new timber because the grades related to the function of the piece within the structure. Thus, a particular piece was graded for specific use as a beam, a tension or compression member, which led to obvious marketing difficulties. In addition, the grade defects did not always fit the range of timber quality which was available, and there was an unacceptable reject rate in attempting to find timber for the higher grades.

In order to overcome the objections to the CP 112 grading rules, BS 4978 *Timber grades for structural use* was first published in 1973. The current edition (1996) relates only to softwoods. It describes two grades which can be used for any structural element, and for which grade stresses are given in the timber design code. A system of identification has been introduced in which the grade and the identification of the grader is stamped on each piece. Since the timber is graded by inspection, this is referred to as a visual grading system. It is necessary for the grader to turn the piece over, and visualise the shape of each knot cluster and the area of the cross-section which it takes up. It is thus known as a knot area ratio (KAR) system, and can only be applied effectively by graders who have been specifically trained in its use.

In the early 1960s a prototype machine was developed which had the potential to grade timber mechanically, at a much faster rate than could be achieved by visual inspection. Grades which are allocated by machine have the prefix 'M'.

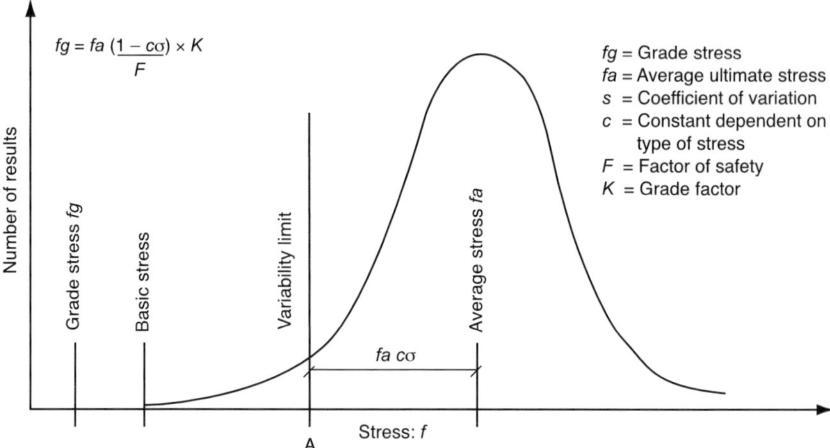

Fig. 3.11 Derivation of grade stress from small clear test results

It relied on the correlation between the modulus of elasticity on the minor axis and the modulus of rupture on the major axis. Following the commercial development of these machines, from 1984 on, BS 5268: Part 2 now includes machine grades which, together with the visual grades, are those in current use.

The derivation of grade stresses

A glance at the permissible stresses in the table from CP 112 shows that they are very much lower than the results of tests quoted previously. It is helpful to understand how the one is derived from the other. Figure 3.11 shows a typical distribution of test results on small clear specimens of redwood in bending. Line A shows the value below which 1% of the results would be expected to fall. A global factor of 2·44 is applied to this value to cover for the effects of size, moisture content and duration of loading, in addition to an overall factor of safety. This gives a basic stress which would be applicable to a piece of full-size clear timber. The grade stresses for CP 112 represent numerically a percentage of that basic stress. The grade stresses in the current code were not related to tests on small clears, but derived directly from tests on structural size timbers, with the aim of providing the same order of safety with a greater degree of reliability.

3.6. The behaviour of timber in fire

The process of burning is a series of rapid chemical reactions between the timber (the fuel) and oxygen (in the air). The process produces heat (and light, as visible flames). For combustion to occur, fuel, air and heat must all be present; the process terminates on the removal of any one.

When timber is heated, gases are released; mainly incombustible carbon dioxide and combustible carbon monoxide. It is the gas which first burns, and not the timber itself. For the vapours to ignite, there is normally a source of ignition. This would happen at around 250–300°C. If there is no ignition source, but the temperature increases, then spontaneous ignition may occur, as happens when a fire radiates heat onto a remote piece of timber. Once ignited, the burning vapours will now heat up adjacent timber, and the process continues. The heat transfer from the flame to unburnt material is mainly by radiation from the flame, and convection from the burning vapours. Changing the orientation of a burning match from the horizontal to the vertical demonstrates the different modes of heat transfer. Because timber is a good insulant, conduction of heat back into the unburnt material plays a minor role.

As the gases burn off, the residue, charcoal, is largely pure carbon. The charcoal intumesces in its formation, expanding in volume and creating microscopic voids. As such, it is an excellent insulant, and the timber a short distance behind the charring layer is virtually undamaged. This has the effect of controlling the rate at which combustion occurs, and many tests have shown a linear relationship between charring depth and time, which, for a particular temperature, is known as the charring rate.

3.7. Commercial supply

The designer or repairer of a building, in the past as today, has certain requirements for any structural timber which is required for the work of repair in terms of its

- species
- strength
- moisture content
- durability
- appearance

and seeks to meet those requirements from the commercially available material in terms of

- availability
- size/quantity/quality
- price.

The specification of timber for repair work is dealt with in more detail in chapter 16, but the broad aim is to specify the minimum requirements of the material, which nevertheless remain within the field of potential supply. The three broad fields of supply are summarised below.

Softwoods

Softwoods became increasingly available from the seventeenth century onwards, being imported from the ports around the Baltic sea, and from America and Canada. While they were not as durable as oak, they were adequate for the predominantly covered applications in which timber was used from this time on and, in addition, they were much cheaper, an advantage which they have held to the present day. The mass of the tree is concentrated in the trunk, which is generally straight, and so the trees produce a relatively high yield when cut for carpentry work. The size of timbers seen in buildings within the UK increases through the eighteenth and nineteenth centuries, culminating in the very large baulks seen in some of the dock warehouses. The increase in size relates primarily to the growth of the technology of transportation and lifting, although the largest pieces are nearly always *Pinus sylvestris* or Baltic redwood. Equivalent cross-sections in this species (up to 400 mm square) are difficult to obtain, and the only species commonly obtainable today in large sections is Douglas fir from North America.

The current supply position is that softwood (generally including sapwood and with mixed species) is readily available in preferred sizes up to 300 mm × 75 mm × 5 m, and this timber will be generally <20% MC. Larger sizes than this, except as noted above, will need to be put as enquiries to suppliers.

Glued laminated timber is available in a range of stock sizes in straight lengths, or can be fabricated to order in a variety of profiles, which can additionally be tapered or curved.

Tropical hardwoods

Few people these days can be unaware that the tropical hardwoods are an environmental issue, although both sides—the environmentalists and the timber trade—tend to simplify what in reality is a very complex situation. In effect we are asking the third world not to do what Europe and America did respectively 1000 and 200 years ago, that is, to clear forests. I have not written further on this subject since, for the reasons given below, only a very small percentage of structures built at any time have made significant use of tropical hardwoods. Particular cases will have to be argued on their merits.

As a generality, the timbers are denser and darker in colour than the softwoods. The most well-known (mahogany, aformosia, teak) have, in addition, a very beautiful figure and, as a consequence, have generally been priced out of the building field, being used mainly for joinery and furniture. They are more diverse in character than the softwoods, but the common species are as strong or stronger—in some cases, such as ekki, keruing or greenheart, considerably so—but large sections and lengths are only available in a few species.

Larger sections may be obtained by laminating, but again checks must be made on the species properties, as not all are suitable. The usual choice for laminated work is iroko, which has very small movements due to moisture content changes, good gluing properties, and is very durable, as indeed are many of the hardwoods. For this reason, their prime use in the construction field is for external structures such as bridges and jetties, which lie outside the scope of this book.

Temperate hardwoods

The temperate hardwoods are also a diverse grouping, but for structural work oak has predominated due to a combination of availability, durability and appearance. It is a beautifully figured timber, stronger than the softwoods, but inevitably, given the alternative uses of the timber, is more expensive.

The supply position for structural sizes is very different to the softwoods. Virtually no stocks are held, and so it must be accepted that the timber normally supplied will be green, or unseasoned. Oak is a medium-movement timber, which means that shrinkage and distortion of the cross-section on drying will be more pronounced than for the softwoods.

For members less than, say, 300 mm × 100 mm × 4 m seasoned material, largely free of fissures, may be purchased from some suppliers and boards of 75 mm or less may be kiln dried. Both these alternatives, however, will increase the supply price by a considerable factor. It is possible to laminate oak from kiln-dried pieces.

Further reading

Hoadley (1980) gives a good account of the properties of timber although he is primarily interested in wood for craft use. The properties of timber for structural use are best covered by Desch and Dinwoodie (1996).

4

Eltham Palace, London. The hammer-beam roof of the Great Hall, begun by Edward IV in 1475.

4

Timber in the building environment

We have seen (in section 3.3) that the MC of timber is a response to the local ambient RH, and that timber which has an MC of 20% or above for an extended period is potentially at risk of fungal attack. Whether the attack materialises or not depends also on the timber's natural durability, and whether or not preservative treatment or a protective coating has been applied, but for the moment let us separate these factors and consider first the risk of attack due to the local environment.

4.1. Hazard classes

Both BS 5268 (Part 5) and EN 335 (Part 1) define a series of *hazard classes*; environments which progressively increase the risk of fungal attack. They are aimed, as are the majority of Standards, at new building, so I have introduced some sub-classes of my own which relate to existing structures.

Hazard class 1

This is the situation in which the timber is under cover, fully protected from the weather and not exposed to wetting.

This class could be summarised as a dry interior situation, with temperatures mainly above, and never substantially below, freezing and with only small air movements that nevertheless prevent a build-up of RH due to occupancy. The design aim of modern buildings, with damp-proof courses and cavity walls, is to put all the interior structural timber into this class, which will render it immune to fungal attack. It is useful to define two sub-classes

- *Class 1A*: areas heated for occupancy, e.g., first floor joists, internally exposed frames, or beams below an insulated roof. These members will normally achieve an equilibrium MC of around 10%, with an annual range of 8–12%.
- *Class 1B*: timber in unheated areas, such as suspended ground floor joists, or timbers in cold roofs (but both in ventilated spaces). The equilibrium

MC of these members will normally be around 12–14%, fluctuating by a few per cent between summer and winter.

Hazard class 2

Here the situation is as class 1, that is, under cover and protected from the direct effects of the weather, but where high environmental humidity could lead to occasional but not persistent wetting.

This class brings the risk of fungal attack. The high humidities could stem from three sources: human occupation, faults in the fabric, or faults in the building services. This leads us to three sub-classes

- *Class 2A*: cold areas with lack of ventilation, such as poorly ventilated roofs with insulation at ceiling level, or suspended ground floor joists, where the air bricks in the external walls have either been omitted, or accidentally covered over.
- *Class 2B*: lack of impermeability of the external fabric. This class is probably the most significant cause of rot in constructional timber. For buildings particularly of the nineteenth century and earlier, three forms of construction are inherently vulnerable

    - parapet gutters
    - solid walls with built-in timbers
    - walls without damp-proof courses.

  Other elements of fabric, while reliable in principle, may contain defects such as

    - cracked or missing tiles
    - blocked hopper heads or broken down-pipes
    - deflective stack flashings
    - cracks in wall render.

  The building-in of softwood joist ends to solid walls is probably the major cause of rot in properties of the nineteenth century and earlier. The damp-proof course and the cavity wall came increasingly into use after the first World War, and resulted in a marked reduction of the decay risk of the internal timber, in effect placing most joist ends in Class 1B. The timber flat roof, however, especially as it was often detailed and constructed in the 1960s (perhaps even in conjunction with a Class 2A environment), placed the whole of the roof structure firmly in Class 2B.

  Since the source of moisture in most cases is related to rainfall or the climate, the timber MC will vary, sometimes going above 20%, sometimes dropping below. Fungal growth is not necessarily inevitable, and may even start, only to die.
- *Class 2C*: leaks from building services, at least those which are minor enough otherwise to escape detection.

It should also be remembered that from the 1960s on, board materials, based on timber, came increasingly into use. The most obvious example is the application of chipboard to domestic floors and some flat roofs. The material is much more moisture-susceptible than solid timber, principally in relation to the binder (which is generally only a moisture resistant glue) with the consequent risk of loss of integrity as well as rot.

Hazard class 3

In this class the wood or wood based product is not covered and not in contact with the ground. It is either continually exposed to the weather or is protected from the weather but exposed to frequent wetting.

This class relates to timber which is exposed to the sun, with constant air movement, variations in temperature which include occasional sub-zero periods, and spells of rain. Naturally, the surface layers of the timber show larger and more rapid changes in MC than timber in Classes 1 and 2, with a tendency for small fissures to develop. The sub-classes relate to the degree of surface retention.

- *Class 3A*: vertical or near-vertical surfaces. These will shed rain rapidly, with a minimum of retention.
- *Class 3B*: horizontal surfaces. Less well-drained, and checks or fissures will retain water for a period.
- *Class 3C*: upward-facing rebates. These will act as a reservoir.

Hazard class 4

Here the timber is in contact with the ground or fresh water, and thus is permanently exposed to wetting.

- *Class 4A*: ground level. For timber in this location, a permanent supply of moisture will retain the MC of at least the contact face above 20%, and fungal attack, in the long term, is inevitable. Most barns which had a sole plate in contact with the earth have had them replaced long ago, or have been lifted up and a few courses of brick inserted.
- *Class 4B*: below ground level. If the timber is not just in earth contact, but driven deep as a pile permanently below the level of the water table, then the almost complete lack of oxygen (and very high moisture content) would virtually inhibit any fungal growth.

  Many well-known structures well over 100 years old are still standing on timber piles, including the High Level Bridge in Newcastle, and Tobacco Dock, London. During the course of the recent refurbishment of the Dock one pile was excavated and found to be in good condition.

Hazard class 5

This situation occurs when the timber is permanently exposed to salt water.

While of only passing interest to builders, salt water introduces the possibility of attack by *Teredo Navalis* (the shipworm) or gribble, which are more active in tropical rather than temperate climates. Greenheart is the species which is most resistant, but metal sheathing (as English ships were copper-bottomed) is sometimes used for protection.

Figure 4.1 illustrates these different classes. The areas of higher risk are generally concealed from view, and it is for this reason that most structural appraisals will require some local opening-up.

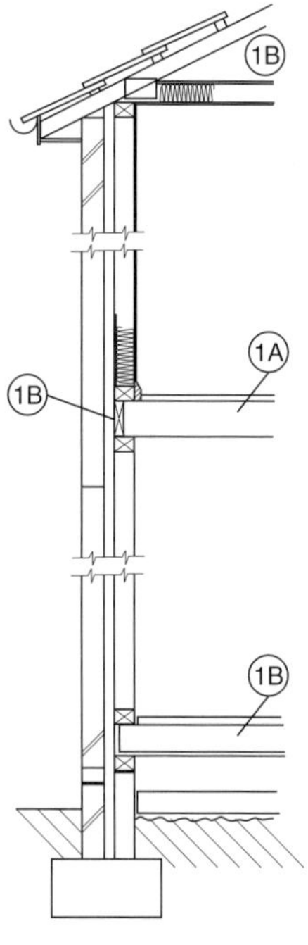

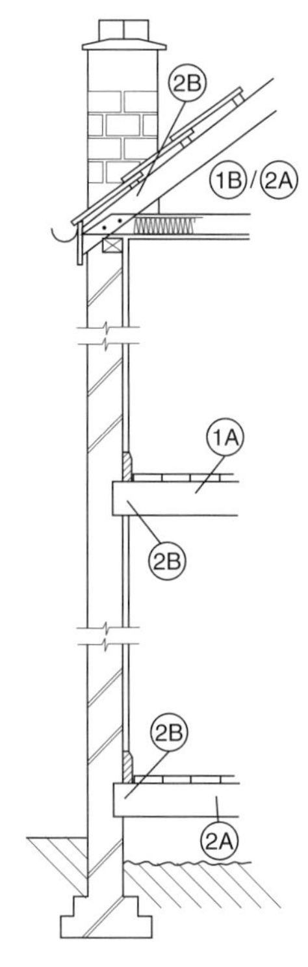

(a)

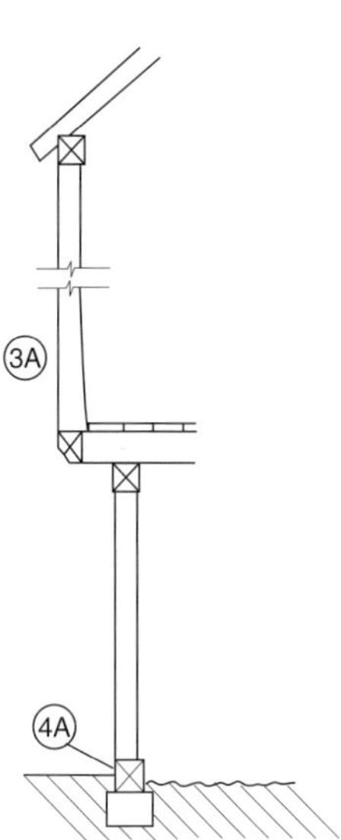

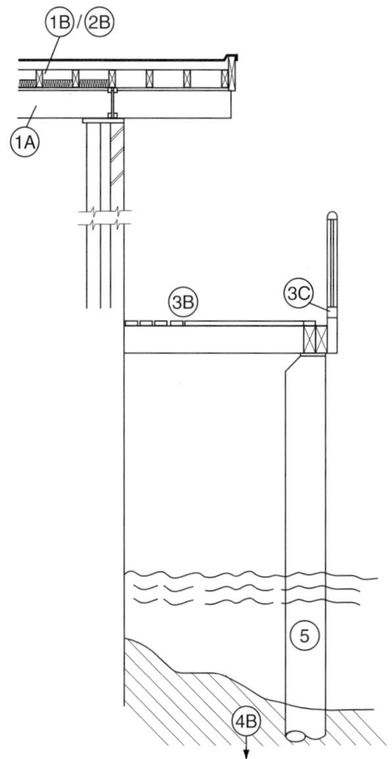

(b)

Fig. 4.1 Examples of the location of the various hazard classes

4.2. Natural durability

As already noted in section 3.4, the natural durability of heartwood varies between species. In the UK, tests were carried out by cutting 50 × 50 mm stakes of selected species, driving them into the ground, and testing them at yearly intervals for failure. This resulted in five durability grades, which are shown in Table 3.1, together with the durability classification of common structural species.

Remember that the durations relate only to the test, and are a basis for comparison only. Remember also that all sapwood is either perishable or non-durable. While it is common to find oak structures built only with heartwood, the possible presence of sapwood must be remembered for most softwood structures. In a few species, such as Douglas fir, the sapwood can be distinguished visually from the heartwood on end section, but it is often difficult to identify sapwood on the face in installed timbers.

4.3. Preservative treatments

For structures of softwood built relatively recently, it is possible that the timber has been treated with some form of preservative prior to installation. The three major preservative types are

- creosote
- CCA (copper/chromium/arsenic)
- OS (organic solvent)

which might have been applied to the timber by

- brush
- immersion
- vacuum/pressure treatment.

Creosote, which is still the most effective preservative, is unlikely to have been used internally, in view of its powerful smell and tendency to bleed following pressure application. CCA generally has a slight green colour, and can be used on externally exposed timber, while OS is colourless but tends to leach out of the timber, and therefore needs, for example, a paint protection when used externally.

Brush application results in negligible penetration of the timber, and immersion only marginally more so, although end grain, as one would expect, is around ten times more absorbent than side grain. Given this lack of absorbency, vacuum and pressure techniques were developed between the wars, which were able to penetrate measurable distances into the timber, and significantly improve its durability. Laboratory tests can be made for depth of penetration and amount of retention of preservative on, for example, small core samples. However, timbers vary in their permeability, shown for typical species in Table 3.1. Those which are extremely resistant cannot be penetrated by preservative to any effect.

4.4. Protective coatings

The lightest protective coating normally applied to timber is a surface sealer. Coatings which actually build up a thickness include varnishes and paints. These act as a water barrier but, because of the moisture-related movements of timber, are liable to local failure and require maintenance on a four- or five-year cycle.

4.5. The performance of timber in relation to environmental conditions

Hazard class 1: means that there is no risk of rot, even to non-durable species or to timber containing sapwood.

Hazard class 2: is the most difficult class to prejudge because of the difficulty of estimating the permeability of the surrounding fabric. It is particularly important, therefore, to check a building for any timber which might be in this class.

Hazard class 3: applies to the exterior of the building. As a generality, timbers which are 'durable' or better (with no sapwood on the external face) should achieve 60 years or more, (considerably more in the case of some timber framed houses) and 'moderately durable' timbers, 40 years. Accurate predictions are not possible, because building details, i.e., the difference between classes 3A and 3C, will significantly affect the service life. The softwoods generally, being non-durable and often with a proportion of sapwood, will start to show signs of decay after 10 or 15 years unless they are painted or preserved. The exception is, of course, western red cedar, a timber of relatively low strength which is sometimes used for domestic structures such as conservatories, verandahs and walkways.

Preserving softwood by pressure treatment (only possible before assembly) will make it 'durable'. However, any cutting or shaping which takes place after preservation will penetrate the zone of the preservative, often at a vulnerable point, such as the framing of an upright into a cill. For preservation to be effective, therefore, it must be applied to the profiled member.

Hazard class 4: ground contact, is the most severe hazard class. Fence posts always fail at ground level—above, the post is too dry, and below ground too wet. The transition zone will inevitably produce at some point the optimum moisture content for the development of rot.

Timber properties and preservative treatments for the design of timber in different building locations are given in BS 5268: Part 5 for structural work and in BS 5589 for non-structural work.

5

The Guildhall, Thaxted, Essex. A medieval three-storeyed frame in oak, with a double jetty on three sides.

5

Building legislation

An appraisal of anything other than the most simple structural problem requires some knowledge of the law relating to buildings. This is a large field, which is currently getting larger, particularly in the areas of health and safety. For present purposes I have confined myself to four aspects of legislation

- the Building Regulations themselves
- loading
- fire
- listed buildings.

5.1. The Building Regulations

Laws controlling the erection and form of buildings have existed, as has been seen, since before the Great Fire of London. For centuries, each major city had its own building byelaws, most taking those of London as their model. In 1976 this system was rationalised, resulting in the issue of the Building Regulations covering England and Wales, with separate Regulations for Scotland and Northern Ireland.

In 1985 the Regulations were radically revised, resulting in the document form that we are familiar with today. The areas of concern are now restricted to public health and safety, energy conservation, and the welfare and convenience of disabled people. The Regulations are expressed as a schedule of functional requirements under a series of lettered headings, or parts (Table 5.1). They apply, as noted previously, to works of building; either new works, extensions, 'material' alterations, or a change of use. It follows from this that existing buildings *per se* are not covered by the Regulations, and neither are routine works of repair, maintenance, nor replacing like with like. Material alterations are defined as any work which by itself would adversely affect the existing structure in relation to parts A, B1, B3 and B4. This would mean, for instance, that if a loft conversion was proposed for a timber framed house which would increase the load on the stud walls, then these walls would then come within the scope of the Regulations (in relation to the parts noted above).

Regulation 5 defines a 'material' change of use, i.e., one which would bring the structure, or elements of it, within the scope of the Regulations. In

Table 5.1. The parts of the Building Regulations. Approved documents

A1	Loading
A2	Ground movement
A3	Disproportionate collapse
B1	Means of escape
B2	Internal fire spread (linings)
B3	Internal fire spread (structure)
B4	External fire spread
B5	Access and facilities for the fire service
C1	Preparation of site
C2	Dangerous and offensive substances
C3	Subsoil drainage
C4	Resistance to weather and ground moisture
D1	Cavity insulation
E1	Airborne sound (walls)
E2	Airborne sound (floors and stairs)
E3	Impact sound (floors and stairs)
F1	Means of ventilation
F2	Condensation in roofs
G1	Sanitary convenience and washing facilities
G2	Bathrooms
G3	Hot water storage
H1	Sanitary pipework and drainage
H2	Cesspools and tanks
H3	Rainwater drainage
H4	Solid waste storage
J1/2/3	Heat producing applicances
K1	Stairs and ramps
K2	Protection from falling
K3	Vehicle barriers
M1	Interpretation
M2	Access and use
M3	Sanitary conveniences
M4	Audience or spectator seating
N1 & N2	Glazing—safety in relation to impact, opening and cleaning

general, a material change of use is defined as one which involves

- the provision of sleeping accommodation
- a use which is not exempt, although the previous use was exempt
- use as a public building.

A change of use which involves an increase in superimposed loading will also bring the load-bearing elements within the scope of the Regulations.

Although I have said that repairs are not covered by the Regulations, this is obviously a matter of degree. The guidance manual to the Regulations, issued originally in 1985, explains that where a whole building has been seriously damaged, perhaps by fire, the local authority may consider that it should be treated as a new building, and the Regulations will apply. If in doubt it is better to make an enquiry.

Each lettered part of the Regulations subject is covered in a separate volume (an Approved Document) which first states the relevant Regulations, and then indicates ways in which they may be met. If, in the context of this book, we look at Part A, we find that the Regulation itself is quite short; so short, in fact, that it may be quoted in full

Loading

A1. (1) The building shall be constructed so that the combined dead, imposed and wind loads are sustained and transmitted by it to the ground:–

(a) safely; and
(b) without causing such deflection or deformation of any part of the building, or such movement of the ground, as will impair the stability of any part of another building.

(2) In assessing whether a building complies with sub-paragraph (1) regard shall be had to the imposed and wind loads to which it is likely to be subjected in the ordinary course of its use for the purpose for which it is intended.

Ground Movement

A2. The building shall be constructed so that ground movement caused by:–

(a) swelling, shrinkage or freezing of the subsoil; or
(b) landslip or subsidence (other than subsidence arising from shrinkage), in so far as the risk can be reasonably foreseen, will not impair the stability of any part of the building.

The rest of the document gives 'deemed-to-satisfy' ways of complying with the basic Regulation.

It is important to realise the distinction between the Regulation itself, and approved ways of complying with it. I have read reports which state that an eighteenth century floor 'does not comply with the Building Regulations' despite the fact that it has transmitted its load safely for 200 years. The demonstration of strength verification is dealt with in more detail in chapter 11.

The Regulations have, of course, changed over the years. Although an existing building may not comply with the current edition, it is more likely to comply with the Regulations as they were when it was actually built. Thus, we would expect an eighteenth century town house to have solid brick walls, with the thicknesses described in the Byelaws of the time for the various classes of dwelling. Even the post-war period has seen significant changes in the requirements, for instance, in the conservation of fuel and power. A timber flat roof built in the 1960s, for example, would probably have only a nominal amount of insulation material built into the construction, which would be well below the current standard. As explained earlier, this 'existing building' does not come within the scope of the later revisions, and the owner is not obliged to upgrade it.

5.2. Loading

Section 4 of Approved Document A lists the loading standards for the design of new buildings.

Superimposed loads

The loadings required under the Regulations most relevant to timber floors are given in Table 5.2. Originally given in Byelaws, they were first published in CP3: Chapter V: Part 1 in 1967, and then in BS 6399: Part 1, without essential change.

These will apply to existing buildings if they are altered or extended, or where there is a change of use. If an eighteenth century domestic building, for instance, is converted to offices, the timber floors would need to be assessed for an imposed load of 2·5 kN/m^2. While it might be possible to justify this level of loading (see section 11.1), the task has been made more difficult in the post-war years by the fashion for proposing much higher loads, in the order of 5 kN/m^2. These were promoted when, in the early days of the computer revolution, it was thought that the equipment was going to become progressively heavier, together with a general ideal of flexibility of use. The proposals were made primarily in the context of new-build offices with floors of reinforced concrete. Apart from the floors in old mills and warehouses, it would be very unlikely that timber could be justified for this level of loading. Fortunately, recent work initiated by Stanhope Properties (1992), together with surveys carried out by BRE, have shown that the Regulation loading of 2·5 kN/m^2 is more than adequate for general use, given that small areas for higher loadings can be made available within the building as a whole. This approach is commended by English Heritage (Hume, 1994).

Snow

Snow loadings were defined for many years in CP3 as 0·75 kN/m^2 on plan over the whole country. BS 6399: Part 3 improved this rather simplistic picture with a snow map graded from 0·3 kN/m^2 in the South of England to 1·0 kN/m^2 in parts of Scotland, together with rules for calculating a possible surcharge from drifting snow, which were introduced following an actual collapse of a lightweight sheeted roof.

As noted in chapter 3, the strength of timber relates to the duration of loading. A 25% lift in design stresses is allowed for snow loads.

Table 5.2. Loadings required under the Building Regulations for floors

Occupancy	*Imposed load (kN/m^2)*	*Concentrated load (kN)*
Domestic	1·5	1·4
Offices	2·5 minimum	2·7
Assembly without fixed seating	4·0	4·5

Wind

Post-war buildings will have been designed to the requirements of CP3: Chapter V: Part 2, now BS 6399: Part 2, using pressures which are normally based on a 50-year return period. The timber code allows up to a 75% lift in the design stresses for the effect of short-term gusts. For pitched roofs, this will mean that the wind load case is rarely critical, but uplift is still a major consideration for flat roofs. Wind loading of the building as a whole would also require consideration of the sidesway resistance.

5.3. Fire

The requirements in relation to fire are given in Approved Document B. They are concerned with the preservation of life, rather than building fabric, under five headings

- B1 – means of escape
- B2 – spread of flame (internal linings)
- B3 – periods of fire resistance
- B4 – spread of flame (external envelope)
- B5 – access for fire fighting.

In the appraisal of timber structures, we are concerned mainly with B2 and B3. As with Part A, the body of the document gives 'deemed-to-satisfy' ways of complying with the Regulations. The 1992 edition also recognised that

> *a fire safety engineering approach that takes into account the total fire safety package can provide on alternative approach to fire safety.*

This is important, for the guidance given in the Document is sometimes rather restrictive, particularly in relation to older buildings.

Spread of flame

In order to inhibit the spread of fire within a building as required by B2, section 6 of the Document defines classifications of wall and ceiling linings in relation to purpose groups. Floors are excluded, since they play little part in the development of a fire until a late stage.

The classifications are based on BS 476: *Method for classification of surface spread of flame of products*. The tests themselves are described in Part 7: *Fire tests on building materials and structures*, and are based on the extent of travel of a flame front in a given time under standard conditions.

The Regulations allow walls and ceilings of smaller rooms ($<30\,m^2$) to be class 3. Larger spaces require lower classes. The surface of most timbers (that is, with a density greater than $400\,kg/m^3$) falls into class 3, but a reduction in class may be obtained by either impregnation or the application of proprietary retardants, although these are varnish-like in appearance, and samples should be checked for visual acceptability.

Period of fire resistance

Regulation B3 requires that a building shall be designed and constructed so that in the event of a fire, its stability will be maintained for a reasonable period (together with other requirements for party walls, compartmentation and cavity stops). These periods are defined in the Document for various elements of structure in Table A2 of Appendix A.

The periods of resistance which relate to conventional timber structures range from 30 minutes for ordinary dwellings, to 60 minutes for two and three storey flats and buildings for public assembly. Roof structures as such are not required to have a minimum period of fire resistance, but if the roof supports other elements, such as walls, then the minimum period of resistance for the supported element must be attained.

The elements of a timber structure will, in general, fall under one of the three headings

- no period of resistance is required (e.g., a roof)
- elements which have applied fire protection (e.g., stud partitioning covered with lath and plaster or plasterboard)
- exposed elements, which are required to have some period of fire resistance.

In this third case the fire resistance of exposed timber structures is covered by Part 4 of BS 5268. Section 4.1 describes the method of calculating the fire resistance of timber members. It is based on the 'charring rate', that is, the rate at which timber would char in the fire resistance test described in BS 476: Part 8. The rate is actually a function of timber density, but for simplicity single rates are quoted for softwood and hardwood. The method is to determine the residual section after a period of fire using the charring rate, and then to check this residual section for strength, using enhanced strength and more generous deflection criteria.

For glulam members assembled with formaldehyde adhesives, the charring rate may still be applied to the full member section, since these adhesives will not lose strength at timber combustion temperatures.

Note that the calculation applies only to simple timber members. No method is given for calculating the period of resistance of joints which depend on metal for their strength, where the metal may be wholly or partly exposed. The recommendation given in this case is to cover the metal with a sacrificial thickness of timber. Fortunately, this condition (apart from roofs, where in general there are no requirements) is relatively rare. The use of intumescent paint on the exposed metal would have to be judged on the individual case.

5.4. Listed buildings

There are around 450 000 listed buildings in England and Wales. The list, or register, is compiled by English Heritage, formally approved by the Secretary of State, and held by the National Monuments Record. The list is arranged by the property address, and each entry includes a short general description of the building.

The list serves the twin purposes of identifying and protecting our inheritance of buildings of special architectural or historical interest. Around 6000 are listed Grade I, defined as of 'exceptional interest', including the great cathedrals and country houses. A further 20 000 or so are listed Grade II*, being of more special interest, and the remainder are listed Grade II.

The demolition or the alteration of the interior or the exterior of a listed building can only be authorised by a specific Grant of Listed Building Consent by the local authority. Penalties for unauthorised demolition allow for an unlimited fine. If the owner allows a listed building to fall into disrepair, the local authority has the power to carry out repairs and charge the owner, or even to take over the building under a Compulsory Purchase Order. These penalties serve to give teeth to a legislation which, for the most part, works by negotiation. It does, however, emphasise that consultation with the local authority is essential for any proposed work to a listed building. This will stand a greater chance of approval if the principles of conservation can be seen to have been understood (see chapter 13).

Further reading

There are several guides to the Building Regulations, including that by Powell-Smith and Billington (1995).

6

St Mary and St James' Church, Wymondham, Norfolk. A spectacular medieval angel roof over Norman arcades.

6

The commission

Most commissions arise out of concern which clients have for particular buildings. It is possible that, in addition, they will have a knowledge and understanding of timber structures, although the balance of probabilities is that they will not. It is most important, therefore, that the concern of a client is properly understood by the engineer, even if it has not, perhaps, been adequately expressed.

6.1. The client's concern

The most common causes for concern can be summarised under five headings: a patent defect, assurance of soundness, proposed alterations/change of use, damage and litigation.

A patent defect

This is probably the most common reason for surveys to be commissioned, with fungal attack being the most common defect. The brief will generally be to determine the nature and extent of the defect, or defects, in some defined area of the building, including necessary investigative work, and to recommend remedial work.

Assurance of soundness

While there may be no evidence of defects, a client requires an assurance as to the condition of the structure, perhaps because it is their intention to purchase or sell the building subject to a satisfactory report. In this case it is implied that the engineer will make a general inspection. To do this meaningfully, even if there are no obvious visible defects, will in most cases still involve some opening-up. The permission required for this will be needed from the owner, who is not necessarily the client.

Proposed alterations, or change of use

In this case it is desirable to have some idea of the client's intentions, since the aim of the appraisal will be to see how well (or how badly) the proposals fit the existing structure. In addition, if the building was constructed before, say, 1850, it will probably be listed, and owners do not then have the freedom to alter the structure as they wish. In this case the commission should include consideration of the possible restrictions which bodies such as English Heritage may impose on any alterations to the fabric.

Damage

Damage may be caused as a result of a storm, an explosion, an impact or, more often, a fire. Damaged structures are often in an unsafe condition which require immediate action to be taken. In addition, the engineer should seek to be informed of the terms of any insurance policy, since they could have a bearing on the options for the remedial work; some policies, for instance, limit the cover on historic fabric to the cost of an equivalent modern building. Insurers may also seek to be informed of any evidence of pre-fire defects, which might be offset against an award.

Litigation

If a client, perhaps through a solicitor, commissions a report for litigation it will mean that, in addition to an appraisal of the defective structure, the engineer will need to comment on the reasons for the present condition and the responsibilities of the parties involved. Work in the field of litigation requires an above average competence and experience, some knowledge of the law, and a willingness, if required, to go into the witness box in court and be cross-examined. Do not take on the work if you do not feel confident on these three points.

Some commissions, while not starting as litigations, may subsequently move in this direction, especially if the survey reveals evidence of possible faulty workmanship in relatively recent construction. It would then be up to the engineer either to accept an extension of the appointment, or to suggest that another expert is appointed for the legal aspect of the work.

6.2. The brief

From all this comes a need, having understood the client's concern, to ensure that the brief is adequately defined. I generally like to visit the building before accepting a commission, and can then, if necessary, clarify the brief in a letter of acceptance. The brief should define the aim of the work, the method of investigation, the scope, and any limitations to the scope of the work such as the level of detail to which the work is undertaken.

It may also be appropriate to obtain the client's agreement to the method of investigation, especially if this involves opening-up, and to inform the client of any limitations to the generality of the conclusions if only a relatively small part of the structure can be inspected. Remember also to keep the client informed during the course of the work if a new direction is suggested, or to seek approval if it appears that the scope of the work (and, hence, the cost) should be extended.

6.3. Conditions of engagement and fees

Most engineers will use the Association of Consulting Engineers Conditions of Engagement, Agreement D—Report and Advisory Services. It provides a simple basis for the contract between the engineer and the client, and should be put forward as such even if, on occasions, clients are unfamiliar with it.

The Agreement allows for fees to be on the basis of a lump sum, time expended, or a combination of the two. Clients these days often ask for a lump sum, and this may be possible to estimate if the scope of the work can be clearly seen and quantified. However, this is not always the case, and most engineers will have a preference for time basis, although it is only fair to give a client some idea of the anticipated costs. This works for both parties, since the client cannot later declare surprise at the fee if it is in line with the budget estimate.

A possible way forward with an intransigent client is to propose that a certain amount of time is expended at an agreed rate to enable the scope of the work to be quantified, and at the end of this period an estimate of the total fee can be given.

7

The Guildhall, Faversham. The arcades of the Guildhall date from 1574. A simple half-lap nineteenth century repair can be seen to the base of the post.

7

The general diagnostic sequence

For all work of appraisal and repair, there is a basic sequence of activities. The sequence is outlined in this chapter, while subsequent chapters deal with each activity in more detail. The appraisal process, like Gaul, is divided into three parts. The first part, the *survey*, is the process of gathering the relevant information. Only then can we make an *appraisal* of the situation, in order to decide what *remedial work* is appropriate. The three activities are generally summarised in a report to the client, who may then give instructions to prepare documents for the repair contract.

7.1. The survey

The aim of the survey is to obtain the relevant information relating to the structure. In general the information falls under three headings

- structural form
- condition
- loading and environmental factors.

The amount of information needed under each heading will relate to the concern which prompted the survey, but it must be sufficient to enable a conclusion to be reached when the structure is appraised. In most cases, the work of survey is initially confined to a visual inspection, preceded by a review of any documentary information which already exists (chapter 8). It is possible that this will provide sufficient information in terms of observed defects (chapter 9), but in the majority of cases some investigative work will be needed (chapter 10).

The condition of the timber in terms of observed defects is often linked to the environmental conditions (chapters 4 and 5), and the defects should not be regarded in isolation.

7.2. The appraisal

From the results of the survey an appraisal can be made; i.e., an assessment of the potential for the various parts of the structure to perform satisfactorily for their expected service life. An appraisal may have to be made under up to six headings

- strength
- stability
- serviceability
- durability
- appearance
- accidental damage.

These headings are considered in more detail in chapter 11.

7.3. Remedial work

When the appraisal has shown that some parts of the structure will not perform satisfactorily for the expected future service life, then remedial work will be required. The different forms are

- repair (locally to a member, or a joint)
- reinforce (add material to reduce the loading on the original frame)
- replicate (new material, in the original form)
- replace (a new, different structure).

Chapter 12 looks at the repair options in more detail, while chapter 13 considers the restrictions which may be put upon the form of the remedial work if the building is listed, and ways of upgrading older structures. A summary of the survey work, the appraisal and remedial proposals is generally presented to the client as a report (chapter 14).

7.4. The repair contract

If the client agrees that the remedial proposals should be implemented, then contract documentation will have to be prepared, and the contract let and supervised (chapter 15). The relatively specialist nature of the work will often mean that quotations will only be invited from contractors experienced in the field, with occasionally a direct nomination.

7.5. Phasing survey work

The sequence given above suggests that all the necessary survey work can be done before an appraisal is made. This ideal situation can perhaps be achieved for an 'open' structure, such as a barn, where access can be obtained to virtually all the members. Even so, there may still be some doubt about the condition of the top face of the rafters if the tiles are still in position.

Most frames are concealed to varying degrees by other elements of fabric, which may, or may not, be capable of removal without causing significant damage, and which may be historically significant in their own right. Thus, in most cases the survey work will be apportioned between the appraisal and the repair contract. This is considered in more detail in chapter 18, although the general principle is that sufficient work must have been done at each stage to warrant the conclusions and recommendations.

8

St John the Baptist's Church, Bere Regis, Dorset. An elaborate and certainly adequate medieval timber roof over largely twelfth century masonry.

8

Initial visual inspection

Even a preliminary walk-around of a building will often give some idea of the general form and construction. Given, for instance, that the property is a late Victorian terrace house, it is likely that the roof is supported by one or two king-post trusses with purlins spanning between them and the party wall. The floors will be in timber, with joists the 'right' way up, and built into walls of solid brick which have shallow corbelled footings. Conversely, a rear extension with a flat roof and stretcher bond brickwork is unlikely to be more than 30 years old.

However, before starting the inspection proper, it is a good idea to see if any information on the building is already available.

8.1. Existing information

As a general rule, drawings were not made for vernacular buildings, and few original drawings exist of most structures up to the early twentieth century. For most post-war buildings some construction drawings, or at least the general arrangements, will have been submitted to the local authority for Building Regulation approval, and it is worth making an enquiry to see if any information is still held. The information may be viewed, but copying will be subject to negotiation. For more recent proprietary timber buildings, drawings may still be retained by the fabricator.

Buildings of significance, such as churches, have often had a basic set of survey plans and elevations made. Fortunately, the idea of measured survey drawings as an aid to maintenance is gaining ground. These drawings, if available, will serve for the general arrangement, but will rarely give construction details such as member sizes and joint details, which will usually have to be determined by inspection.

8.2. The inspection

The extent and level of the information which it is aimed to record will depend upon the nature of the commission. An investigation of a specific defect, or a strength assessment, will require local, detailed information, which could then be put in the context of the building as a whole. A general survey will obviously need to build up the whole picture of the building, but perhaps with less quantitative detail.

Remember that the aim is to determine the form and condition of the structure. General information headings for form would be

- the form and age of the building (chapter 2)
- the general arrangement of the timber elements, leading to
- the principles of stability.

More detailed information would be

- the species group
- member dimensions and gross defects
- joint form: timber/metal/adhesive.

A third level of detail would be

- the member species
- the member grades
- measured joint details.

The condition of the members is normally recorded at the same time, but it is a good discipline to record them as separate concepts. Remember that 'in good condition' is meaningful, but 'in poor condition' is not, unless the defects are described. Condition should be specifically defined by the type and distribution of defects, under the headings listed in chapter 9

- fungal and/or insect attack
- instability
- deterioration
- structural inadequacy
- deformation
- noise transmission and vibration of floors
- accidental damage.

Since very few buildings consist entirely of timber, it is usually necessary to extend a defect survey to the relevant non-timber elements.

8.3. Recording techniques

It is possible that the initial enquiries have produced some drawn information, which can be photocopied for site purposes and checked against the built structure. If not, some drawings will often have to be made at site. For a large repetitive structure, an *ad hoc* grid system is a useful means of reference. There are, in general, four levels of drawings

- general arrangement (location and elevations)
- assembly sections (how elements fit together)
- components (e.g., roof trusses)
- details (e.g., joint profiles).

I work in a fairly conventional manner, drawing on A4 or A3 sheets on a clip-board. If it is appropriate I sometimes draw details to scale, as it provides a check on the work before leaving site.

Accurate recording needs a high level of illumination. Even a good hand torch may be insufficient in a large building, and it is sometimes worth hiring commercial lights for the day, with a portable generator if an electricity supply is not available, or has been switched off.

The modern camera is an invaluable aid to surveying, together with flash gun, although if the light is at all adequate, I prefer to use a stand and long exposures. Again, there are levels of photographs, from the general view to the detailed shot. Have in mind also photographs which would be useful for the report. Remember that, contrary to popular belief, the camera can lie, or at least not tell the whole truth, and it should be used to supplement the visual survey, not replace it.

8.4. Concealed elements of structure

The scope of a purely visual inspection is generally limited in some way, since some elements of the structure may be concealed. The medieval barn is a relatively open structure; however, in a modern timber-framed house only the roof trusses can be seen directly, and even this operation will need access to the loft. Chapter 4 showed that the concealed areas of a frame are the more hazardous environments. For most properties of the eighteenth century and later a purely visual inspection will be heavily qualified unless some opening-up is done. It is important to make the client aware of this, and to seek the necessary permissions.

To minimise permanent damage done to the building by opening it up, the following points should be observed

- capitalise on any existing openings, such as floor boards which have already been lifted and replaced, perhaps for the installation of services
- aim for critical locations, lifting the floorboards against the wall, to allow inspection of the beam ends
- use locations where a repair can be made, such as flat areas of plaster, or behind an architrave or panelling
- maximise the information from small openings, by the use of a car mirror on a stick, or a Borescope (chapter 10)
- cut out where an element has already been damaged.

8.5. Level of inspection

In principle, the level of detail to which the inspection is carried out should be that necessary to achieve the aims of the commission. For a local defect, where some investigative opening-up has been possible, the inspection may have been sufficiently detailed to come to a conclusion on the condition and scope of the remedial work. For a general inspection with limited opportunity for opening-up, the client should be made aware of any limitations to the generality of the conclusions (as already noted in 6.2), together with a way ahead. This might be by further investigative work, either (as noted in 15.1) pre-contract work, or the first phase of the actual contract.

9

St Andrew's Church, Cullompton, Devon. Seven-cant trusses above, with a barrel vault below.

9

The range of possible defects

Timber is a potentially durable building material, as is illustrated by the many framed houses and church roofs of the medieval period which still retain the majority of their original timber. However, an inspection of the structure may reveal defects, some original and some time-related, such as

- fungal and/or insect attack
- instability
- deterioration
- structural inadequacy
- deformation
- noise transmission and vibration of floors
- accidental damage.

9.1. Fungal attack

We have seen (in section 3.4) that the spores of fungi are present in the atmosphere in great quantities, and that there is the possibility of some spores germinating when in contact with moist timber. Examples of timber locations within a building where germination and fungal growth could occur are given in chapter 4. The species of fungi capable of so germinating can botanically be described as white or brown rots. However, for the purposes of structural appraisal they can best be considered under the headings of wet rots, dry rot and the non wood-rotting fungi. Descriptions of the various rots are given in Desch and Dinwoodie (1996), and they are illustrated in Bravery *et al.* (1992).

The wet rots

Those listed below are the most common rots to be found in buildings. They may cause a darkening of the timber (brown rot) or a bleaching (white rot).

- *Coniophora Puteana* (the cellar fungus). A brown rot, which can attack both hardwoods and softwoods. It favours wet conditions, such as those produced by a persistent water leakage. The timber becomes darker, and cuboidal cracking may occur. Mycelium is only present in conditions of high humidity.
- *Fibroporia Vaillantii* (and other *Poria* species). Brown rots, which prefer higher temperatures, and which commonly attack softwoods. Shallow

cuboidal cracking of the wood occurs. The mycelium appears as white or cream sheets, and strands (aggregations of hyphae) remain flexible when dry.

- *Donkioporia Expansa*. A white rot, which attacks hardwoods, particularly oak. Prefers damp conditions, such as the ends of oak beams built into external walls with permeable masonry. The mycelium is a yellow to red-brown thick felted growth.

There are other species than those noted above, and it needs considerable experience and expertise to make a positive identification on site, especially since more than one rot may be associated with a particular outbreak.

As a building defect, however, all the wet rots may be grouped together. They all indicate that the MC of the timber on which they are growing has been well in excess of 20% for a considerable period. Wet rots are unable to colonise any area away from the wet timber. If the source of moisture can be eliminated, then, as the MC gradually drops below 20%, the rot will become quiescent, and eventually die.

Dry rot (*Serpula Lacrymans*)

A brown rot, which for optimum growth requires a 30–40% MC in the timber (somewhat less than the wet rots), although it will not attack timber below 20% MC. It is sensitive to high temperatures (over 25°C) and drying, and is therefore rarely found on exposed timber where fluctuating conditions are likely. It develops on timber in concealed situations, such as non-ventilated suspended floors and behind panelling, adjacent to a source of moisture such as a solid brick external wall. In damp conditions, the developing hyphae appear as fluffy white masses; in drier conditions, they appear as thin grey skin. The fruiting body is plate-like, yellow when young, changing to rust-red as the spores are produced.

In addition, the hyphae are able to form strands, sometimes as thick as a pencil, which can penetrate or grow across timber away from the food source. Although the rot cannot colonise dry timber, it has the ability, from an established growth, to wet timber locally by secreting drops of water from the air (the weeping effect of its name).

These last two properties of dry rot mean that it is much more adept than wet rot at propagating itself, and of surviving attempts to eradicate it which are too localised. For this reason it is generally necessary to distinguish between wet and dry rot.

9.2. Wood-boring insect attack

Relatively few insects are able to use sound timber building components as a food source, and these species are noted below. In addition, some insects are able to feed on damp wood rotted by fungi. Such an infestation would be dealt with in the course of the wood rot treatment. Occasional evidence is sometimes seen of damage caused by insects before the timber was seasoned, which will require no further treatment. As before, they are all described in Desch and Dinwoodie (1996) and well illustrated in Bravery *et al.* (1992)

- *Anobium punctatum* (the common furniture beetle). Can attack softwoods and hardwoods. When the timber is dry, activity is normally confined to the sapwood.
- *Hylotrupes bajulus* (the house longhorn beetle) attacks the sapwood of softwoods. In the UK, it is sufficiently active in and around Surrey to have preventative measures prescribed in the Building Regulations.
- *Xestobium rufovillosum* (the deathwatch beetle) only found in older hardwood timbers, where some moisture has allowed previous fungal attack to take place.

Since beetles are less inclined to attack dry timber, water penetration is still the most significant contributory cause of insect attack, as well as fungal decay.

9.3. Instability

The majority of medieval frames are stabilised by means of triangulating members. Thus, a frame may be potentially unstable if a bracing member is inadequate or missing, or if reliance is placed on tension at a pegged joint.

Domestic construction of the seventeenth century and later generally relies for stability on the interaction between the timber and masonry elements. The walls take the vertical load of the floors and roofs, which in return stabilise the walls horizontally through their diaphragm action. Boards, if double-nailed, function reasonably well as a diaphragm, although an extension of the principle to larger industrial buildings sometimes overstretched the limits of the system.

Relatively recent structures may be stabilised by the diaphragm action of panels of board material fixed along their edges—a form of construction which generally has a high degree of rigidity. Finally, there are elements which are diaphragms by default, such as the infill to the external wall of a frame, although if this is of brick, it is potentially quite rigid.

Roofs normally require some form of bracing—tiling battens will suffice to keep rafters in line, but in aggregate they are a mechanism rather than a diaphragm. Hipped roofs may get sufficient stability from the hips themselves, but gables of masonry, far from stabilising the roof, generally have to be stabilised by it, through the purlins and ridge board. The building-in of purlins often leaves much to be desired, and they may be able to mobilise little more than frictional resistance.

In the early days of trussed rafters, the potential in stability of the gable wall was often overlooked; the components may have been sound, but the stability of the assembly was neglected. The gables were sometimes held only by the oversailing tiling battens, and some failures occurred. Positive ties, with a tension capability, are required both at rafter and ceiling levels. In addition, trussed rafters are themselves very slender. In Scotland it is still the fashion to overnail sarking boards to the rafters—diaphragm action again—but in England and Wales stability is usually achieved by triangulating members nailed to the soffit of the rafters (against 'pack of cards' collapse), and horizontal battens to stabilise slender truss members in compression. Standard bracing arrangements for trussed rafters in housing are given in BS 5268: Part 3.

Potential instability is generally marked by some amount of lateral movement. This may well invoke passive resistance from another building element, which effectively stops the movement, and stability is restored. The critical cases are those where a potential lateral movement would be unresisted, or partly resisted, so that gradual further movement could ultimately lead to failure.

9.4. Deterioration of joints

Joints in most frames are critical areas; there are likely to be concentrations of stress around the fasteners, and the joint itself may be located in an area of high risk. Joints fall into three categories: timber-to-timber, metal fasteners and adhesives.

Timber-to-timber

In profiled joints load concentrations occur around the tenon shoulder, or on the bearing end of a tenon (see Fig. 2.7b). These may show local crushing, if the joint is highly loaded. Joints on the external face of a building can take up water more readily on faces with end grain, which are sometimes subject to local degradation. Timber ends are more prone to splitting, which can sometimes pass through a dowel or bolt hole.

Metal fasteners

Nails, screws and, particularly, bolts are all points of stress concentration, which under load may generate local crushing (more probably, for the larger diameters, across the grain) which is seen as joint slip. Corrosion of both iron and steel is again related to the hazard classes. Those metals in hazard class 1 should show no more than slight surface rusting, but the higher classes will bring with them the increasing possibility of profile loss on the exposed surfaces, or, depending on the timber MC, of the embedded metal.

The pressed metal plate fasteners used for the joints of trussed rafters are only around 1 mm thick, although they are fabricated from galvanised strip. They have generally performed satisfactorily, given that the roof environment has remained in hazard class 1.

In addition to the effects of the contained moisture, green oak is highly corrosive to metal due to the effects of the extractives. Timber freshly treated with CCA preservative is also corrosive. However, both these actions cease when the timber has dried.

Adhesives

Most structural adhesives are used in a factory, as part of the fabrication process of components such as glulam and plyweb beams. This is as it should be, since the essential requirements of any gluing process—the preparation of the surfaces, the ambient temperatures, the pot life of the glue and the contact pressures—are all difficult to control at site. The types and classifications of modern (i.e., post-war) adhesives are given in BS 5268: Part 2. All should perform adequately in hazard class 1 where they are normally used. Urea–formaldehyde (a light-coloured glue line) is only moisture resistant. Hazard classes 2 and 3 require a phenol or resorcinol–formaldehyde (a dark glue line), as well as timber which is at least moderately durable.

If there is evidence of failure, the moisture content of the timber should be checked in relation to the adhesive type. If this is satisfactory, a clean break along the glue line probably indicates an inadequate standard of workmanship in the original assembly. Glued joints are intended for use primarily in shear, and can fail prematurely under direct tension.

9.5. Deformation

All structures deform to some degree under load. Deformation takes several forms; from the simple vertical deflection of a beam, to the horizontal spread of a truss with a raised tie, or the lateral sway of the columns which support it. In assessing the present profile of an element in bending, remember the inherent variability of timber, its E-value, and that creep deflection may be many times the elastic deflection. It is also possible that a medieval frame, either pit sawn or adzed, might not have had originally the mechanical straightness of modern machine-out timber.

Deformation is a serviceability criterion, and is to be distinguished from strength, which is a safety criterion. In general, the Regulations are concerned with the latter, but not the former. In other words, the engineer may be a little more relaxed about deformation *per se*, but not where it might indicate

- associated lack of strength, or overload, requiring a separate strength evaluation
- lack of serviceability in the element itself, e.g., where a floor has deflected to an extent which causes a hazard
- distress in another element, e.g., where a long lintel has deflected and cracked the glass in a window below.

If possible it should also be noted whether the deformation is load-related, or appears permanent. If the principal beam of a floor still shows considerable deflection when cleared of all superimposed load, then it is most likely to have undergone creep. Large deflections are associated with lack of safety by most clients, but for timber this is often not the case.

9.6. Noise transmission and vibration of floors

These factors may sometimes be perceived as defects by owners, and stem from the fact that timber, compared to concrete or steel, is a relatively lightweight material.

Noise transmission

The main sources of noise are surface impact and airborne sound. The medieval open floor, especially with butted boards, gives very little attenuation. Later floors, with a ceiling below, are somewhat better, but many floors of the larger eighteenth and nineteenth century houses have a built in pugging layer of sand or shells laid on boards supported by runners on the main joists, at least for the principal apartments (section 2.3). Some London town houses at the turn of the century even abandoned timber for steel joists with clinker concrete infill, since attenuation of medium and low frequencies is mainly achieved by mass.

The Regulations contain a series of prescriptive assemblies which apply only to party floors (those which separate one dwelling from another). No requirements are given for floors within a dwelling.

Vibration of floors

Judgement as to whether a particular floor has an excessive vibration is, to a large extent, subjective. Although BS 6472 gives acceptability criteria for acceleration (i.e., rate of change of velocity) of the human body in various positions, and it is possible to use an accelerometer and recording equipment to measure the acceleration of a floor under a standard heel-drop test, most people will sense that they are on a timber floor and be more tolerant of vibration than they would be on concrete.

Broadly speaking, the liveliness of a timber floor increases with the span, and with high span-to-depth ratios. The 14 mm limit on floor deflection in BS 5268: Part 2 is an indirect attempt to limit the vibration characteristics of the thinner floors. The conventional floor, with joists spanning in one direction, has a very low stiffness in the transverse direction, and this increases the tendency to vibrate. Thus from the nineteenth century on, herringbone strutting was introduced with the object of increasing the transverse stiffness, and such strutting is required currently by the NHBC for longer span floors. The struts have to be well fixed to be effective. The alternative method is to introduce blocking pieces between the joists, which also need to be tight fitting.

There are several analytical approaches to the calculation of the characteristics of vibration of a timber floor, one of which is contained in Eurocode 5 (DD ENV 1995-1-1: 1994). The difficulty with this method (as with others) is that it is necessary to establish the floor stiffnesses in both directions, and to make an assumption of the damping factor of the whole assembly. In addition, the method is intended for the design of new work and the acceptability criteria may not be appropriate to a particular existing floor.

Complaints of excessive vibration more often stem from some form of slackness in the construction, which gives rise to impact noise under foot traffic. Examples include inadequately fixed floorboards, or board panels with fixings at large centres (an endemic fault of domestic timber construction). It is also possible that the joists have been inadequately built into the walls, or that one joist has been ‘lifted’ by the floorboard fixings and only drops onto the support when loaded.

9.7. Accidental damage

This is a rather general grouping, since, strictly speaking, some of these causes of damage might on occasion have been deliberately conceived. However, they all fall under the heading of events which would not have reasonably been anticipated by the original designer or builder, such as

- overload
- impact or explosion
- strength-reducing alterations
- fire.

Overload

The three basic load cases for most structures relate to superimposed loads, snow and wind. By the middle of this century, these loadings had been reasonably well defined in Codes of Practice. The assumption would be that they had been used for the design of relatively recent structures, unless a survey showed otherwise. Older structures, of course, relied more on rules of thumb and general experience. In these cases, overload may on occasion be caused by a load which today we would define as statistically predictable.

The structural elements of timber which are most vulnerable to wind damage are flat or shallow pitched roofs, when the uplift forces can approach or exceed the dead weight. Failure can then occur if the tie-down straps are inadequately fixed, or have an insufficient dead load anchorage.

Impact or explosion

Impact sufficient to cause structural damage is most likely to be the result of a blast wave emanating from the source, which produces an impulse pressure for a very short period. The pressure is obviously highest at the source of the explosion, dropping proportionately with distance. The response of the various elements of fabric to an impulse depends upon their ductility and their mass. Glass, being brittle and lightweight, is most likely to be damaged. Timber cladding elements, although having some elasticity, are still lightweight and are more likely to suffer damage. Brick walls, although brittle, are less likely to be totally demolished because of their mass, but are vulnerable to cracking.

Strength-reducing alterations

The ease with which timber can be worked becomes something of a disadvantage in the completed building. Holes on the centreline and small notches near the supports of beams may be accepted under the deemed-to-satisfy rules in BS 8103: Part 3: Table 1, but larger interventions, up to the removal of a diagonal member, perhaps to enlarge a window, all need to be recorded and appraised.

Fire

The damage sustained by a building after a fire can be broadly attributed to five causes

- the fire itself
- smoke

- extinguishing water
- other fire fighting activities
- the post-fire condition.

A fire is the most common form of accidental damage. When the fire itself has been put out, the remaining structure may well be in a dangerous condition. Needless to say, the initial survey must be done with caution. The use of a cherry-picker is sometimes a way of surveying with safety.

There is also a need to ensure that members of the public generally are not put at risk. Usually, there are three approaches to making the building safe

- demolition of dangerous elements
- temporary propping
- prevention of access.

Where it is obvious that a dangerous element is damaged beyond repair, then rapid demolition is the simplest option. If, however, the structure is historic, and the degree of damage is not immediately obvious, temporary propping will allow a more detailed inspection to be made. Prevention of access is always a prudent measure, but any barrier should be robust and continuous, and not merely a plastic tape.

Referring back to the building damage

- *The fire* will initially cause charring of unprotected timber members, and then actual loss of section. It is generally held that the timber below the charred layer has not lost significant strength, and could be considered undamaged.

  The movement of the fire (see section 3.6) is determined primarily by convection currents. There is therefore always a strong tendency for the fire to move upward, and it is unusual to find fire damage below the source, unless as a result of structural collapse or of burning material.
- *Smoke* results in the deposition of soot, which is largely carbon. While this will not cause any structural damage, it may be difficult to remove without damaging any applied finishes.
- *Extinguishing water* During the course of a fire large quantities of water will find a way down the building, often well below the seat of the fire, and will be retained by absorbent elements, such as carpets, ceiling plaster and, to a lesser extent, wall plaster.
- *Other fire-fighting activities* The Fire Brigades' first duty is to extinguish the fire, and they may cause incidental damage, such as the breaking down of locked doors, in the pursuit of that aim.
- *Post-fire condition* If some otherwise undamaged timber elements, such as floors, become wet due to extinguishing water, and the building remains closed for some length of time, there is an increasing risk of an outbreak of rot, or perhaps the reactivation of quiescent fungus.

10

Bessie Surtee's House, Newcastle-upon-Tyne. A multi-storey glazed frame – of the seventeenth century.

10

Investigative techniques

Few appraisals can be completed solely on the basis of a visual inspection. It is normally necessary to carry out some form of investigative work, either during the course of the inspection or on a later visit. Some of the techniques require specialist knowledge and/or equipment. If the engineer decides that he does not have one or the other, he can either contact the Building Research Establishment (BRE) or the Timber Research and Development Association (TRADA) who, in addition to their own specialist services, could recommend other testing houses or consultants.

10.1. The Borescope

The need to examine members which are normally concealed has already been mentioned. The Borescope was originally developed to examine cavities in brickwork and consists, in effect, of a small periscope, which can be inserted through a 10 mm hole. At the tip is a powerful light source, fed through optical fibres, which illuminates the cavity to about a 1·5 m radius (Fig. 10.1). The instrument can also be used to examine similar cavities in timber framed work, such as suspended floors, flat roofs or stud walls, either by direct viewing, or (with an adaptor) to take record photographs. Holes should be resealed if they have penetrated a vapour membrane.

10.2. Moisture content

Two forms of instrument for measuring the MC of site timber are available. Both measure MC indirectly, one by measuring electrical capacitance, and the other measuring electrical resistance.

Capacitance instruments measure over the full range of moisture content and are, for practical purposes, independent of ambient temperature. They are applied to the surface, with no penetration. However, the readings will only give values of MC if the density of the wood is known. Since this is a difficult parameter to measure, readings can only, in practice, be based on the species average density, which not only will affect their accuracy but also will give a result at some indeterminate depth.

The meter type in most general use, the Protimeter, is based upon the measurement of electrical resistance between two probes put into contact with the

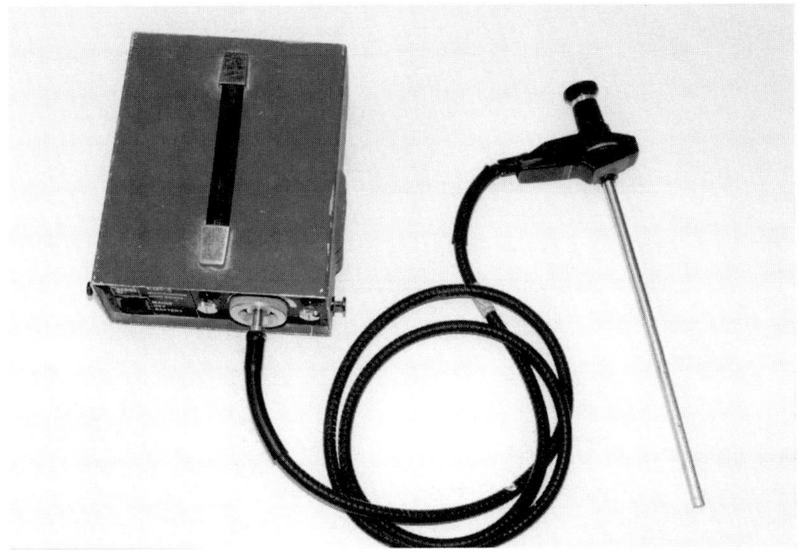

Fig. 10.1 The Borescope

timber. The correlation between resistance and moisture content varies slightly between species, but the meter has differently calibrated scales, from which the MC can be read directly. The meter is only accurate between around 6% and 25%, but this is the range which is of most interest.

The main limitation of the standard probes is that they take relatively shallow readings, at most 6 mm below the surface. The surface of even freshly felled timber quickly dries down to 20% MC or less, while deeper readings may still be far higher. Additionally, a surface layer of water or, more importantly, some preservatives or fire retardants will reduce the electrical resistance between the probes, and give falsely high readings. To overcome these problems, 'hammer probes' are provided, with insulated shafts which can be driven approximately 30 mm below the surface. Both probes can be used through surface finishes such as paint, although the test should only be carried out where the resulting pin-holes can be accepted. For readings at greater depths, two separate electrodes can be used in predrilled holes.

The Protimeter is quick to use, and creates minimal damage. If, however, there is some residual doubt about the result a definitive value can be found by the oven-drying method. A small solid sample of the timber is taken, usually by core-drilling, and placed in a sealed container such as a polythene bag until such time as it can be tested. The sample is then weighed, dried in an oven, and re-weighed. This process is, if necessary, repeated to establish a constant residual weight. The moisture content is found from the weight of water (i.e., the loss of weight) expressed as a proportion of the weight of the (dry) timber.

10.3. Auger drilling

We have seen that the areas in which the condition of the timber is most critical are often the least accessible, such as the ends of large principal

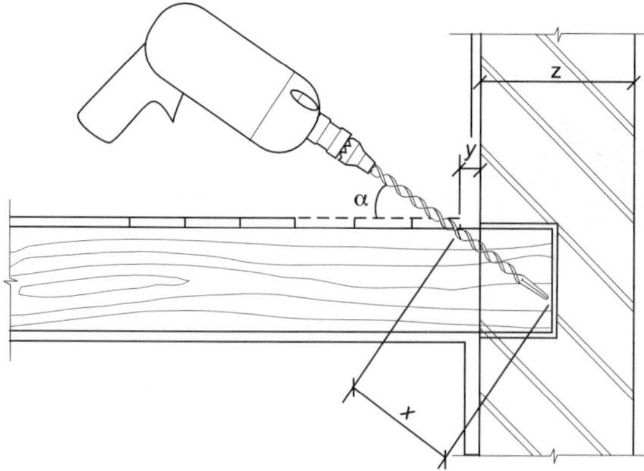

Fig. 10.2 Auger drilling

beams built into a solid external wall (Fig. 10.2), or the end of a roof truss in the eaves. In such cases a long auger bit may be used, mounted in a power drill and run at slow speed. The shavings can be cleared regularly, and their position in the timber defined by plotting to scale the angle of the drill and the depth of penetration. If the pitch is judged correctly, the end of the beam can be located. This is useful, because it can be used to establish the brick cover to the beam end; something to be taken into account in judging the risk of future rot.

The condition and smell of the shavings will also give an indication of the beam end condition, and they can be collected and oven dried for moisture content as noted above, although the weight collected would have to be borne in mind when considering the accuracy of the result.

10.4. The Sibert drill

The Sibert drill is essentially a more sophisticated version of the technique described above (Fig. 10.3). The drill bit is only 3 mm in diameter, but is nevertheless able to penetrate up to 200 mm into timber. The rate of penetration of the bit under a constant load is recorded as a trace on paper mounted on a drum (Fig. 10.4). Less dense timber is detected by faster penetration of the drill. In the figures the drill is being used to establish the residual profile of sound timber in some roof trusses over a barn, which in the past have suffered severe insect attack. The trace can be calibrated by drilling into obviously sound timber at some other point on the member.

The drill should ideally be used in an approximately radial direction. Tangential drilling can allow the bit to travel along a growth ring and give a falsely low reading. Since the drill hole is only 3 mm, and tends to close slightly, it can almost be considered a non-destructive technique of investigation.

10.5. Non-destructive testing

The most useful form of non-destructive testing developed to date is the technique of mechanical strength grading, referred to in section 3.5, although

Fig. 10.3 The Sibert drill

Fig. 10.4 Trace showing the rate of penetration of the bit under constant load, and showing the jump in alignment as the head passes through the split

it cannot be used on members which are built into a framework. The main areas of research on the subject lie in the field of acoustic wave propagation, in which the progress of a mechanically or ultrasonically induced compression wave is tracked as it passes through the timber. The wave can be made to travel along or across the timber, and two sensors are used to measure the speed of the wave and the degree of attenuation. The speed of the wave is related to the modulus of elasticity of the timber. Areas of rot affect the modulus and, hence, change the wave characteristics.

The method is therefore indirect, as are most of the non-destructive techniques, but has the added difficulty of the interpretation of the results.

Therefore, it should not be used by itself but in conjunction with other forms of test. It is most useful on a large population of broadly similar elements which enables some sort of datum reading to be established, such as the planks of a marine deck.

10.6. Dendrochronology

To conclude this chapter, two techniques are outlined which are used more for the purpose of dating ancient timbers, rather than for repairing them. Occasionally, however, this is an essential part of an appraisal.

Dendrochronology is the science of dating a piece of timber by studying the pattern of growth, as shown by the annual rings, and comparing it with a base chronology for the region. The annual growth of a tree is not constant, but a response to the climatic conditions over the year—principally rainfall, but to a lesser extent temperature and sunshine. The growth rings, therefore, vary in width and mark the response of the tree to the year's climate. By taking the average of several trees in a region, a base chronology can be built up, giving each year an index, relating to 1·00 (e.g., 0·75).

This chronology can then be extended backward in time by using overlapping samples obtained from buildings which have a known date of construction. The technique was discovered by an Arizona astronomer named Andrew E Douglas in the 1920s using samples taken from the long-lived bristle-cone pine.

A small core is taken from a particular timber by the use of a borer, which produces a sample about 4 mm in diameter, drilled close to the radial direction. The technique is not always successful—it obviously requires a principal beam rather than a common joist, and the original tree may have been 'complacent', e.g., a tree growing close to a river which gave it a relatively constant water supply. As a consequence, the annual rate of growth would be fairly constant and unresponsive to annual variations. The technique has, however, been used successfully on many medieval buildings.

10.7. Radiocarbon dating

Radiocarbon dating is a method of assessing the age of relatively ancient organic material, and became possible following the developments in atomic physics made in the post-war period. Radiocarbon (often written as C-14) is a rare variety of the common element carbon (C-12). It is a little heavier—as the reference numbers indicate, radiocarbon atoms weigh 14 units instead of the usual 12 units. Such varieties are known as isotopes, and there is only about one atom of C-14 in the atmosphere for every million atoms of C-12, a ratio which has been shown to be constant through time.

The carbon in trees is derived from the carbon in the atmosphere by the process of photosynthesis, (as noted in chapter 3), and so this carbon has the same minute proportion of C-14 as does the atmosphere—while the tree lives. However C-14, unlike C-12, is radioactive. When a tree is felled, the C-14 is no longer renewed, but decays slowly, again at a constant rate, giving off electrons and changing to a different element, nitrogen. Thus, a measure of the residual proportion of C-14 in a particular piece of wood, related to the norm proportion by the rate of decay, will give an estimate of the age of the sample.

Much use of this method is made in the general field of archaeology, and timber, being largely carbon, is amenable to the technique. In 1955 W F Libby published a paper which showed the known age of selected samples of timber (mostly from Egypt) plotted against the age predicted by radiocarbon dating, which gave confidence in the general method.

The test is looking for small differences in small quantities, and so it is only effective on timber more than 200 or 300 years old. It should also be remembered that it gives the date of the cutting of the tree, which may not neccessarily be the date of its incorporation into the building.

The method is, like any experimental procedure, subject to inaccuracy, and a plus and minus deviation is generally given for any predicted age. It is also necessary to ensure that the sample is uncontaminated by, say, later fungal growth, which would alter the C-14 ratio.

11

Arkwrights Mill building at Cromford Mill, Derbyshire. Dating from around 1780, this is possibly the world's first factory, with stone walls supporting timber floors of large redwood principals.

The appraisal

From the results of the survey an appraisal of the condition can now be made. The aim is to decide if the building is capable of performing adequately for the expected service life, or whether some form of remedial work will be needed.

Service life is a phrase which is often used, but rarely defined. If we are dealing with a basically well-built structure which is protected from the weather, i.e., it is in service class 1 or 2, there is really no reason why it should not be put into a condition in which it will last indefinitely, given periodic inspection and appropriate maintenance. For a structure which is partly in service class 3, then there may be some limit to the service life, although this will depend very much on the balance between the degree, or severity, of the exposure, and the durability and/or finish of the timber.

There are some five headings under which performance can be judged:

- strength
- stability
- serviceability
- durability
- appearance

with occasionally the need to consider

- accidental damage.

Only one, or all, may be relevant, depending upon the brief and the survey findings. An initial appraisal under the separate headings is a useful starting point.

11.1. Strength

Almost any appraisal will have to address the question of strength. There are three approaches to strength assessment, which can be used separately, or in combination, depending upon the circumstances.

History of performance—or the 100-year rule

If a building has performed well for a considerable number of years, then it would be foolish to ignore the evidence that the structure is sound, in the sense that it can cope with what is required of it. The period of compliance—100 years—is suggested both because it can be deemed in practice to include all structures built before the 1914–18 war, and because this return period gives something like a 95% chance that the building has sustained the designed wind and snow loads. For younger buildings a judgement would have to be made.

The rule cannot, of course, be used simply as stated; it would mean that no structure has ever collapsed, which is obviously not true. 'Why are you so worried about that building,' said the architect to the engineer, 'when it has stayed up for a hundred years?' 'Well,' replied the engineer, 'I think it's tired and would like to lie down.' Ensure buildings are not tired by observing the following provisos to the rule:

- The principles of stability can be seen and there is no evidence of current movement or distress—in other words, the structure is not hanging on by a thread.
- Defects which might have gradually reduced the strength over time must be made good. This would mean that all decayed members or joints, for instance, must be repaired.
- The loading regime will not be worse in the future than in the past.

Whether acknowledged or not, this is the method of assessment most often used for domestic frames. If the building fulfils all the conditions of the rule, then calculations are not necessary.

It is important to realise that the rule does not demonstrate, for instance, that a floor is capable of supporting the appropriate loading defined in BS 6399: Part 1, but only that it can continue to support the load regime sustained in the past. (The difference has been discussed in section 5.2.)

Some wood scientists have pointed out that there is an apparent incompatibility between the 100-year rule and the loss of strength of timber under sustained load. It would be possible to take a rather contrived example, such as a permanently full water tank, supported by some undersized joists subject to a permanent stress level which was over half the long-term failure stress. These joists would, at some time, fail but a glance at Fig. 3.9 shows that failure would almost certainly take place within a year or two. Moreover, the majority of our structures have relatively low permanent stress levels—floors in normal usage, roofs without snow, frames without wind—and so the ability to ride the occasional peak is generally sufficient assurance that the loading regime can be sustained indefinitely.

Analysis

There is sometimes a need to establish the strength of a structure in absolute, rather than relative, terms. Indeed, this is often the reason for the appointment of an engineer. The 100-year rule may conclude that the structure is 'strong enough' but not 'how strong' it is. If we wish to increase the loading on a structure, or justify a change of use to a heavier imposed loading, then we will have to attempt some form of analysis. The usual approach is to

- prepare an analytical model of the structure
- analyse the model under the relevant load cases
- determine the applied member stresses, and then
- compare them with permissible limits.

Permissible stresses for the design of new structures are contained in BS 5268: Part 2. Since this is the only material code still based on permissible stresses, remember that all analysis is done at working loads, and that the permissible stresses include a global factor of safety. The new Eurocode 5 is a limit state code, with the factor of safety divided between the loads and the material stresses (appendix 1).

The principal problems in the analysis of existing structures are the preparation of a meaningful analytical model, and the determination of the member and joint strengths. Simple elements, such as beams and columns, and triangulated frames may be modelled without undue difficulty. Redundant structures such as a crown post roof, where the 'fit' of the members can radically alter the distribution of forces, present more difficulty, and the assumptions behind any model which is then analysed by computer must always be carefully understood, since a print-out of results is often regarded as Holy Writ.

Having determined some applied stresses, of greater or lesser accuracy, they have now to be compared to permissible stresses. If the members do not contain gross and obvious defects, a conservative assumption may be made for softwoods by taking the lower (GS) grade from BS 4978. If these stress are nevertheless greater than the applied stresses, then all is well and good. If they are not, and the surface characteristics of the members can be seen on at least three sides, then the visual grading rules of CP 112 can be used to allocate grade stresses, which, in general, will be higher than the minimum. The method is explained in appendix 3.

If the structure still cannot be justified by analysis, we should not rush to strengthen or condemn the structure, especially if it is of historic value, since it may be possible to carry out a load test.

Load tests

There is a load testing procedure described in BS 5268, but it is designed to establish the load at failure of a prototype assembly and, therefore, cannot be used for a structure which is to continue in service. A procedure for the load testing of building elements is given in appendix 2. Tests must be carried out in safety, and in a controlled manner, and they should not be regarded as a cheap option. However, in certain circumstances they may be economic when compared to the cost of remedial work, as is shown in 18.2 and 18.3.

In practice loads can only be applied vertically, and so load tests are most often applied to floors, and occasionally to roofs.

A load test should not be proposed unless there is a reasonable expectation of a positive result. The applied stresses, if calculable, will give some idea of the likelihood of success. For simple floor beams these can be established relatively easily but, as stated in the previous section, highly redundant structures, with many joints, are often difficult to analyse meaningfully.

11.2. Stability

If lack of strength can result in a building falling down, lack of stability may cause it to fall over. For any framed structure, it is necessary to check stability.

The survey will have determined the way in which the building is stabilised—by triangulation or diaphragm action—and the engineer can decide if this is adequate. Triangulation is relatively easy to assess, but diaphragms are more difficult to analyse.

The 100-year rule may apply, if it can be shown that the structure is stable; that is, if it has reached equilibrium, and there is no on-going movement.

Most historic structures show some evidence of movement that has taken place in the past, and this will have been noted during the survey, but these movements are not always progressive. If the present alignment of elements is not unsafe, then the situation can simply be monitored. If there is no further movement, no remedial works are necessary. If movement is evident, the rate at which it occurs will suggest a programme for remedial work.

Monitoring the movement of a structure is generally carried out by establishing datum points which are related to the anticipated movement. As a rule, horizontal movements are caused in the main by outward thrusts, perhaps from roof trusses of an arched form, and vertical movements by foundation settlement. Instability relates primarily to horizontal movements, but vertical movement, as a trigger of horizontal movement, should not be ignored. The measuring points should be robust, and the accuracy of measurement sufficient to determine trends in the movement.

11.3. Deformation

The aim of the survey has been to note those deflections which appear to be significant, and to link them to a possible cause. The aim of the appraisal is to decide whether these deflections can be accepted and, if not, what remedial work might be appropriate.

In most cases, deformation would more appropriately be regarded as a serviceability, rather than a safety limit state. (Nevertheless, we have already looked at the instance of sidesway of an inadequately braced assembly as a reason to check for instability.) Since the modulus of elasticity of most timber is in the order of 8 000–12 000 N/mm^2—around 1/20 that of steel—and can, under some circumstances, appear to be even lower due to the effects of creep, it is not surprising that deformation is often a subject for appraisal.

The creep deflection of members in bending

BS 5268 gives moduli of elasticity for timber in the dry and wet state, and implies that it behaves elastically. For the majority of modern structures—built of seasoned timber with a relatively small cross-section and installed in service classes 1 or 2—this is more or less true. However, timber does have a tendency to creep, that is, the deflection of a beam under a constant bending moment will increase with time, albeit at a gradually decreasing rate. If the MC of the timber remains constant, the creep will be very small.

If the MC changes, then the creep component of the deflection will become more significant. While the MC of any structure will fluctuate slightly with time, the most significant change occurs when a large member is installed green, or only partly seasoned, and then dries out under load. It is not uncommon, especially for a beam with a high span/depth ratio, to find creep deflection in such a case which is of the order of span/100, five or six times greater than the simple elastic deflection. The creep component of the deflection is non-recoverable and the beam, when dry, will behave elastically. It follows that attempts to straighten the beam may produce stresses which are too high for comfort.

It is sometimes necessary to distinguish between creep deflection and incipient failure, since clients often assume the latter. An approximate analysis may have already been done for the purpose of strength appraisal, and this might show that the beam is not overloaded. It may also be possible to unload, or greatly reduce the load on, say, a floor beam, and demonstrate the permanent set characteristic of creep deflection. The beam may then be judged on the criterion of strength alone.

Deflection limits

The Code, from the first edition in 1951 onwards, recommends that

> *The dimensions of flexural members should be such as to restrict deflection within limits appropriate to the type of structure, having regard to the possibility of damage to surfacing materials, ceiling, partitions and finishings, and to the functional needs as well as aesthetic requirements.*
>
> *For most general purposes, including domestic flooring, this recommendation may be assumed to be satisfied if the deflection of the member when fully loaded does not exceed 0·003 of the span.*

These are rules for the designer and recent structures would be expected to comply formally with them. When appraising structures which were built before the Code was written, particularly where issues of safety are not involved, it is very much a question of the 'live-with' principle—can the building, or the occupants, live with the deflection? If so, then there is no need for remedial work.

There are many different conditions under which deflection becomes critical, and some common instances are given below. Most are static conditions. The liveliness of floors as a dynamic condition is treated separately.

- *Appearance* is perhaps the most subjective condition to judge. Structures which have been designed to span/330 should have no noticeable deformation. However, it does not follow that a noticeable deformation is unacceptable. For old structures, it is possible that the reverse will be true. There is always a strong incentive to accept the *status quo*, in view of the difficulty of reversing creep deflection. Any remedial work would either involve a very extensive intrusion, or modification of the structure.
- *Alignment* The deformation of a timber element may affect the alignment and, hence, performance of other elements. A combination of elastic and creep deflection on longer span flat roof structures which have a minimal fall could cause ponding, since outlets are nearly always close to supports. If the ponding is minor, then it may possibly be accepted, but significant ponding will increase the permanent load and, perhaps, progressively

increase deflection. If a prop or even some kind of secondary support from below is not acceptable, or possible, the top surface and waterproofing layer may have to be reset. Some structures of this kind have performed so poorly that they have eventually been covered with a pitched over-roof.

The deflection of floor surfaces, due again in older properties to creep deflection of the structure, may also be tolerated, particularly in domestic buildings where the occupier can become familiar with the shape.

For public buildings where the deformed surface could be considered unsafe, it may be possible to lift the floor covering and fir up the joists to a safe level. In domestic buildings, however, many owners may be happy to live with the deflection.

Spreading roof trusses can be seen in many parish churches where the roof, intentionally or inadvertently, is acting as an arch and pushing out the masonry. Monitoring the situation, in the first place, may establish that the roof and the walls have been able to come to an agreement, in which case no action is needed. If, however, the movement is progressive, or there are signs of distress in the roof, then some reinforcement may be needed (see 18.4).

Roof tiles may show a pronounced ridge, or 'hogging', as they pass from a timber structure across a relatively rigid party wall. If this is bad enough to cause leaks, the tiles will have to be lifted and the battens locally reset.

- *Load shedding* Creep deflection of a beam or truss may shed load onto a rigid element below, such as a partition or sliding door. While this will relatively rarely cause structural distress, the performance of sliding doors, for instance, may be adversely affected.

11.4. Durability

The survey work will have determined the general form and age of the structure, the species or species group, and the hazard class of the various elements. If rot is found, then the type and extent of the attack will need to be determined, together with the environmental conditions in that area. The aim of the appraisal is to find an explanation for the outbreak in terms of the origin and timescale of the moisture source in relation to the durability of the timber, in order to determine effective remedial work.

The remedial work would cover the following points

- elimination (if possible) of the moisture source
- (for wet rot) evaluation of residual member strength
- (for dry rot) evaluation of the area of influence
- member repairs
- (if necessary) application of preservative to adjacent members.

The moisture source

If the source of moisture is due to a defect in the external building envelope, such as a leaking parapet gutter or a missing tile, then obviously the defect must be repaired as part of the remedial work package. It is more difficult if the moisture results from the form of construction, such as joist ends built into a solid external wall. Applying a render would generally not be feasible, and so the remedial strategy would have to recognise the continuing risk, either by using only treated timber for wall contact, or by using metal shoes or splice plates (either galvanised or stainless) to break the contact between the timber and the wall.

Remedial work

In an appraisal of damage due to rot, it is first necessary to identify the source of moisture, to establish if it can be removed. The member would then eventually dry down to an equilibrium MC below 20%, and suffer no further damage. It is necessary to define the area of timber affected by rot by, for instance, auger penetration. (The Sibert drill can be useful for this purpose, by comparing the drilling rate for timber under test with rates for timber which is obviously undamaged).

Sections of structural timbers which are significantly affected by rot will generally require some form of repair, to be selected from the range given in Chapter 12. If the source of moisture cannot be completely eliminated this will determine the form of the remedial work, which might be to:

- use preserved timber for the repair
- use corrosion-resistant material for the repair (e.g. 12.2)
- establish a moisture barrier in the relevant area.

Beetle damage may, on occasion, be confined to sapwood on the arrises of the timber. When this 'frass' is scraped off, and the heartwood can be seen to contain no flight holes, then an analysis of the residual section may show that it is sufficient. For more general infestations, assuming that they are still active, a specialist in applied treatments should be consulted.

Residual risk

It may be that the survey reveals areas which are sound but where, nevertheless, there is a risk of rot in the future. Inevitably, we return to the previous example of the joists built into an external wall where a sample survey, perhaps using the technique shown in figure 10.2, had indicated that the joist end condition was generally good, but that there was a potential for moisture ingress. If general remedial work such as that described above was not feasible, considered to be too expensive, or conflicted unacceptably with conservation principles, the client should be made aware of, and agree to, the decision to accept the current condition. Some arrangements for monitoring the condition in the future should then be built into a maintenance strategy.

11.5. Accidental damage

Accidental damage brings several additional factors into the appraisal sequence. It is likely that some parts of the structure are potentially unstable, and the 100-year rule most certainly does not apply. First of all, it is generally necessary to form a quick overview of the whole structure, identifying areas which are unsafe and, if necessary, commissioning some temporary propping or local demolition. Preventing access is one way of making a building safe, but this must be done very positively; a simple notice on an unlocked door is not sufficient, as noted previously.

Of course surveyors must consider their own safety, and this may need some *ad hoc* assessment of conditions—a wall which is now free-standing, for instance, may not be a risk if the wind speed is low.

Other factors also make the survey difficult, such as the general presence of debris, and the need for a certain amount of detective work to decide what the structural form was, or could have been. Thus, at the Tyne Theatre (section 18.6), the trusses over the stage were badly damaged, but could still be seen to be similar to the undamaged trusses over the auditorium.

For these reasons, it is often appropriate to carry out an appraisal of a damaged structure in two phases. In the preliminary phase, the survey is done at the equivalent level to the medical process of triage, separating the elements into

- badly damaged (beyond repair)
- some damage (possible to repair)
- superficial damage (basically still sound)

and building up a first broad picture of the aggregate damage, which would then give a direction for more detailed survey work.

Such a picture will often be needed for the purposes of an insurance claim, another factor which will affect a fire appraisal. Most owners insure their property, and in the case of a significant claim the insurer will appoint a loss adjuster, whose job is to assess the total value of the claim in terms of direct and consequential losses.

A surveyor should seek to be informed of the relevant conditions of the insurance in relation to the form of repair covered, and any cost limits. Some insurance policies, for instance, limit the cover on old buildings to the cost of the equivalent new construction, and this may be relevant when assessing the options for new work. The extent of the remedial work may also be determined by a requirement to deal with all aspects of the damage. If, for example, some concealed roof trusses had been lightly charred, but the residual section was adequately strong, the loss of section would still be regarded as fire damage. For historic buildings, there may have to be a balance struck with conservation requirements to maximise the retention of original fabric. Thus, while many owners of medieval houses proudly display smoke-blackened rafters, caused before the building of a fireplace, most owners of modern buildings would argue that charred roof timbers would reduce the value of their property on resale, and would require them to be replaced.

It is often useful to organise an initial contract for the removal of debris, temporary protection and the dismantling of elements clearly beyond repair. In historic buildings, the debris may be of significance, and would then have to be examined in detail, for evidence of original material and form.

Temporary protection may be appropriate, to avoid further damage from rain, but such a provision would have to weighed against the period of risk, and the restrictions which a cover might place on remedial work. Following a fire, free circulation of air is the primary aim, to disperse any build-up of extinguishing water and to discourage mould growth. For timbers which are in still air, such as floor joists, and which on examination are found to be wet, it would be prudent either to lift occasional floorboards, or remove areas of ceiling, whichever does the least further damage. If dampness is going to last for some while, a fungicidal spray on the timber surfaces is a good idea. Timber, as mentioned before, is not a good absorber of moisture, and if the sources of additional water can be minimised and air circulation encouraged the timber itself will dry out fairly quickly, and no permanent damage will be done.

The main aim in the repair of accidental damage generally lies in reconstructing damaged elements, either as a replica or in an alternative form. The main problem areas are the boundaries with undamaged structure, e.g., the floor joists which have been burnt at one end only.

Most contracts begin with the insurer agreeing to fund a series of work packages for the preliminary items outlined above. The contract may well continue in this way, or the owner and the insurer may come to an agreement on a lump sum settlement. At this point, the insurers would have no further interest in the contract, and the owner may sometimes propose a radical change in the direction of the work.

The potential significance of claims for consequential losses (loss of profit, alternative accommodation, etc.) may dictate whether a fast-track approach is appropriate for the remedial works in order to reduce the total cost of the claim.

Further reading

The issues of timber decay and beetle attack, including a balanced view on remedial work, is comprehensively covered by Ridout (1999).

12

Concourse roof, Main Railway Station, Copenhagen, Denmark. Europe's best bolted laminated roof; one hundred foot span arches dating from 1901.

12

Timber repairs

The aim of this section is to outline the principles of the different forms of repair, and the factors which govern the choice of form for a particular application. In general, repairs can be categorised under the following headings.

Repair form
- member replacement
- part replacement (generally an end)
- patches

Repair type
- all timber
- metal with timber
- adhesives

Design parameters
- member loading and joint capacity
- hazard class
- appearance
- historic significance.

12.1. Repairs to exposed members

Member replacement

The need to replace complete members occurs most often in cill plates which have been in direct contact with the ground (Fig. 12.1(a)). Indeed, it would be true to say that most medieval frames have either already had replacements fitted, or have been lifted up and put on some form of plinth, in order to reduce the moisture content level of the plate. Since the foundations to timber frames are generally shallow, and sometimes even non-existent, differential settlement is quite common, resulting in a cill plate which is neither level nor straight. If the distortion is not too severe, and the building is a simple framed structure such as a barn, then it may be possible to improve the line by propping and jacking (b). For a domestic structure, with internal plastering, it is normally wiser to accept the *status quo*. This may mean sawing the cill plate to a curve, the precise shape of which can be established by cutting a template.

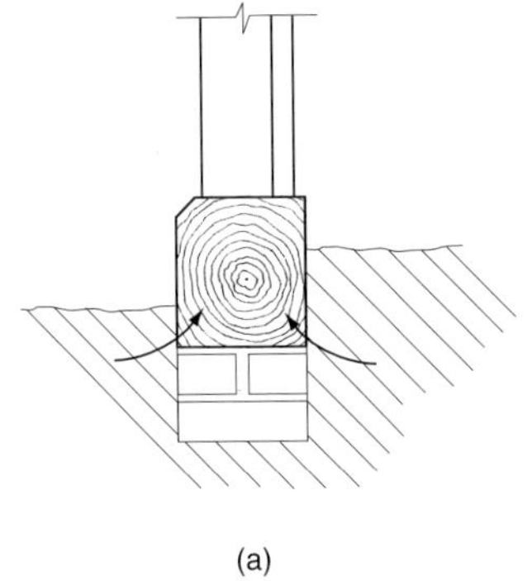
(a)

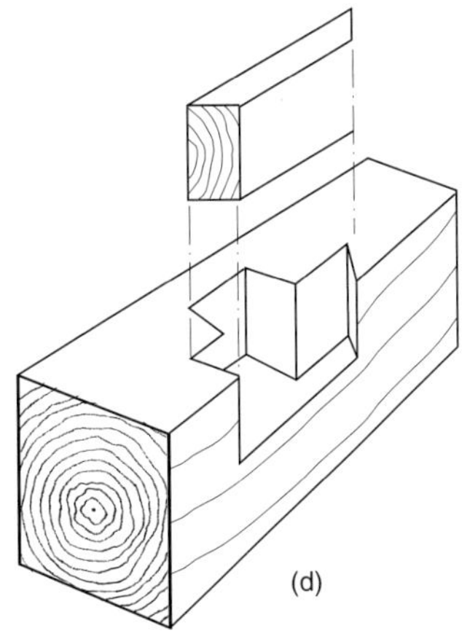
(d)

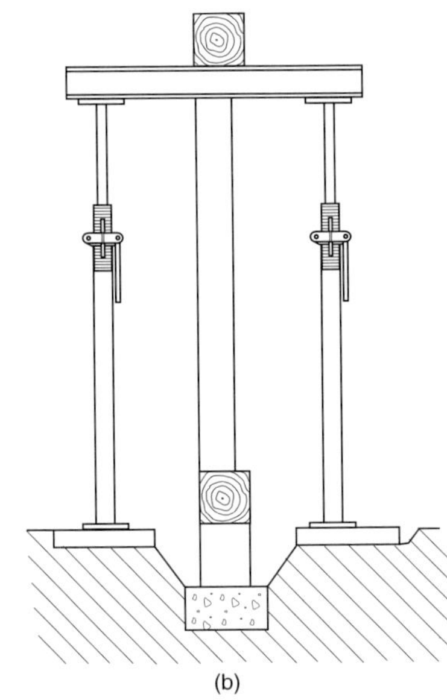
(b)

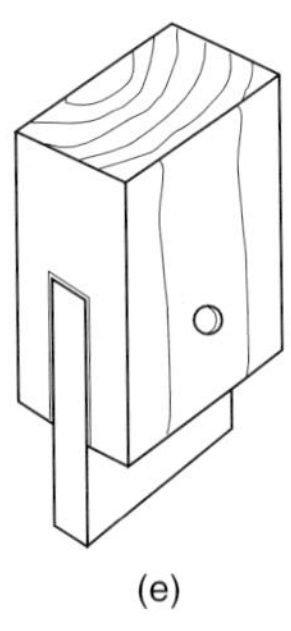
(e)

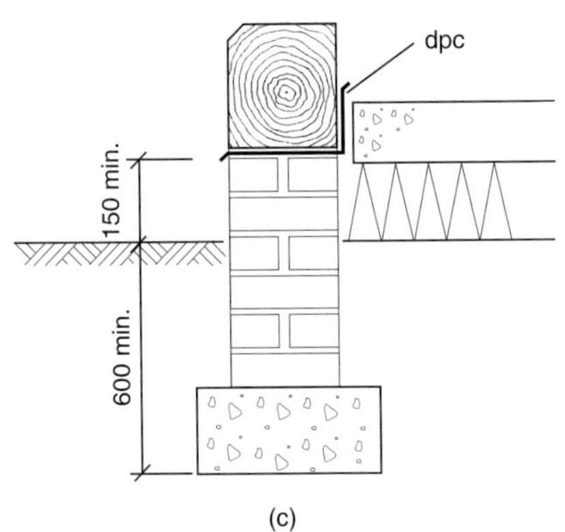

(c)

Fig. 12.1(a) Cill plate in direct contact with the ground; (b) Propping and jacking of the first floor beam over cill plate; (c) Deepening of the foundations; (d) Studs closed by wedged filler pieces; (e) Studs modified and fitted with slip tenons

The replacement of all, or part, of the cill plate will need local temporary underpinning of the superstructure. If the foundations are very shallow, and there is evidence of seasonal, or progressive movement, it may be a good idea to take the opportunity to deepen them (c). This would also allow the cill plate to be offered up onto the stud tenons. In all cases the cill plate should be laid on a dpc and, if necessary, consideration given to locally modifying the immediate ground level, so that the plate is raised 150 mm or so above it. The aim of this work is to put the new cill plate into hazard class 3A and to render the frame stable. Conservation arguments about interfering with a relatively minor part of the original fabric should not be allowed to compromise the aim of durability.

If the foundations are not to be replaced, then the cill plate will have to be offered horizontally into position. This may be done by cutting open mortices to receive the stud tenons, which are then closed by wedged filler pieces (d). Alternatively, the studs may be modified and fitted with slip tenons (e).

Occasionally the complete replacement of other frame members is necessary, because of rot or beetle attack, damage, or removal at some time in the past. It is generally necessary to make some modification to the original joint, usually the mortice, to enable the new member to be offered into position.

Scarf repairs

The majority of timber repairs involve the replacement of one end of a member. If the member is visible, the new section is generally aligned with the existing to replicate the outline of the original. The principal problem, therefore, is to form an in-line joint between the two sections. Within the traditional building vocabulary such joints exist, in order to form long continuous members such as cill plates and wall plates, and are generally referred to as scarfs. The number of different scarf types is very large indeed; the choice will mainly depend upon the principal and secondary forces or moments to which the joint will be subject, but will also be affected by the decision either to restrict the repair materials to timber alone, or to include metal components.

All timber scarfs

It is obvious that a scarf joint made entirely of timber cannot be as strong as the original unjointed member. It is important, therefore, in the more critical cases, to make some quantitative assessment of the joint loading, i.e., the moments and forces.

Bending

The repaired beam as a whole has to sustain the applied bending moment, (Fig. 12.2(a)), and so the function of the joint is to transfer the bending moment locally from the original member (A) to the new member (B). This is most efficiently done by tapering the sections (b), although it can be seen from section x–x that the capacity at the centre section (M_{jnt}) can only be half the capacity of the unjointed section (M_{orig}). In addition, (b) is

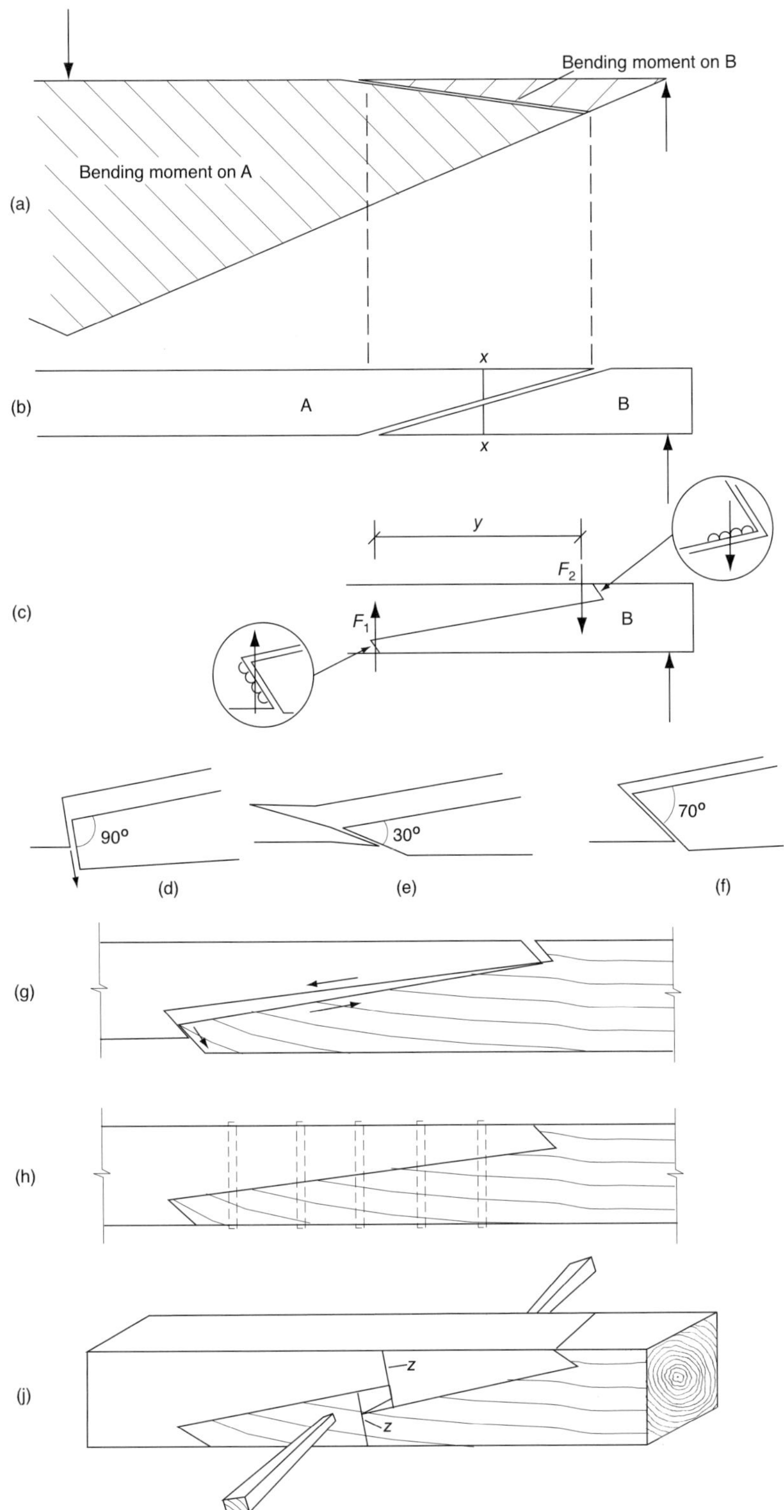

Fig. 12.2 Transfer of the bending moment

not yet a joint, because there is no mechanical connection between the two parts. This could be done by undersquinting the abutments, as in (c). The two bearing points allow restraining forces to be developed (F_1, F_2), separated by the distance y. The couple $F \times y$ is the resistance moment of the joint, and for this to reach the potential capacity limit of M_{jnt}, y will be in the region of $3d$ to $4d$, where d is the beam depth.

The squint angle α on the tension side is important: if $\alpha = 90°$, no restraint is offered at all (d). For $\alpha = 30°$ or less, there will be an early local failure of the two thin wedge sections (e). A value of $\alpha = 70°$ is about the optimum (f). Even then the wedge action of the squints will push the two parts apart (g) unless they are locked together with dowels (h), or the scarf face tabled. The table can be fitted with a folding wedge, as shown, (j), which helps to make the whole joint tight, and takes up any lack of fit, although it does reduce the potential joint strength (compare z–z in (j) with x–x in (b)).

Joints such as these cannot achieve much more than one third of the strength of the unjointed section, and locally the stiffness of the beam is reduced to about one third of the unjointed stiffness.

This example has been dealt with in some detail, because it is important to understand the way in which such joints work. It is one of a range of traditional scarf joints which can be used for a repair. Some others are shown in Fig. 2.4.

They all require

- an adequate overlap scarf length
- end connections to the blades
- some reserve of strength for moments on the other axis

and for splayed scarfs

- a mechanical lock to prevent slip failure.

A large range of traditional scarf joints is illustrated in Hewett (1980) although many of these are too complex to be used in repair work—hence the shortlist above. Remember that even the simplest joint needs to be cut accurately, and that the original end must be cut *in situ*. Thus, a reasonable working space around the repair will be needed.

Compression

At its simplest, a compression joint may be formed by directly butting two faces (Fig. 12.3(a)). However, in practice, most compression members are prone to buckling, and so some resistance must generally be provided to secondary bending about major and minor axes. For light duties, an open mortice and tenon may be adequate (b); for more significant lateral loads a step in the bearing surface (the scarf principle again) is more appropriate (c), although cutting inaccuracies will probably mean that one surface predominates for bearing. A slight squint on the bearing surfaces assists buckling resistance (d). If you are very confident of the standard of workmanship, the scissors scarf (e) gives a fine virtuoso effect, providing very high resistance to lateral bending, but with some loss of direct compression capacity (due to the potential splitting effect of the scissor ends).

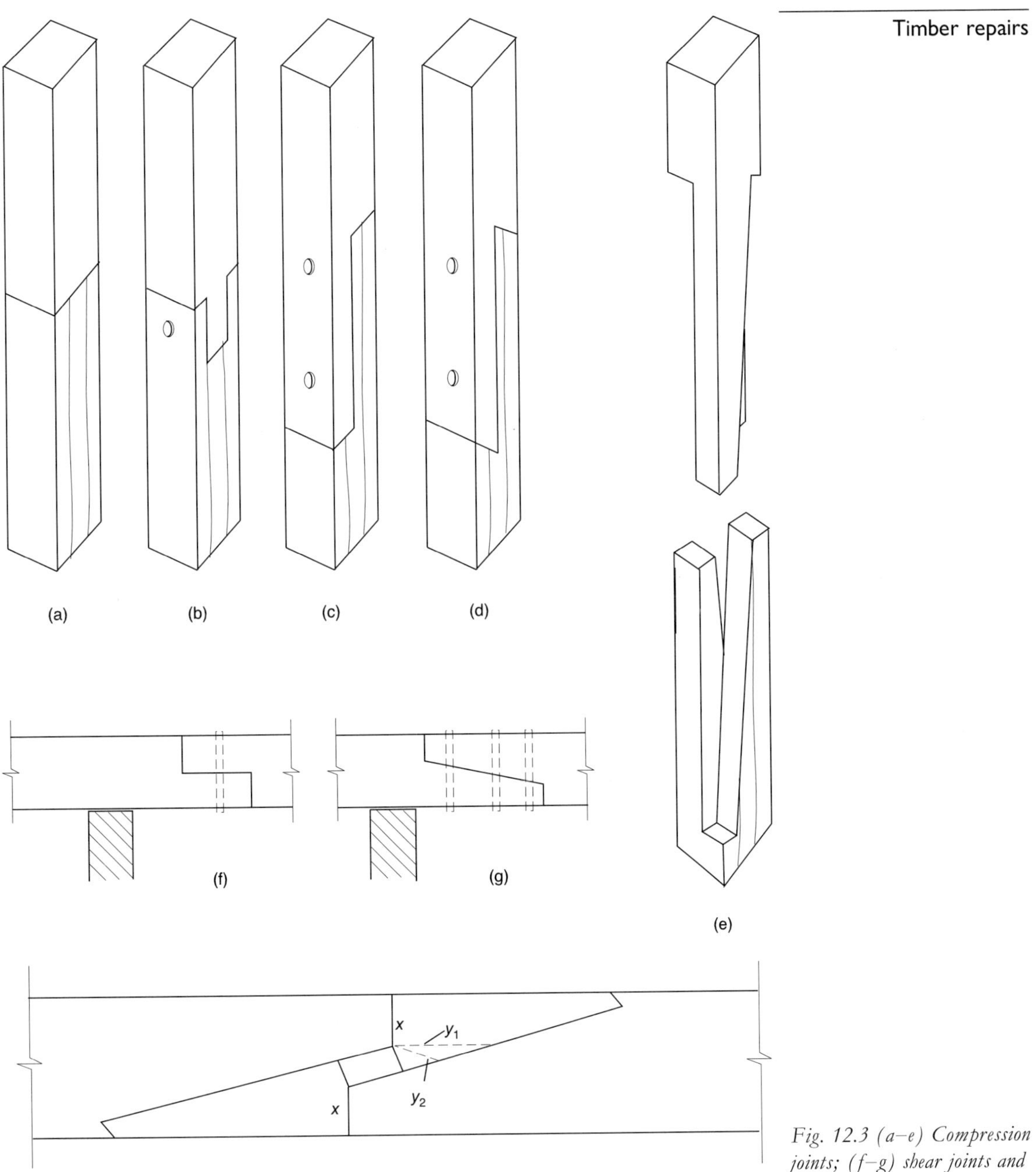

Fig. 12.3 (a–e) Compression joints; (f–g) shear joints and (h) tension joint

Shear

For light duties, a simple face-halved scarf (f), with retaining pegs, will suffice. For more significant loads, it is prudent to splay the scarf surface slightly (g), due to a tendency for splits to develop at the base of the scarf. The joint will then, however, need more positive retention by pegs.

Tension

Some interlock in the longitudinal direction is again needed, and the tabled splay scarf is probably the best way of achieving this (h). The design aims to balance the residual tension capacity of the scarf at section x, against the shear capacity of the potential failure line y_1. Straightness of grain is important in both members; the slope of grain shown at y_2 will considerably reduce the length of the potential shear plane and, hence, the joint strength. Dowels can be added to increase the shear resistance but, given the existence of some secondary bending, the joint is unlikely to achieve much more than one quarter the tensile strength of the unjointed section.

The reduced strengths of all these repair joints are not in general the problem they might seem. Tension members in medieval and later structures are, as a rule, generously sized, and beams are usually repaired near to the support, that is, not at a point of maximum moment. Having stated that, it is always important to see that the strength of the joint is not unduly reduced by grade defects in the joint area, perhaps by an adjustment in the line of cut.

Scarfs with metal fasteners

The use of metal fasteners enables joints of higher strength and stiffness to be made. This is due partly to the increased shear strength of a steel bolt over a timber dowel, but is also due to the tensile forces that can be developed in the bolt by using washers, and the large shear capacity of the range of metal connectors (Fig. 12.4(a)–(f)).

Bending

A splayed scarf can now have simple stopped ends, and the restraining couple can be developed between the bearing point F_1 and the tension bolts F_2. The value of F_2 is determined not only by the bolt strength, but also by the details around the bolt head at the scarf end. A washer will be needed for each bolt to spread the load over an area large enough to prevent crushing of the timber perpendicular to the grain. The washer can either be surface mounted (b), recessed (c), or recessed and plugged (d), depending on visual acceptability, or required fire resistance (section 5.3). The net section x–x has to be capable of taking the bolt force in shear.

As before, the joint can achieve a bending strength of about half the unjointed section, although this could be increased if the members have very few defects in the joint area.

The joint can be further strengthened by the addition of top and bottom straps (e), since this introduces an additional restraining couple F_3–F_4. In order that the couple can be considered as acting together with F_1–F_2, it is important that there is very little bolt slip; shear connectors are recommended.

Metal fasteners also enable a strong joint to be made using a simple edge-splayed scarf (f). In this case all the load is transmitted by the fasteners (which, as timber pegs, would give a relatively weak joint). The restraining couple is simply that developed by the bolt groups, which can be fitted with split rings

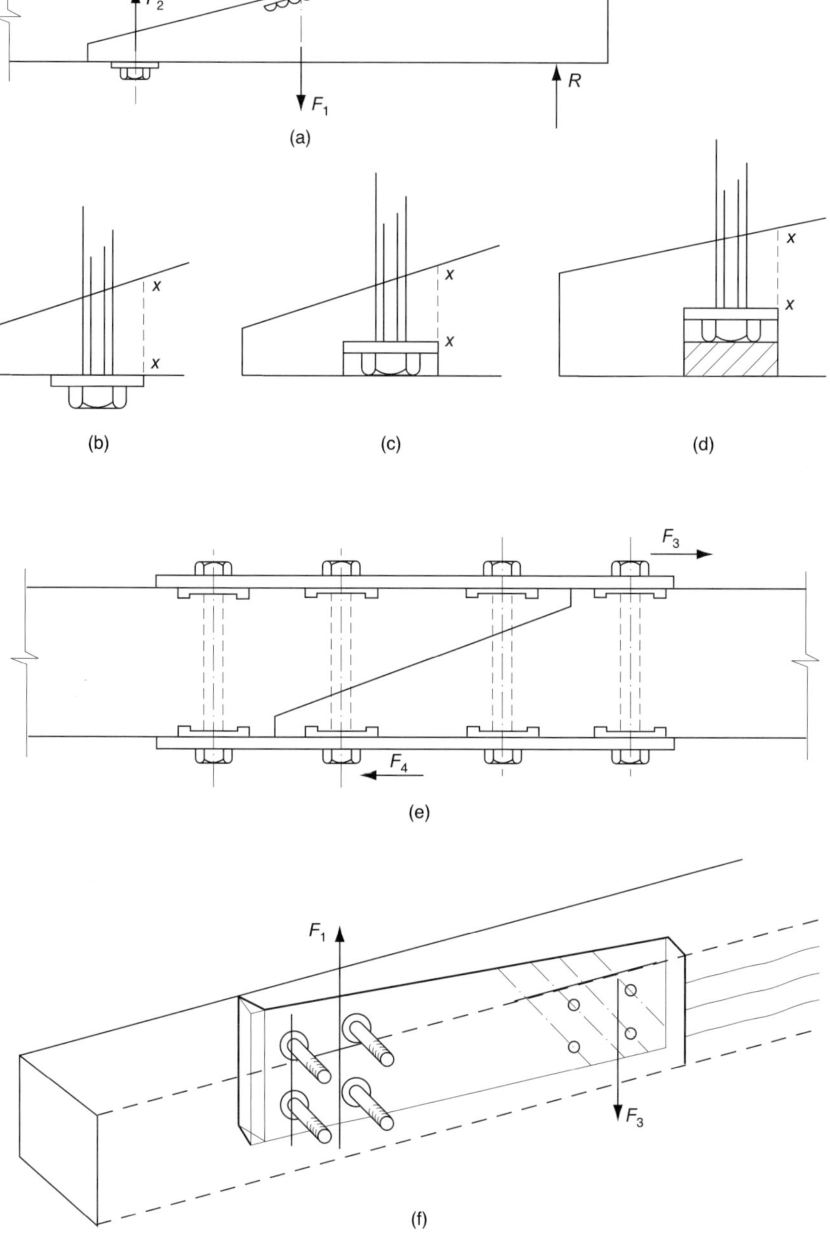

Fig. 12.4 Scarfs with metal fasteners in bending

for increased capacity. The moment capacity can approach 70% to 80% of the unjointed section, since the two scarf sections always retain their full depth (although the scarf length may need to be $5d$–$6d$). For this reason also, (if split rings are used) there is a negligible loss in stiffness. The effects of shrinkage will however be more noticeable, and if there is more than one

Fig. 12.5 A vertical splayed scarf with bolts and split rings used in Cranbrook Church, Kent. (a) The joint before assembly, showing the bolts and split rings. (b) The assembled joint. (The boltholes are still to be plugged, and the bottom moulding added)

row of fasteners, the distance between them will be fixed by the original (seasoned) piece. Thus, for a green oak repair, two rows of split rings may bring the risk of a central split developing due to drying shrinkage. An example of the joint is shown in Fig. 12.5, where the beam has moulded sides, and a conventional face-splayed scarf would have been impractical. In this case, the new section was cut from reclaimed (i.e., seasoned) timber.

Compression

Easily made with a simple half lap. One or two bolts with washers will give adequate resistance to secondary bending.

Shear

A simple splay or half-lap, with bolts to provide continuity.

Tension

Again, a simple splay or half-lap, with all the load transmitted through the fasteners.

The joints referred to above may be designed using the Code, since all that is needed are estimates of the timber and the fastener strengths.

12.2. Metal reinforcement

If the repaired area cannot be seen, or is not normally seen, in the completed structure, then there is the possibility of choosing a repair from a large range of metal reinforcement techniques. These repairs can be thought of as 'reinforcement' because the metal is added to, and lies partly outside, the original member profile. They have the following advantages

- in general, they require less original timber to be removed
- member strengths can be increased
- some estimate of strength can be made using Code rules.

Although, as has been stated, these repairs are normally concealed, there is no reason why they cannot be visible, if they have been neatly detailed, and if they can be acceptably 'read' in a historic structure.

Splice plates

Plates applied to each side of the member, generally metal (although solid timber or plywood can be used), and placed across a simple butt joint (Fig. 12.6(a)). The plates take all the load and can be designed using nails, screws, bolts, or bolts with connectors. If greater strength is required, sections such as angles or channels can be used. This is a useful detail if the splices are to be extended into a wall to provide end bearing where rotten joist ends have been cut off (b). This detail is appropriate where it is not possible, or practical, to cure the dampness in the wall. The steel should, as a minimum, be galvanised. It may be necessary to replace a 'dummy' member, in order to provide fixing for the floorboards or the ceiling. Of all the repairs shown in this chapter, this one is probably used more than any other.

A single splice plate can also be used to strap joints, e.g., where the end tenon of a joist has partly pulled out of a mortice (c).

Flitch plates

A flitch plate lies inside the timber (d) and is usually employed to add strength or stiffness to a heavily loaded member. If a blind slot can be cut from above, the flitch will be completely concealed. Fixing by side bolts is difficult, because

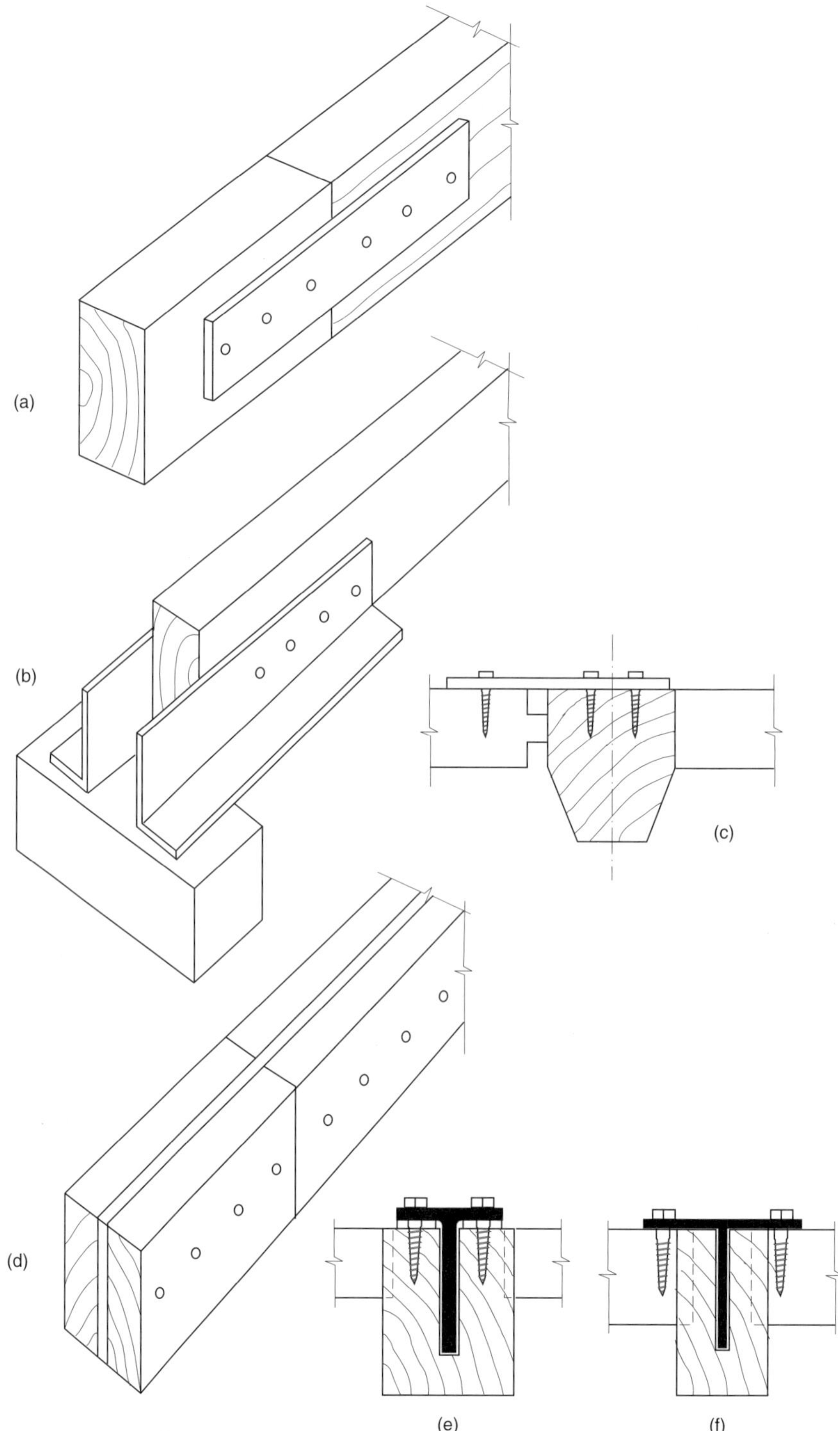

Fig. 12.6 Joints made with metal reinforcements (a) splice plates (b) splice angles (c) top plate (d) flitch plate (e) and (f) flitch tee piece

of the problem of accurately drilling the timber to hit the holes in the steel. Any enlargement to correct the alignment obviously reduces the effectiveness of the connection. For very thick timbers, the better approach is to drill the timber first, fix the steel flitch in position and spot the hole centres on it by drilling though the timber holes. The flitch is then removed, and the bolt holes drilled in it. This is not as difficult as it might seem, if a modern magnetically-attached drill is used. Alternatively, a plywood template may be used.

If space permits, a tee-section can be more easily fixed by means of coach screws though the top flange (e). Packs may be needed if the timber beam has a permanent sag, and if this is very pronounced it may be necessary to survey the top surface and fabricate the tee-section accordingly. If the beam is actually loaded by a series of joists (f), the tee-section can be arranged to pick up the joists directly, and no connection to the principal beam will be needed, except to ensure that the reaction in the steel can be transferred to the beam support.

Frame reinforcement

It is also possible to reinforce timber frames by adding steel members. Examples are shown in Fig. 12.7, where a bottom tie is added to an A frame roof truss (a), and strut and members are added to a beam to convert it into a bowstring truss (b). The principle of tying the feet of a roof truss is also described in section 18.4, and if the supports are unable to provide the lateral restraint necessary, then this may be the only feasible way to ensure stability. The steel members are visible, but are small in cross-section as they are simple tension members. Intermediate supports may be necessary to avoid sag in the ties. The steelwork should be detailed so that its function is clear, and it can be read as a later addition to the original structure—the idea of clarity that is referred to in 13.2, where I suggest that repairs should represent the time at which they were done.

It should be remembered that the steel rods have no significant period of fire resistance, and that intumescent paint is not effective on such small cross-sections. In general, this is not a problem for roof structures, but floor beam reinforcement may have to be justified on the basis of a fire calculation without the exposed steel.

12.3. Adhesives

There are, in fact, relatively few situations in which adhesives can be successfully used for in situ repair work. This is due to the number of stringent conditions which have to be met in order to ensure a sound joint, and which are not always adequately appreciated.

There are two broad classes of adhesives; those based on synthetic resins which are condensation polymers of formaldehyde with either urea, melamine, or resorcinol (or mixtures of these individual types) which are listed in the Code for structural work, and certain grades of epoxy or polyurethane adhesives, for which there are no application standards.

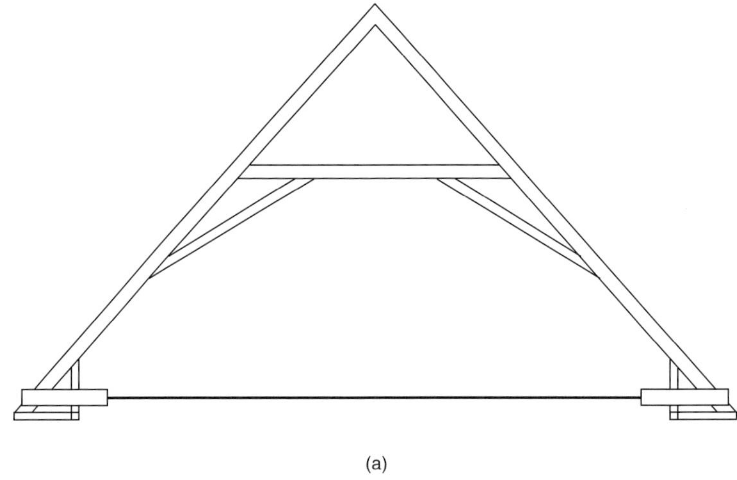

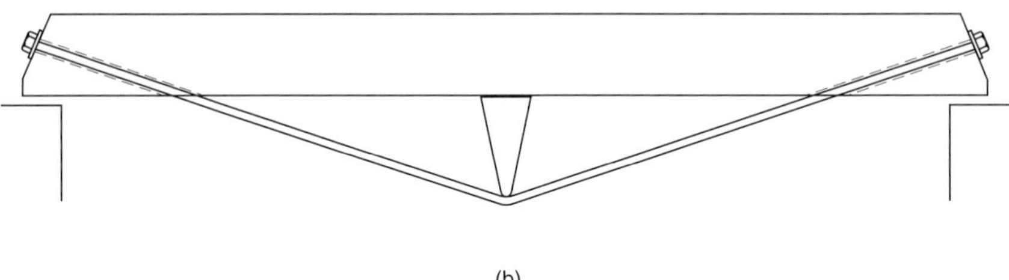

Fig. 12.7 Examples showing the reinforcement of timber elements by adding steel members

The formaldehyde adhesives

The most commonly-used generic types are

- urea–formaldehyde (UF) and
- phenol–formaldehyde (PF)

which are marketed by various manufacturers. They were specifically developed for timber and have been available for over 50 years. For softwoods and medium-density hardwoods, it can be assumed that, in a correctly made joint, the adhesive is stronger than the timber itself, and that eventual failure will take place in the timber behind the glue line. The shear capacity of parallel grain joints can be estimated from the appropriate shear strength for a species given in the Code. Where the grains are at right angles, however, rolling shear values should be used, which are roughly 30% of the parallel-to-grain values. These values should also be used for plywood splices, since even if the face grain is parallel to the grain of the solid member, failure could occur in the outer core veneer. It is also important to remember that the strength of any mechanical fasteners which pass through the joint cannot be simply added to the glue strength, because the glue line would have to fail before the fasteners took their load in bearing.

The glued joint is potentially, however, a very strong and rigid connection between two pieces of timber. The problem, as mentioned above, is to meet the necessary conditions listed below.

Mode of application

The glued joint is designed for use in shear (since any significant tension component will rupture the timber behind the glue line). Glued scarfs should not have a greater slope than 10, and glued end-to-end butt joints have a negligible strength, as the essential overlap of the fibres has been lost. It is quite difficult to ensure that joints are in pure shear, and it is usual to use metal fasteners to cope with possible tensile forces.

It is also inadvisable to use adhesives for members much above 75 mm thick, since distortions of the section caused by moisture content changes could again result in a failure in tension perpendicular to the grain of the timber behind the glue line. (It is for this reason that the thickness of the laminations in a softwood glulam beam is limited to 50 mm.)

Moisture content of the timber

The range for optimum bond strength is 8–12% MC. Above 20% MC there is an increasing risk of inadequate bond. Thus green timber cannot be glued, both on this account and for reasons of drying-out distortion. Timbers should ideally be within 5% of their equilibrium MC, and adjacent surfaces should not differ by more than 3%, more particularly for grains at right angles. Manufacturer's instructions will give more details. Obviously, the work of gluing must be done under cover.

Ambient temperature

While curing, thermosetting adhesives are temperature-sensitive. Again, manufacturers will recommend limits, but as a guide resorcinol formaldehyde glues will need at least 20°C although other formulations can accept lower temperatures. Remember that these temperatures apply to the timber as well, and for the stated curing period, which, of course, is extended by low temperatures. In a UK climate, these temperatures would be difficult to achieve on site for much of the year without some protective measures.

Surface preparation and fabrication tolerances

It is often thought that a rough surface increases bond, but this not so. Any surface contamination such as dirt or grease will reduce bond, and so cleanliness is more important than roughness. Surfaces should be planed, to give an undamaged surface, ideally not more than 24 hours before gluing, and the surfaces should be a close fit. This is another point of misunderstanding, for these adhesives are described as gap-filling. However, this is a material scientists' gap, and not an engineer's gap—in other words, about 1 mm, which demands a high standard of workmanship.

Contact pressures

In order to achieve the glue line thickness given above, manufacturers generally specify contact pressures within the range 0·7 to 1·2 N/mm^2. In aggregate, these are large forces, and the odd cramp here and there is quite inadequate. Screws or nails, with bolts for thicker timber are recommended (and will deal with any tension force on the glue line).

Given the conditions which have to be satisfied, the role of the formaldehyde adhesives in repair work is at best limited. However, timber (or more conveniently plywood) splice plates can be glued over fractured members, or inadequate joints, in more modern structures.

Epoxy resins

Some of the limitations noted above could be overcome by the use of epoxy resins, which can accept much thicker build-ups without cracking, and which will also bond to steel as well as timber. Epoxies were originally developed in the 1960s for aerospace applications, and today are used widely throughout the industry. They are generally supplied in a two-part resin/hardener formulation, and can be mixed either to a liquid, or to a putty consistency, which could be used where pouring the adhesives was not feasible. Since they are very expensive, they are usually pre-mixed with fillers—generally micro-silica or cellulose fibre—which also improve the toughness, or resistance to crack propagation. They are all proprietary materials and so the conditions of use, such as the allowable ambient temperature range and curing times, are subject to the manufacturer's instructions.

Some early applications of the material were misguided, including attempts to dub out exposed but weathered members to their original line, but a consensus is gradually emerging on the most appropriate uses, which generally involve the bonding of steel into timber members.

If a beam has some rot in the centre, which makes it inadequate, or it is required to increase the bending capacity, then an epoxy may be used to bond steel into a slot cut along the centre of the beam from above (Fig. 12.8). The steel can either be in the form of reinforcing bars (a), or a vertical blade (b). Individual rods are easier to handle, and will adapt to the line of the beam, but a higher section modulus can be achieved with a blade.

Beam ends can be repaired by drilling holes in the sound material after the decayed end has been removed. Resin is injected into the hole and then the metal bar inserted. If the decayed section is entirely concealed, say, within the wall, then the original profile could be made out with resin (c), which would solve any problem of moisture penetration. If the repaired section was visible, then a new piece of timber could be drilled and bolted in place (d).

Epoxy-bonded steel can also be used for general strap or tie purposes, e.g., at joints, if movement has occurred which reduces the joint strength (e).

In all these applications, it must be remembered that there are as yet no general design rules. In particular, we do not know what bond strength can be achieved between resin and steel, and what is the optimum surface treatment. Most installers opt for threaded rod which would achieve a mechanical interlock between the steel and the resin, and have an additional

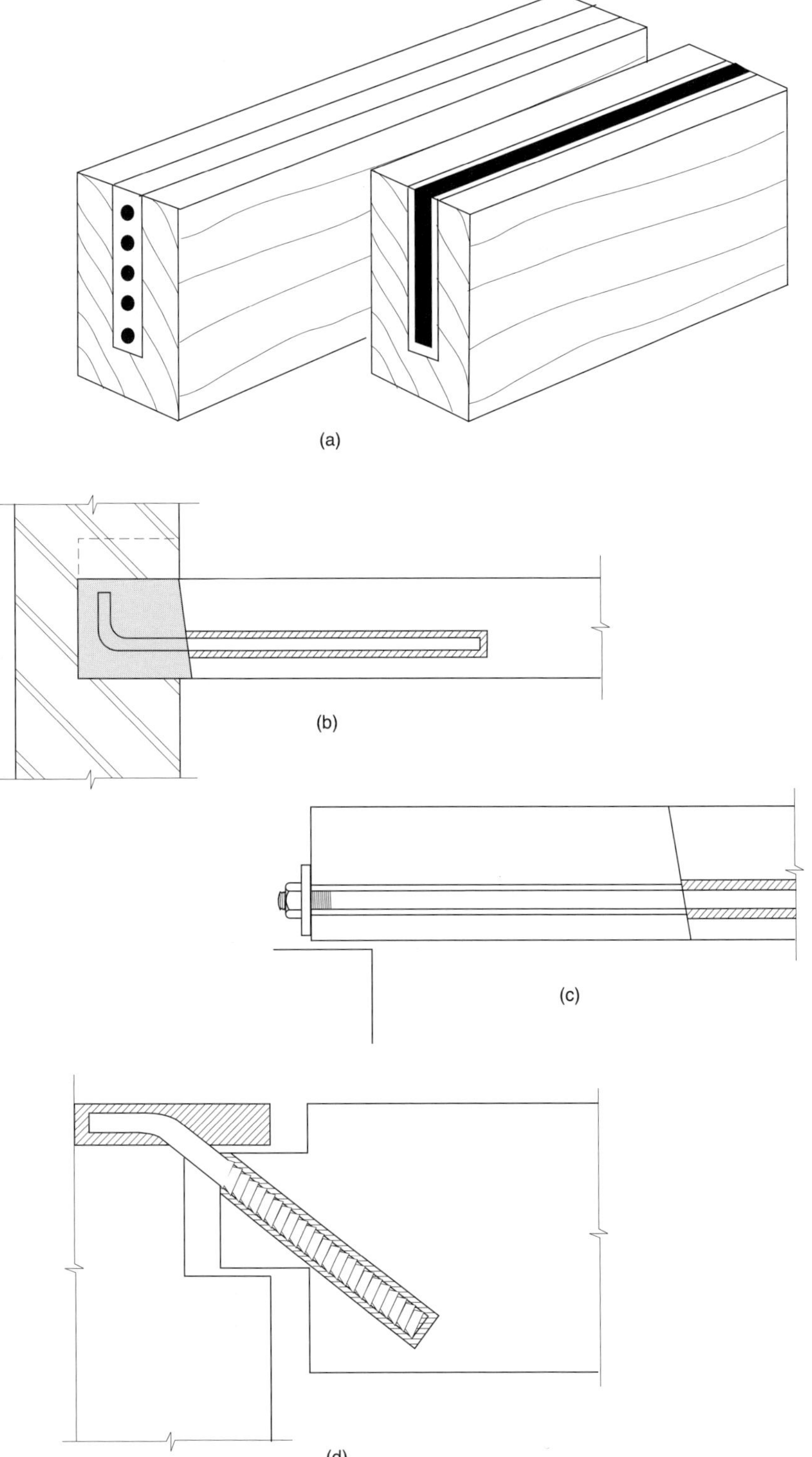

Fig. 12.8 Repairing rot in the centre of a beam by using steel and epoxy resin

benefit in terms of end connections such as those in (d) above. The bond strength between the resin and the timber is also not known, although it could be argued that the position is the same as the formaldehyde adhesives, where it is assumed that the bond is stronger than the shear strength of the timber. For the moment it would be advisable to take a conservative view in this respect. The third area of ignorance is the question of creep characteristics in epoxy resin, which might, for instance, result in a long-term reduction of the composite section modulus of the bonded-in rods in (a). Research is currently underway, however, which will hopefully result in design information becoming generally available in the near future.

13

Littledown Sports Centre, Bournemouth. A forty metre span roof of three-pin glued laminated arches, with a boarded roof of solid timber, built in 1984.

13

Historic buildings

Many of the buildings illustrated in this book, in addition to being old, are more properly described as historic. Most historic buildings, at least those built before 1840, have their status formally recognised by being listed. As already noted in section 7.4, any work to a listed building is subject to approval by the local authority. So, just as it is necessary to understand how a structure works in order to repair it effectively, we also must understand what makes a particular building historic, in order to decide what forms of remedial work are best suited to it.

In general, historic buildings are important because they record our past, that is, they are culturally significant. The concept of cultural significance has been developed in various publications of ICOMOS (the International Council of Monuments and Sites), although in somewhat formal phraseology. The following section is a fairly free interpretation of their principles.

13.1. Cultural significance

The cultural significance of a building can be assessed under several headings

- *aesthetic*: the appearance, form and scale of the building, and its general architectural qualities
- *technical*: for instance, framing or jointing techniques
- *historic*: the age of the structure, or its association with a period of history
- *social*: association with a cultural group, or individual.

Some structures may qualify, for example, under more than one heading. The Duxford hangars (section 18.1), for example, have primarily a technical significance which relates to the superb Belfast trusses and the sliding-folding doors. In addition, the buildings have a historic and social significance, since they were built in 1917 by German prisoners of war, and they are also handsome structures in their own right, although completely without ornament.

Significance is relatively easily assessed if, like the Duxford hangars, the building appears to be all of a piece. Even here, however, the original roof covering has been replaced by profiled aluminium, since the cardinal rule for a timber frame of softwood is to keep it dry. Mostly, in day-to-day work, our concern is with buildings which have been altered, to varying

Fig. 13.1 The Frigate 'Unicorn' at Dundee. A conservator's dream—all original timber from 1824

degrees, since they were built. It is then necessary to make a cultural audit, which, in simple terms, means taking stock of the structure and its history, and building up a picture of the changes with time. Again, there are several headings under which the elements may be grouped.

Original structure

The starting point of an audit is to determine which part of the structure is, or might be, original. The frigate *Unicorn* is admittedly an unusual example of a timber structure, but a glance at the framing, bound in by the iron straps, indicates that it must all be original, since replacement of individual members is virtually impossible (Fig. 13.1). A closer inspection shows that this is indeed so, despite the fact that the ship has been in the water since 1824. The reason for the high significance allocated to original structure is that we can then be sure of the form in relation to history—later replications always bring something of their own age with them.

Later additions

Buildings which are equivalent of the *Unicorn* are in the minority—most have been extended with time, as has happened to many of our parish churches. Occasionally, the extension may be equal to the original building, as at Stratford House, Birmingham (Fig. 13.2).

Modifications

Timber is a material which can be easily modified on site, and many structures will show examples of

- the addition or removal of subsidiary structure, such as partitions, ceilings, or minor frame members

Fig. 13.2 Stratford House, Birmingham. The front part of the house is seventeenth century, with exposed timber frames. The rear is eighteenth century, with brick walls and a concealed timber first floor and roof. Neither part is more significant than the other—the real significance of the house is the clear delineation of the two periods of construction

- the addition or removal of finishes, such as wall or floor linings, or externally, weather boarding or render
- service-related notches, holes, etc., cut for the installation of heating pipes and wiring, and often without a thought for the effect on member strength.

The purpose of the audit is to determine where, for a particular structure, significance really lies. Listing is of itself no guidance, for it applies to the complete building but the accompanying notes my be of help. Original fabric is generally more significant than recently-introduced material—the audit of Alderham Farmhouse (Fig. 18.5) shows plasterboard partitions and skirtings of the 1960s overlaying a 300-year old frame. The rule is not absolute, however, for in some medieval churches most significance might attach to nineteenth century restoration work. Contemporary elements may not be equal—in an eighteenth century property the concealed floor structure is generally considered to be less significant than the visible joinery work.

13.2. Remedial work

Having determined the significance of the building, the aim of the appraisal is to retain this significance as far as possible when deciding on the form of remedial work under the other headings of safety, durability, etc. The case studies in chapter 18 are all examples of the choice of remedial work which attempted to keep the significance of the building. The Tyne Theatre and York Minster both had their timber roofs destroyed by fire. The primary significance of the Tyne Theatre, the stage machinery, which included the roof trusses, could be regained by replicating the original. The original York trusses were already repaired and strengthened at the time of the fire, and new trusses which attempted to replicate a previously repaired form would be meaningless.

Thus if the significance can be defined, any one of the 'four R's' in section 7.3 could be the most appropriate. However, there are a few general guide lines, such as

- *maximise the retention of original material*
- *allow the original form to be seen*: the significance of the structure lies in the material and the form. Good repair solutions allow the original structural form to 'come through'.
- *do the minimum*: putting it the other way round, there must be a reason for everything which is done. Remember that the aim is to make an old building sound, not to make it a new building.
- *consider 'reversible' remedial work*: reversibility has been a much vaunted concept in conservation work, but the principle requires closer consideration. The all-timber traditional repairs to medieval structures are not fully reversible, because some original timber has to be cut off to make the joint. They are, however, replaceable. An example of an irreversible repair would be to epoxy resin a metal blade into the centre of an original beam, the removal of which would involve the virtual destruction of the member. The most obviously reversible repairs also use metal—the eaves tie to the roof trusses at Sandwich (section 18.4) (for strength), and the props to the Duxford trusses (section 18.1) (for serviceability). Both leave the existing structures essentially unmodified, and can be removed if required. This could only be done, however, if some alternative way was found to prevent the subsequent movements of the structures, and so in practice they are unlikely to be reversed. They could, however, be replaced by another construction, if somebody can do better. This, then, seems to me to be the central idea, which is to allow future conservators an option.

True reversibility can be achieved with additions to a building, such as partitions to divide up an open space in a barn or a warehouse, and which, to some extent, interfere with the significance of the original structure. These should be designed so that they can be removed, and leave the structure as it was before.

In attempting to keep remedial work to the minimum, consider the use of the 100-year rule, and the possibility of load tests, where they are feasible. For medieval structures, the use of the repair types shown in section 12.1 allows the retention of the original connections, for there is no doubt that part of our appreciation of such structure lies in following the logic of way in which the frame is assembled. However, on occasion, a simple metal strap may allow much original material to be kept (Fig. 12.6(c)).

Remember also that we are unused to seeing fissures in the relatively small members of modern structures, but they are almost inevitable in larger, older members, especially in oak. They only affect shear strength, and very rarely warrant remedial work. Filling with an incompressible material may cause further splitting, if the MC of the timber increases.

In later structures metal may be used more freely, and does allow stronger joints to be made. My own view is that a repair should honestly represent the time at which it was done. Thus new member sections should be sawn, and not artificially adzed for effect. Repairs should be inconspicuous at a distance (to enable the original form to be seen) but discernable at close range, if possible explaining, or hinting at, the method of connection.

13.3. Upgrading historic structures

So far remedial techniques, aimed only at putting the building into a safe and serviceable condition, have been described. But there is often a desire to upgrade some aspect of a historic structure, perhaps for economy or as part of a change of use. The areas of concern are usually

- strength
- thermal insulation
- fire resistance.

Upgrading is in general more intrusive than simple remedial work, and the retention of significance becomes more difficult.

Floor strengthening

A change of use often brings with it the need to establish a formal loading capacity for floors, most often when large domestic properties are converted to offices. Charlotte Square, Edinburgh (section 18.2) is an example of a load test justifying the floors in this situation, and the results are not untypical of the reserve of strength of older timber.

If load tests are not feasible, then some of the repair techniques shown in Fig. 13.3(a)–(c) can also be used to increase floor capacity, although they involve a considerable intervention in the floor structure which is generally irreversible. They can, however, be used where the floor structure is judged to have a relatively low significance within the building as a whole.

For floors which are based on principals and common joists, the arrangement shown in (a) may be used. After lifting the floor boards, a slot is cut through the joists and notches formed, which allow two channels to be dropped into place and then moved sideways to pick up the cut ends. This halves the load on the principal beams, and thus doubles the floor capacity.

The critical member of many older floors is usually the principal beam, and the capacity of the floor as a whole can be increased if the principal beam can be strengthened. This can be sometimes be achieved with splice plates or channels (b), if the common joists allow sufficient depth. A flitch plate, perhaps in the form of a tee, is another way of increasing strength (c) but may be considered to be too intrusive. In these cases, it is sometimes possible to increase strength by building a second steel beam at right angles to the principal. Figure 13.4 shows such a beam, used in the Bell Inn at Gloucester.

In this case the client required the floor to be upgraded to take a superimposed load of $4\,kN/m^2$, which was asking too much of the principal beam, particularly since it was elm. The beam had actually suffered creep deflection in the order of 130 mm, and the floorboards had been relaid on tapered firring pieces. The two halves of the new beam lie between the common joists. One side is, in fact, a double channel due to the lack of alignment of the joists. To provide central continuity, the compression force is transmitted though a top plate lying in the zone of the firrings and the tension force passes through two high-tensile threaded rods set in holes drilled in the principal beam. Thus damage to the floor framing, which had a high standard of carpentry, was kept to the minimum (and was certainly less than the holes which had been cut for service installations).

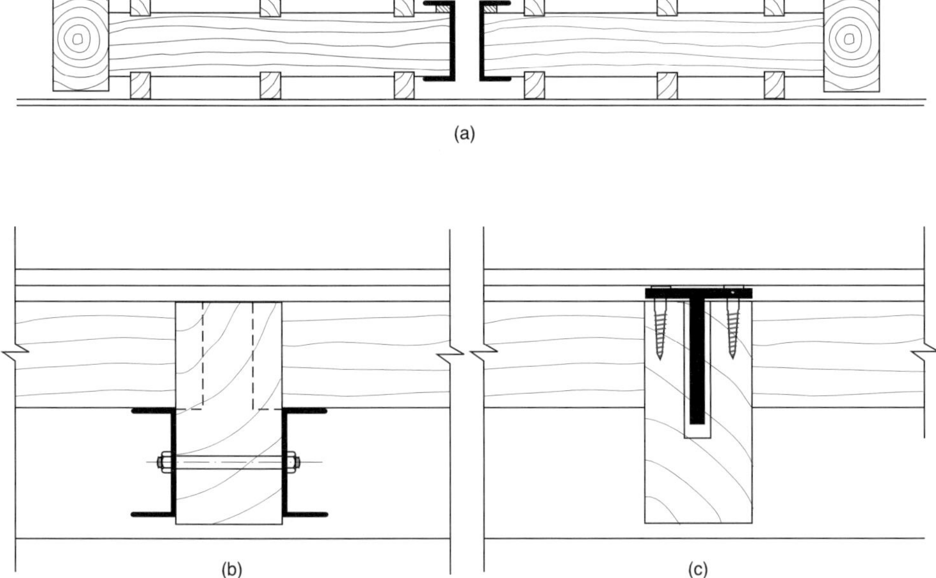

Fig. 13.3
A traditional repair to a barn

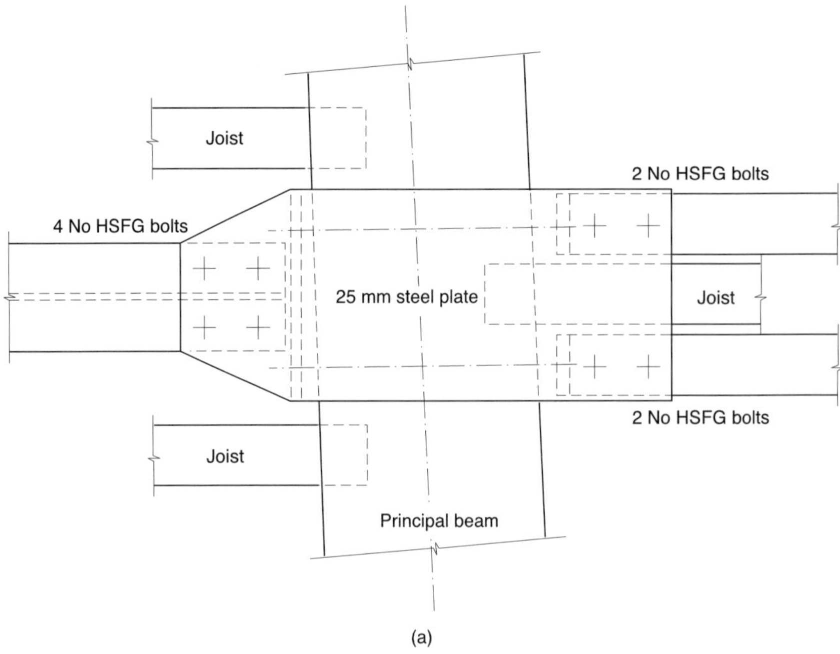

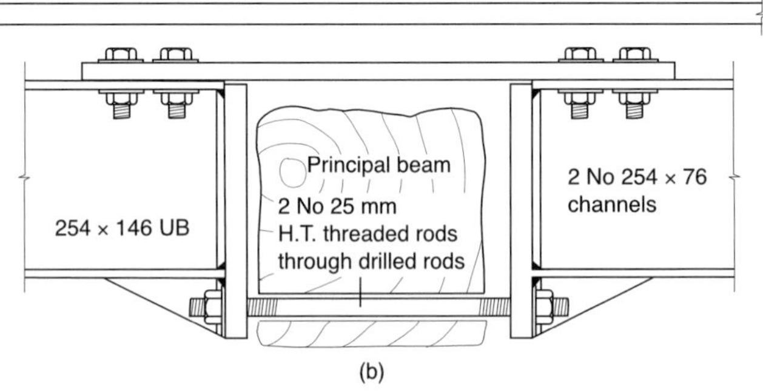

Fig. 13.4(a) and (b) The Bell Inn, Gloucester. The floor was strengthened by providing a second 'principal' beam in steel at right angles to the original

Additional insulation

Although insulation is not of itself a structural issue, it may be a factor to be taken into account in the appraisal, together with the increased risks of condensation. Adding insulation to walls is difficult, unless a fundamental reconstruction of the facade is being made. An example is given of Alderham Farm (section 18.5). The most effective place for additional insulation, however, is in the roof.

Closed roofs, i.e., trusses with a ceiling below, can be upgraded easily with insulation above the ceiling. Since this will be a 'cold' roof, ventilation is important, the more so if the ceiling is not an effective vapour barrier.

If it is visually acceptable to conceal the rafters, they can be underlain with, e.g., foil-backed plasterboard, and insulation set in between the

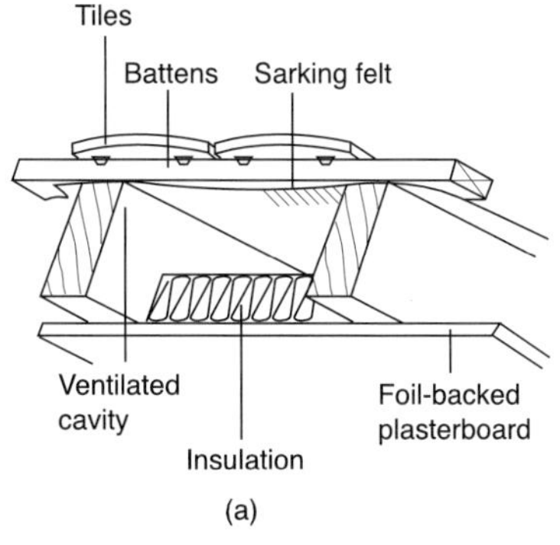

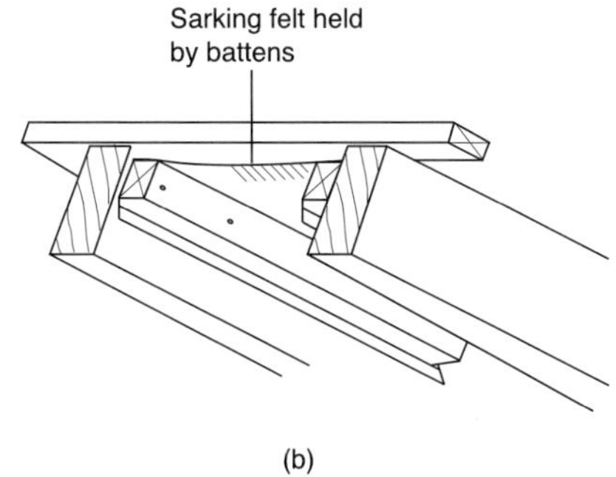

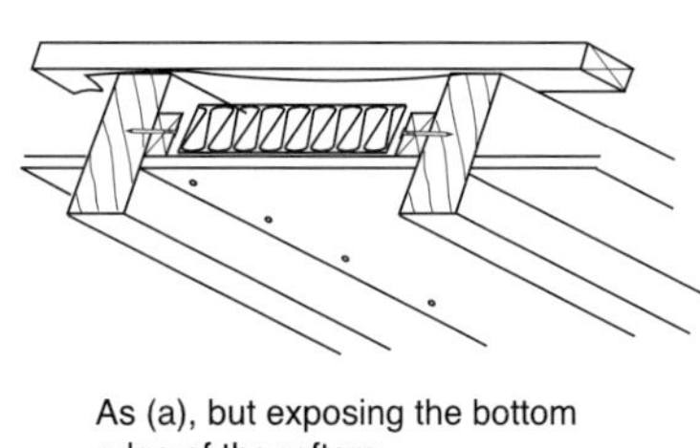

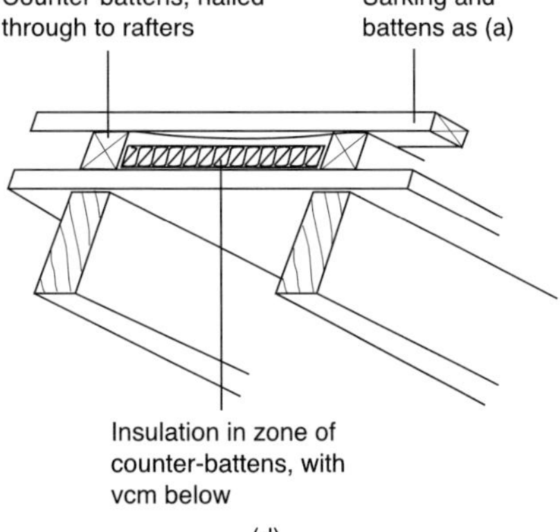

Fig. 13.5 Adding insulation to a pitched roof

rafters (Fig. 13.5(a)). If there is no sarking felt, it would be prudent to introduce it as shown, although this is an imperfect form, and the tops of the rafters are still at risk (b). This is still a cold roof, and relies on a good vapour control membrane, and trickle ventilation though the laps in the sarking. The arrangement is often used for the conversion of lofts into habitable spaces. Detail (a) can be recessed as in (c) to allow the rafters to be seen in part if they have sufficient depth to accommodate the insulation.

Where the rafters and boarding are significant, e.g., in an open roof, the best arrangement is to work from outside, as shown in (d). The removal and replacement of the tiles (or slates) is of course a major consideration, and in many cases would mean that the work would only be economic at a time when the roof covering itself was the subject of general repair.

The increase in height of the roof would need to be taken into account, and the gutter realigned. It is generally not feasible to use insulation much above 30–40 mm in thickness.

Additional fire resistance

There is sometimes a need to improve the period of fire resistance, more particularly when a framed building is being opened for public use. As an

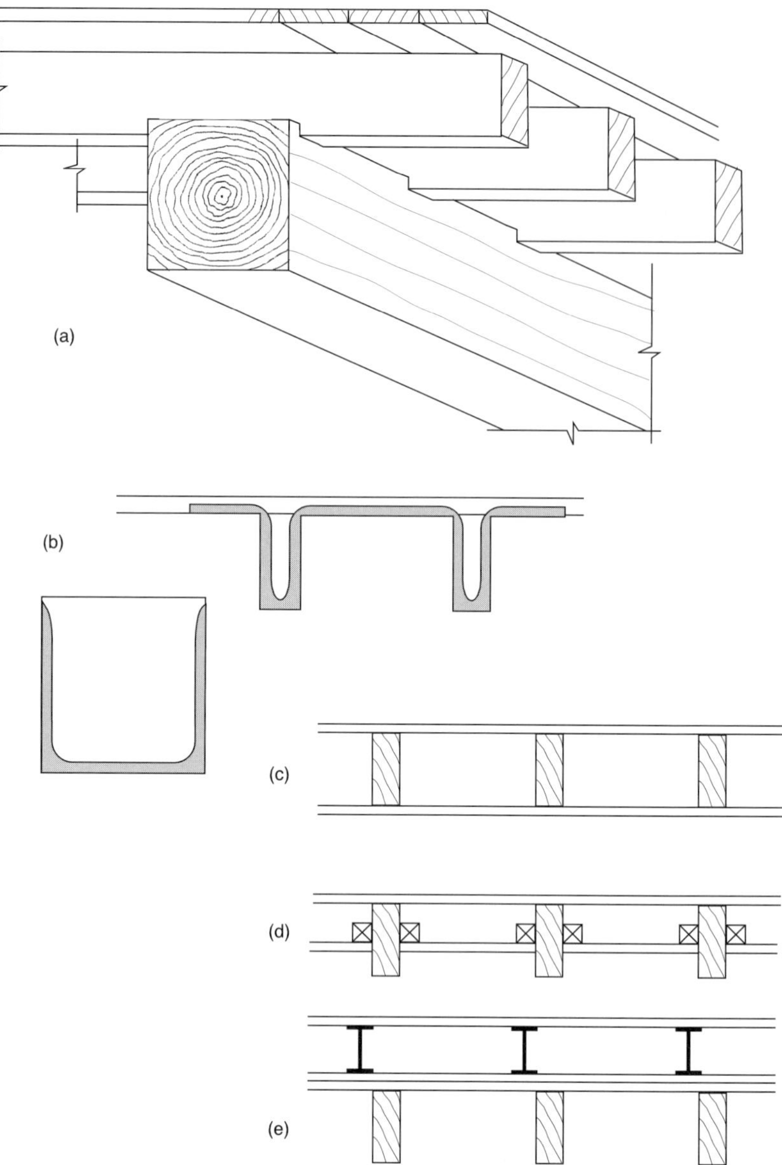

Fig. 13.6 (a) A typical warehouse open floor. (b) The effect of the same charring thickness on the different elements. (c) to (e) Options for additional fire resistance

example let us take a mid-nineteenth century warehouse with large principal beams, common joists and boarding (Fig. 13.6(a)). Given a charring rate of 40 mm per hour, the principal beam will obviously have a period of resistance in excess of two hours (b). In contrast, the joists could achieve about an hour, with less than half an hour for the planks.

The options run broadly in parallel with those suggested for insulation. The joists could be underlain with a fire board to achieve any required period of resistance (c). If concealing the joists is not acceptable, the board can be fixed between them (d). This reveals the joist rhythm, but the proportions are altered. If the whole of the underside of the floor was considered to be significant, then an independent floor could be constructed, spanning between the principal beams with fire protected steel joists (headroom permitting), creating at the same time a service floor (e).

14

Burrell Museum, Glasgow. Softwood glulam frames, glazed externally and neatly turning the corner of the restaurant.

14

The report

Most appraisals are concluded by the presentation of a report to the client. In the broadest sense, the report will address and answer the concern of the client which gave rise to the original commission. If it does not, the reason must be clearly stated, together with an outline of the way in which the commission could be concluded. The client should always be given a way ahead.

14.1. Report layout

The appraisal sequence given in chapter 7 can be used again as a report sequence

- brief
- construction
- condition
- appraisal
- remedial work.

A typical sequence of headings and subheadings for a report on a patent defect, or damage, which is very flexible, and which can, if required, be extended to a third or fourth level for very large reports is shown in Fig. 14.1. An introduction sets the scene, followed by a restatement of the brief, which should be quoted in the form that was agreed with the client (who may possibly have forgotten what that was). The restatement of the brief is also a useful discipline for the report-writer.

If the report is a very large one, or if the spectrum of readers may include those who do not need to know all the details, a summary is useful. If there is a significant amount of information already available, it should be itemised. If it is bulky, consider an appendix.

Before going into detail, it is a good idea to give a brief general overview of the building as a whole—age, form and general condition. This would then be followed by the main part of the report which gives a more detailed assessment of the area of concern. In the example, 'construction' and 'condition' have been separated (perhaps the defect, dry rot, affected all the construction elements), but they could be dealt with under one heading. Choose whichever gives the clearer picture.

MAIN TITLE (building, location)
SUB-TITLE (keyword aim)
for (CLIENT)
AUTHOR (or Company)
DATE

1. INTRODUCTION
2. BRIEF
(3. SUMMARY)
(4. INFORMATION AVAILABLE)
5. THE BUILDING
6. THE ROOF CONSTRUCTION
   6.1 Trusses
   6.2 Purlins and rafters
   6.3 Tiles, battens and gutters
   6.4 Ceilings
   6.5 Services
7. THE ROOF CONDITION
   7.1 The timber structure
   7.2 Tiles, battens and gutters
   7.3 Ceiling
8. STRUCTURAL APPRAISAL
9. REMEDIAL WORK
   9.1 Options
   (9.2 Approximate costs and programmes)

Appendix 1: Specialist report on fungal attack
Appendix 2: Calculations for the purlins
Appendix 3: Photographs (individually titled)
Appendix 4: Drawings:
   1. Roof layout
   2.–4. Details
   5.–6. Remedial options

Fig. 14.1. Example of the layout of a report on a patent defect

The appraisal, in many cases, will have to take into account elements other than the timber frame. This would lead to recommendations for remedial work or, as is sometimes the case, remedial options. Clients may say that they are not interested in options, but as has already been shown in chapter 12 there is nearly always more than one form of remedial work, perhaps with significantly different costs, and it is only right to present these to the client, together with the factors which should be taken into account when making a decision. The costs and outline programme for the works may or may not have been part of the brief, but a brief comment should generally be included, particularly if the client is not knowledgeable in the building field.

Engineers will have to decide their own competence in giving costs. Quantity surveying is, after all, a discipline in its own right. An added difficulty with repair work is that it is not so amenable to costing by the conventional build-up of quantities and rates. I personally prefer to set out the sequence of work in an operations format and, if appropriate, obtain an informal estimate from specialist firms who may later be included on a tender list.

Element	Construction	Condition	Repairs
1. ROOF 1.1 Covering 1.2 Gutters 1.3 Chimneys			
2. EXTERNAL WALLS 2.1 Frame 2.2 Fenestration 2.3 Foundations			
3. ROOF STRUCTURE 3.1 Trusses 3.2 Purlins and rafters 3.3 Ceilings joists			
4. INTERIOR 4.1 Structure 4.2 Ceilings 4.3 Walls 4.4 Floors			
5. MECHANICAL SERVICES			
6. ELECTRICAL SERVICES			
7. EXTERNAL WORKS			

Fig. 14.2. An example of column format for general survey work

The format outlined above concentrates on a particular area of the building. When the brief is for a general assessment of structural condition, a column format can often be used with advantage, as shown in Fig. 14.2. Of course, the sequence of elements and sub-elements must be tailored to the particular structure, but the format allows the general condition to be easily assessed. The repair column relates to work of routine maintenance, such as 'clean and repaint gutters'. Where remedial works are more extensive, or are cross-linked to other elements, it may be necessary to refer to a later section, in conventional format.

Engineering assessments often involve calculations, which may not be fully understood by all the readers. Nevertheless the report should outline the calculations which have been done, and what the results mean. The calculations themselves may be presented in an appendix, as indeed may any item which would have a limited readership or which would hold up the flow of the main report.

14.2. Drawings and photographs

The body of the report will obviously consist of words, but drawings and photographs are often an effective way of communicating information. Drawings will generally be based on the sketches made on site. Prints of photographs may be mounted directly into the report, to give the best quality, but laser copies may be acceptable in many cases. The most important point to remember, however, is that each illustration should have been included for a specific purpose, otherwise it will appear to the reader as padding. Remember also that features which are obvious to yourself may not be so obvious to the lay reader. A photograph of 'dry rot in the roof void' may benefit from the explanation that rot can be seen 'at the eaves on the bottom tie of the truss'. Beware of creating a false impression of the extent of the defects from a range of photographs which are defect-biassed. Somewhere in the report the correct assessment must be given. Having said all that, drawings and photographs are a great help to the reporter, particularly if the reader is not familiar with the building, and the costs of A3 reductions of drawings, which may be folded into an A4 report, and standard 150 × 100 mm colour prints are not high. However, these methods are rapidly being overtaken by the development of electronic cameras and computer editing programmes which make it even easier to build images into the report.

14.3. Report style

Perhaps 'style' is to high-sounding a word—I mean no more than an effective mode of writing; effective in the sense that the reader clearly understands what the writer wants to say. Much good advice is given in Gower (1973). I personally believe that comprehensibility depends on three factors

- order
- precision
- clarity.

Although these factors are to an extent interdependent, it is worth considering them separately.

Order

The order in which ideas are presented to the reader is vitally important to the understanding of the report as a whole. I normally start a report layout by scribbling a series of headings, much as those in Fig. 14.1. Then each heading is filled in with a series of points, which will be subject to much alteration as they are gradually sorted into the most logical order. Only then would I start to write using the report plan as a guide.

Although I still use pencil on paper, keyboard skills are becoming more general. Certainly it is much easier to read and proof text when it has been typed. The order of points within a heading should follow the logic of the headings, dealing with the general before the particular, and dealing with the more significant before the less significant.

Precision

Precision involves not only providing correct information, but also giving it the correct weight. Information comes from various sources

- documentation
- direct observation
- from a third person
- inferred
- estimated.

Information sources should generally be quoted; this will also act as a reminder of the weight of the information.

It is also easier to be more precise about the form of construction than the condition. As stated before, 'in good condition' is meaningful but 'in poor condition' is not, unless it is qualified by the type, degree and distribution of the defect. These may be given in qualitative terms as, for example, for degree

- slight
- moderate
- severe

and for distribution

- occasional
- significant
- general.

For a major defect, however, these terms should be replaced by a more quantitative description, such as 'the dry rot has affected the bottom tie for approximately one metre from the wall, as shown in figure X.'

Clarity

Clarity—making the sense clear to the reader—depends in the first place on order; or to put it the other way round, elegant prose cannot make up for a poor structure. Something which is clear should be able to be spoken aloud without effort. A comma would indicate a short pause, and the full stop a breath. This will avoid an over-long sentence. The sentence can be seen as a unit of thought, and the paragraph as the discussion of a topic.

Thus the whole arrangement of the report—the headings and subheadings, right down to the punctuation—should be helpful to the reader, so that the eyes may move continuously through the report, without having to stop and go back for a second look. In addition, words like 'in addition', 'therefore' also help by suggesting that what follows is a continuation of the same thought. 'However', 'in contrast', 'on the other hand'—on the other hand—indicate that the other side of the case is being considered. The field of grammar and syntax, so often the engineer's Achilles heel, is outside the scope of this work, but again useful advice is given in Gower (1973).

Further reading

A glossary of terms used to describe the components of a timber frame is given in Alcock *et al.* (1996). Advice on technical report writing is given in Cooper (1964).

15

York Minster, South Transept Roof boss. Carving one of the vault bosses from a block of glued laminated oak.

15

The repair contract

When remedial works have been recommended, a client will generally request some estimate of costs, in order to decide whether or not to implement the recommendations. It may be useful to allocate priorities to the work, and to distinguish between what is essential, what is desirable, and what is optional.

This might allow the development of a phased contract, with less immediate demands on a client's purse or his accommodation. Generally speaking, however, phased contracts are more expensive than a single campaign.

15.1. Precontract work

The scope of the remedial work is often only outlined in the report, because there is often more than one option, and because at this stage the client is not necessarily committed to proceeding, and has not paid for a detailed design. There is often, therefore, a need to make a more detailed survey, especially of the concealed elements, as a preliminary to the detailed design of the repair scheme.

Further opening-up could be done on a day-works basis by a small contractor. The advantages are

- a confirmation of the appraisal or, perhaps, an indication of a slight change in direction
- better quantification of the scope of the works and, hence, a reduction of the price risk
- (if the work can be left open) better on-site information for tenderers.

The disadvantages may be

- that the occupier would be unduly inconvenienced
- that access requires disproportionately expensive temporary works.

While there is always a preference for the maximum amount of information, these factors will have to be balanced against one another. If no pre-contract work is done, then any further investigation work will have to be, in effect, the first phase of the main contact. The detailed survey work for St. Mary's church (section 18.4), because of the cost of scaffolding, was done in this way. Alderham Farm (section 18.5), as an unoccupied domestic property, was opened up before the main contract under a small day-works contract for relatively little cost.

15.2. Tendering

Most clients expect that any contract for remedial works will be let by competitive tender. It must be remembered that the tendering process is about cost, or rather the minimisation of cost, and not quality. It is important therefore that all the tenderers can be seen to possess the necessary skills to carry out the work, and that its scope and nature are clearly set out in the tender documents.

In practice this usually means that a short list of approved firms is prepared, whose competence is, in so far as possible, checked by the engineer. This can be done by an assessment of past work (with some assurances about continuity of employment of the personnel involved), together with an inspection of their workshops. Craftsmanship as such cannot be instructed, but must be in the minds and hands of the tenderer's staff. It is sometimes difficult to find a large number of suitably qualified firms, and in my view three or four is sufficient. There may even, on occasion, be a case for a single nomination. Consider specifying sample pieces, if this is appropriate.

15.3. Contract documentation

The aim of the contract documentation is to set out as clearly as possible

- the basis of the contract (the conditions)
- the scope of the work (drawings and specification)
- the basis of payment (bills of quantities or, as a preference, a schedule of work).

Overall, the JCT Forms of Contract still provide, in my view, the best framework for works of repair; select the one which is most appropriate to the scale of the works. If the project work can be well defined and the contractor will be doing most of it personally, the Minor Works contract will be adequate, and is mercifully brief. More complex projects will need to have more comprehensive Forms.

Drawings are the best way of describing locations, assemblies and members. The type and quality of the materials and workmanship are best expressed in words. The choice and specification of timber for repair work is considered in chapter 16.

15.4. The specification

The specification is normally divided into

- preliminaries, and
- materials and workmanship for each work section.

Some larger firms have developed their own standard specifications. A published specification library, the *National Building Specification*, is available in loose-leaf file format (with user notes) and with the text on software. While it is aimed primarily at the new-build contract, it provides a useful vocabulary for both the preliminaries and the various work sections. The material specification, as noted before, is covered in chapter 16. The notes below relate to preliminary items for works of repair.

- *Programme*: the current vogue for 'fast-track' programmes may have some justification for the construction of speculative office blocks, but it is not really compatible with good craftsmanship and complex repair work. Try to establish a contract period which allows the work to be done properly—you will, after all, not be able to stand aside from any arguments over quality of work and delays caused by an unrealistic programme.
- *Boundaries, accesses and restrictions*: these could be called the 'edges' of the contract. An existing building is often close to other buildings and to highways. Time spent defining the precise area of the site, where it can be entered, and any limitations on free working such as restrictions on working hours, or noise, help the contractor to understand what will be required, and mitigate claims.
- *Temporary works*: the functions of temporary works may be described under the headings of

    - support
    - protection
    - access.

    The different approaches within the contract will be to give

    - no specific instructions
    - performance criteria and/or general arrangement
    - a detailed design.

    For contracts of a domestic scale such as Alderham Farm (section 18.5), most contractors will need no specific instructions for conventional support and access scaffolding. When temporary support is needed, perhaps for the replacement of part of a truss member, this will generally be specified by performance requirements of position and capacity (see section 18.4). Only rarely will a detailed design be prepared by the specifier, but this might be appropriate if the main work was being carried out by a timber specialist, without a general contractor in attendance.

If it is decided to protect the whole works with a temporary roof, this should be specified, since it is normally an expensive item. The need for a temporary roof is generally determined by the vulnerability of the fabric below. If the repair works need components to be craned in, then the temporary roof is a severe restriction and may have to be designed to be moveable (see sections 18.6 and 18.7).

16

York Minster, South Transept, new roof boss. A representation of the 'green man', carved from a block of laminated oak.

16

The specification of timber for repair

The specification of the timber for repair work is as important as the repair scheme itself, and should be thought of as the qualitative aspect of design. A balance must be struck between the quality of timber needed to fulfil the project requirements on the one hand, and the economics and availability of the supply on the other. The classic 'all timber shall be fully seasoned, true to line, and free of all defects such as knots, splits and shakes' is ultimately meaningless, since if such timber could be found, it would certainly be priced out of the structural market.

In specifying timber for structural repair, a designer will have one or more of the following criteria in mind

- species
- dimensions and finish
- the form of the member in relation to the log
- strength
- moisture content at installation
- durability
- applied treatments.

16.1. Softwood

Species

The softwoods generally available for structural work are listed in table 3 of BS 5268. For conventional structural repairs these would include redwood, whitewood, spruce, firs and species combinations. Douglas fir and pitch pine are more expensive timbers, and are used when their properties are specially required as, for instance,

- to match the species of an existing historic structure (a check on site with samples may be worthwhile)
- for member size (see *dimensions* below)
- for member capacity (see *strength* below).

Dimensions and finish

The basic sizes of sawn softwood, which are available ex-stock, were formerly given in BS 4471 (BSI, 1987), and are now transferred to the National Annex of BS EN 336 (BSI, 1995). Basically, these include pieces up to 75 × 300 mm in section and up to 6 m long. For pieces greater than 100 mm in thickness, special enquiries would have to be made, unless Douglas fir is specified, which can still be obtained in baulks up to 400 × 400 mm in cross-section, and around 12 m in length. The availability of this material may diminish in the future.

Timber is normally supplied sawn. If required, it may be fine sawn or planed, although planing will reduce the member dimensions by 3 mm (or 5 mm if the width/depth is >100 mm).

In repair work there is often a need to match the dimensions of the repair pieces to those of the existing members in the structure. This is generally done by cutting them from the next largest standard size.

Strength

The designer has two options within the Code

- specify a Strength Class with the selection of timber species and grade being left to the contractor
- specify the species (with origin where necessary) and the grade.

The grading rules for new timber are given in BS 4978 (see appendix 1). The defects covered (for visual grading) are

- knots
- slope of grain
- rate of growth
- wane
- fissures
- resin pockets and bark pockets
- distortion.

If the member is visible in the finished structure, it is usual to override the grade allowance for wane, and specify that the piece will have a full section throughout.

Moisture content

A maximum moisture content at the centre of, say, 20% is generally specified. For thicker members, although this limit would still be desirable, it must be expected that moisture content will be higher, and a small amount of shrinkage as the timber dries out should be accepted as a factor in the design. This may mean that periodic tightening of bolts after assembly has to be specified.

Durability

It should be assumed that all commercial supplies of material 75 × 300 mm or less will contain a proportion of sapwood, and must therefore be classified as perishable (see section 4.2). An exception could possibly be made for Douglas fir and pitch pine, since they are available in large sizes, and there are colour differences between the sapwood and the heartwood. However, if 'heartwood only' is specified there will be a small cost penalty for the selection and cutting involved. Alternatively, the strategy for the design of repairs in softwood should either be to place the timber in hazard class 1, in which case there are no durability requirements, or to treat the timber with preservative.

Applied surface treatments

For timber that will be visible in the repaired structure, there are normally three options for applied treatment

- *a surface sealer*: untreated timber is very prone to staining, particularly where it can be touched. For internal work it is usual to apply a surface sealer, so that the surface can be cleaned. The brave do nothing and regard the result as texture. Sometimes this is successful.
- *paint or varnish*: any surface treatment to repaired timber will generally be determined by the existing structure.
- *retardant*: the need for the control of surface spread of flame will be determined by Part B of the Regulations (see section 5.3). Some clear retardants are hydroscopic and will stain if exposed to rain. Application should be left until the building is sealed.

16.2. Temperate hardwood

The supply position for temperate hardwoods is very different to that of the softwoods. Merchants are predominantly concerned with supplies for joinery work, compared with which the demand for structural repair material is very small indeed. As a consequence very little stock of structural sizes is held, and most is supplied freshly cut, i.e. green, with implications both for the design of the repair scheme and the specification of the timber.

Species

This section is written in the context of European oak (*Quercus robor*), but the principles will also apply to elm and chestnut.

Moisture content

It has to be accepted that timber which is green, that is, with a MC of 80–100%, will still be green on installation. The old carpenters' rule for seasoning—'a year for every inch of thickness'—is simplistic, but it does give some idea of the period of time needed to achieve an MC of around 20%. Inevitably, even green timber is going to dry out in service, with the resulting distortions of profile shown in Fig. 3.4. These distortions must simply be accepted (as, of course, they were by medieval carpenters) with the additional proviso that repair timbers are often framed into seasoned timbers. Drying distortions in the length will obviously be more significant as the slope of grain increases, and some limit should be specified when the maintenance of line is significant.

For thickness up to 100 mm, some merchants keep seasoned planks perhaps up to 4 m long. Intended primarily for joinery, they will comply with a very high structural grade, but will cost considerably more than the price of unseasoned timber.

For thicknesses less than 75 mm, kiln drying is a possibility, but for oak the process will take some time, and will also result in a significant increase in the supply price.

Position in the log

By reference to Fig. 3.4, it can be seen that pieces from different parts of the log will move in different ways when drying out. For smaller pieces (say, less than 150 mm) it is possible to exclude boxed heart, with a reduction in the amount of splitting which will take place. For larger pieces, it is usual to allow the inclusion of boxed heart.

Sapwood

This can be accepted for internal work and for the inner face of external pieces. Prohibiting it entirely increases the cost, since larger logs have to be used.

Wane

If all pieces are required to be full section for reasons of appearance, wane should not be permitted.

Strength

If the repair members need to be designed for strength, then one of the grades from BS 5756 (BSI, 1997) may be used (in conjunction with the 'wet' stresses in BS 5268 if the timber is used green).

When there is no formal need for a design strength, the grading rules may still be useful to give some minimum assurance of quality.

Finally, it should be remembered that a specification is written as a generality, and that a craftsman's eye can, and should, override in areas where joints are to be cut.

Further reading

The specification of (new) softwood is covered by Baird (1990).

17

Frensham Heights School, Farnham, Surrey. The Performing Arts Centre auditorium, framed in redwood glulams.

17

Moving timber frames

It is obvious that a medieval frame is capable of being dismantled and re-erected elsewhere, and there is much evidence for this happening in the past, and for the reuse of framing members within a later structure. In the present century, the movement of frames has been primarily for conservation reasons. The Weald and Downland Museum, near Singleton, and the Avoncroft Museum in Cheshire, are both collections of framed buildings that, for one reason or another, were not required on their original site, and were then dismantled and re-erected.

As the conservation movement has gained ground, fewer frames have become available for moving, and conservation officers would generally hold the view that moving a listed building is not acceptable unless it is the only way of preserving it. This chapter is therefore limited to a brief overview of the two methods available—dismantling and re-erection, and, in certain instances, the possibility of a 'lift and slide' move.

The lift and slide method involves the creation of a rigid frame under the building, which is lifted up, if necessary, and then slid along a prepared track to a new location. For longer distances, the building and its frame could be put on a prepared trailer. The great advantage of the method is that the building remains unaltered, although there would need to be an evaluation of the risk of cracking of in situ finishes. Particular equipment and expertise is necessary, and it is usual for the detailed design and the move itself to be carried out by a specialist company. However, for either method, a very detailed appraisal is necessary before any work is put in hand.

17.1. The survey

In addition to the normal survey evaluation of construction and condition, it will be necessary to consider

- the frame joint details for general robustness, and feasibility of disconnection
- the fabric components such as tiles, or joinery, which have the potential to be stripped and refixed
- the in situ fabric such as brickwork, where it would only be possible to build new walls with the original bricks, or plaster, which would have to be redone with perhaps small decorative elements cut out and refixed

- the context and environment, to decide what significance would be lost if the building was taken out of its surroundings (or, perhaps, gained in a new location).

This would allow a balance sheet to be made up for the two options, which might favour one or the other, or suggest that a move of any kind was not feasible.

17.2. Dismantling and re-erection

If the frame components are, overall, in reasonably good condition, and the in situ finishes are either a relatively minor part of the whole, or are not significant, then the dismantling and re-erection of the frame is technically feasible.

An accurate survey of the frame, particularly at sole-plate level, is needed. Many frames suffer differential settlement, and it is generally prudent to prepare the new base as a replica of the old, unless it can be established that a rectified assembly will fit together. Identify and reference each member with a firmly fixed label before dismantling. Member repairs are best done in the disassembled state. For an end repair, the original length must be carefully recorded, in order to ensure replication.

A case study is given in section 18.5.

17.3. The lift and slide method

If the condition of the frame does not appear to be conducive to dismantling, or if in situ elements and finishes, such as brickwork and plaster, are of major significance in the overall structure, then only a lift and slide move may be feasible. Although the costs associated with such a method are obviously considerable, they will depend upon the size of the structure, and the distance moved. The details of any scheme will depend on the particular circumstances, but the following is an outline of the general sequence of work (Fig. 17.1).

1. The installation of internal and external bracing, related to obvious weaknesses in the structure and the possible lateral forces associated with the move.
2. The installation of a robust bearing frame under the load-bearing elements. Sometimes this may be done in steel, but it is usually more feasible to consider a concrete frame, installed in short sections by underpinning techniques, with lapped reinforcement. The stiffness of the frame has to be assessed to keep the distortion of the structure within acceptable limits under the various support conditions associated with the move. Realistically, it has to be in a single plane, and so any basement structures have to be cut through and left behind.

Then EITHER, for short distances at the same level

3(a) A running track is constructed below the bearing frame, leading to the new location, with prepared top surface.

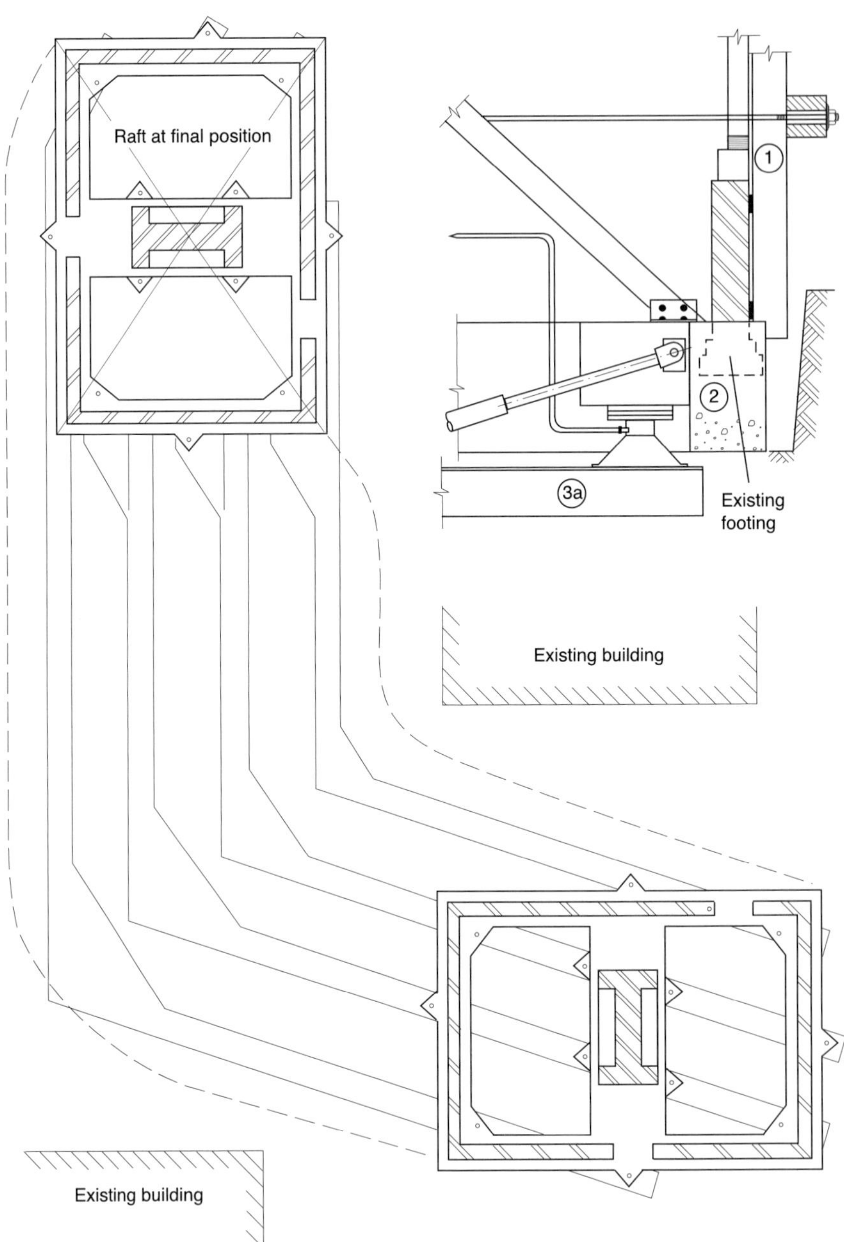

Fig. 17.1 General sequence of work in the 'lift and slide method'

4(a) The building, on its bearing frame, is slid along the track to the new location. The move may be made by the use of simple rollers, e.g., scaffold tubes, or proprietary sliding bearings, which need a metal plate surface to the track, and operate on the hovercraft principle, with grease instead of air. It is possible to change the orientation of the building, and to 'steer' around other buildings.

OR, for longer distances, or change of level (Fig. 17.2)

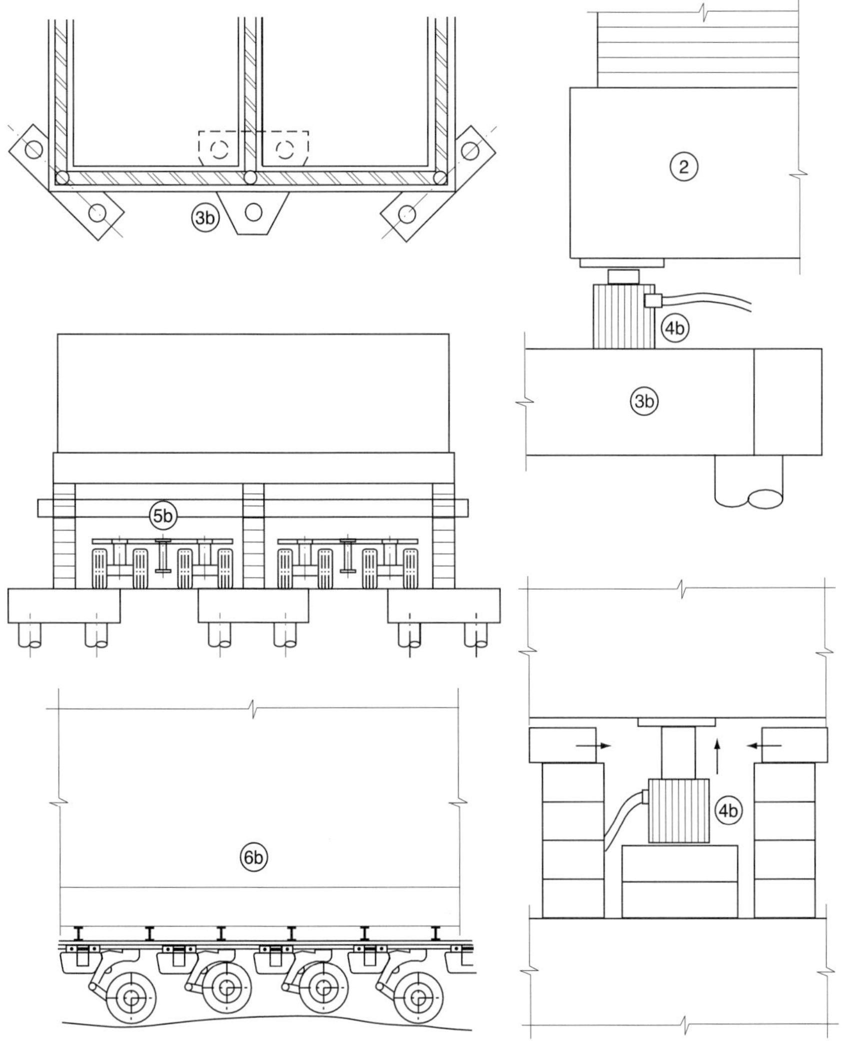

Fig. 17.2 Construction sequence for longer distances or a change of level

3(b) Foundations using pads, or mini-piles, are installed below the frame to provide jacking points.

4(b) Using jacks and blocks, the frame is jacked up to the new, or travelling level.

5(b) The transport rigs are introduced below the frame. These rigs are usually built up from wheeled modules, and the assembly is steerable and self-levelling, and can be raised to lift the frame off the blocks.

6(b) The rig is towed to a new location, over a prepared track. A slight incline in the track may be feasible. When the building is in its new position, the lifting procedure is reversed to lower the frame onto new foundations.

18

The courtyard roof of Portcullis House, London. A diagonal lattice vault in American white oak, with stainless steel nodes.

18

Case histories

18.1. The Belfast truss and the Duxford airfield hangars

Chapter 2 described the radical effect which the mass production of metal fasteners had on the construction of timber frames and, in particular, the roof truss. Timbers of relatively small cross-section (produced quite cheaply by power saws) could simply be lapped, and then nailed or bolted together. These fasteners, with their dowel action in shear, would resist tension or compression in the joint, and so make possible fundamentally different structural forms.

The Belfast truss is a particularly elegant example of such a form, which uses small cross-section timbers and a large bag of nails to make trusses which span up to 30 m. The truss form is very efficient, although without ornament of any kind, and it can be seen at its best in the First World War hangars at Duxford Airfield, a part of the Imperial War Museum (Fig. 18.1.1).

Each truss is fabricated in two halves (Fig. 18.1.1), which are then joined together by nailing through the diagonals. Each bottom tie is made up of four pieces nailed together, with staggered laps, and the top boom of two square pieces, slender enough to be pulled to the required curvature. The diagonals are in the sophisticated form of an orthogonal lattice, canted over towards each end of the truss, and engineers can spend hours debating the merits of this arrangement. The trusses are spaced at approximately 3 m centres, and joined by purlins and cross-bracing. It is likely that the original roof decks were made up of diagonal boards covered with bituminous felt, replaced at some time with corrugated iron. In 1990 the Museum began a programme of roof covering replacement, using a proprietary insulated profiled aluminium system.

All of the surviving three hangars at Duxford are of a similar form (the fourth was burnt during the making of the film *The Battle of Britain*). Each hangar (Fig. 18.1.3) has two halls, with trusses spanning onto brick walls. The ends of each building are closed by pairs of sliding–folding doors, which in themselves are significant pieces of carpentry. Each door is made up of 18 leaves hinged onto sliding uprights. Each leaf is framed, often

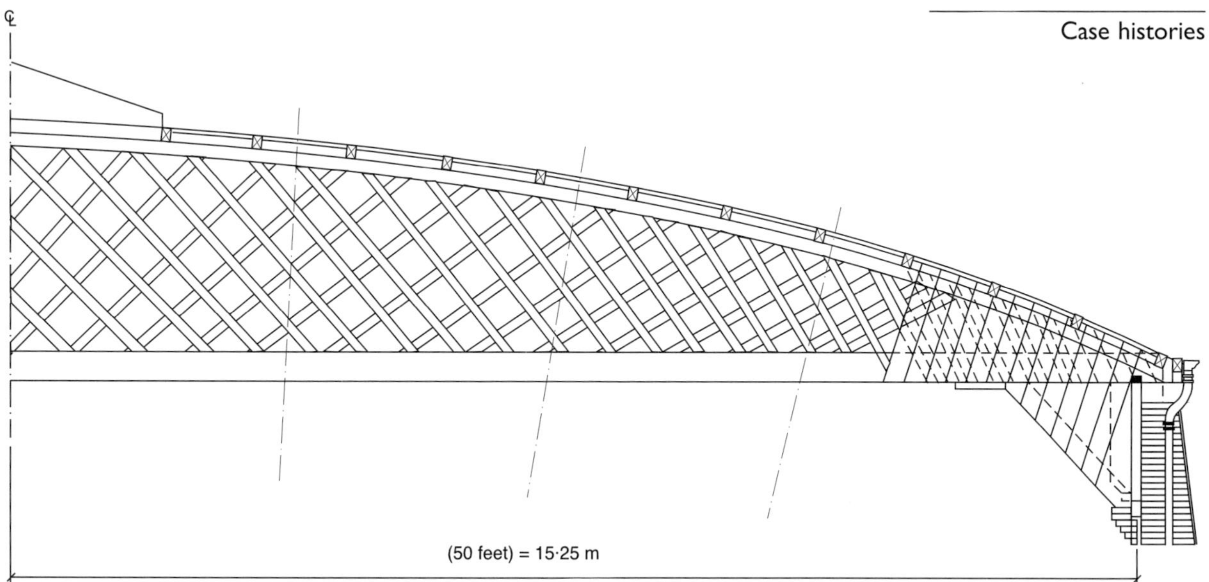

Fig. 18.1.1 Duxford Hangar: half elevation of roof truss

with full-height stiles, and infilled with diagonal tongued and grooved boarding. The leaves are linked by folding steel straps, to prevent over-opening. Two pairs of leaves have fixed straps, to stabilise the assembly and prevent overturning.

The weight of the doors is carried on wheels which run on a metal track embedded in the floor, while the uprights are stabilised by horizontal rollers engaged between steel-faced timber guides attached to the end truss (Fig. 18.1.5).

In 1992 the Museum asked Ove Arup and Partners to investigate the condition of the roof and doors in relation to two problems.

- Deflections of the trusses with time had caused some of the head guides to bind on the tops of the doors, making them difficult to operate, even though some of the individual leaves had been eased in the past by notching (Fig. 18.1.6).
- The large air gaps at the door heads meant that the internal ambient conditions could not be controlled to the degree which was desirable for the repair of aircraft, which nowadays are made of metal, rather than timber.

Some means of lifting the door heads slightly and controlling future deflections was required, so that the air gap could be controlled and reduced to an acceptable minimum.

The trusses are relatively shallow, with a span/centre depth ratio of 9:1. Although their strength is still adequate (a sample number were load-tested a few years before). A survey of several guide rails (Fig. 18.1.6) (that would originally have been set to level) showed a mid-span deflection of around 70 mm to 80 mm, which would represent the creep component of deflection.

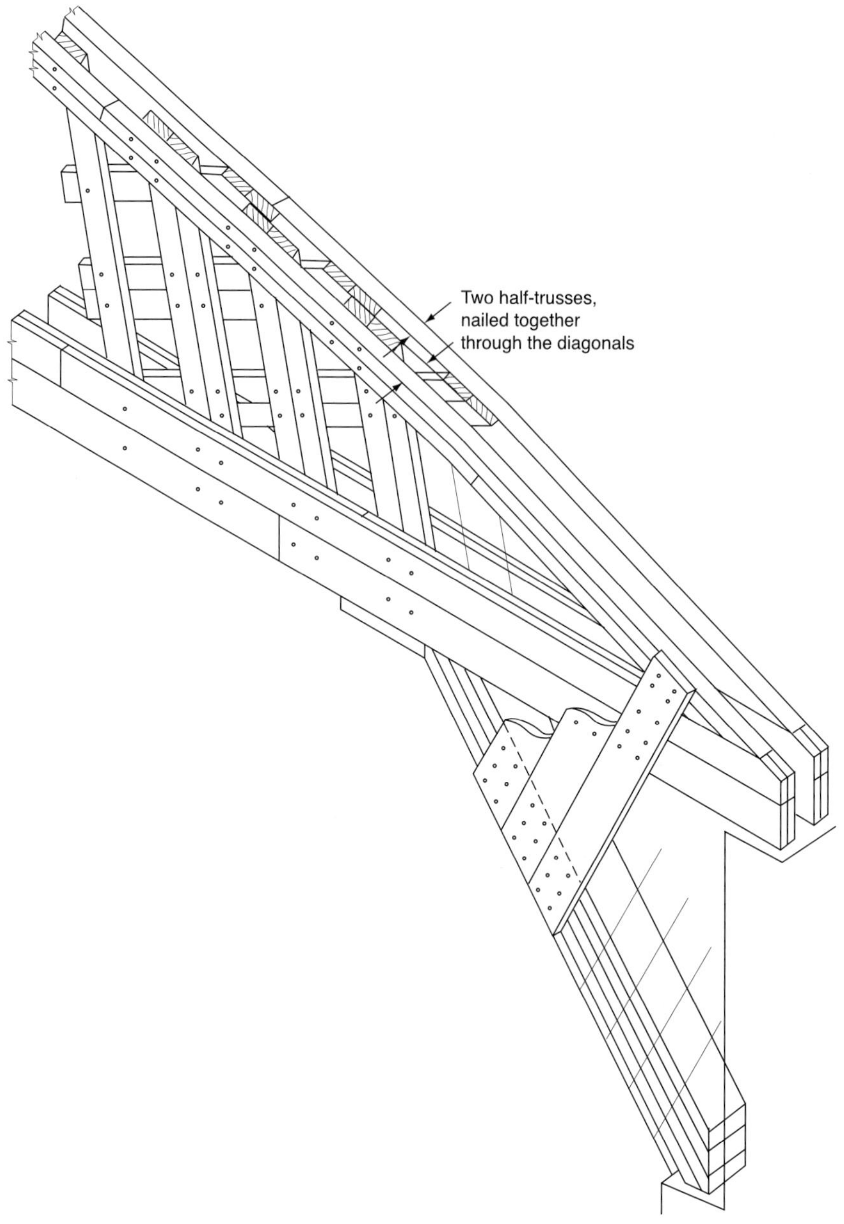

Fig. 18.1.2 Truss construction

Although it is not large in relation to the truss itself (span/400), it was much larger than the clearance over the doors, and it was for this reason that they had been notched. Some guides were binding despite the notches, so it was clear that creep deflection was on-going.

Thus some method would have to be found of eliminating creep deflection. In addition, it would be desirable to reset the guides to line. Initially it seemed difficult to deal with the creep deflection: in practical terms, it would be impossible to modify the end truss, and the only answer would be to build

Fig. 18.1.3 Interior

Fig. 18.1.4 Exterior view of doors in the fully open position

a steel truss adjacent which took over its duties. However, the study of the doors immediately showed that they did not open to the full span of the building. Props could be placed at the limit of the opening, which would reduce the truss span by a third (Fig. 18.1.5). Since deflection is proportional to the fourth power of the span, the influence of creep would be reduced by one hundred fold, and would, in effect, be eliminated.

Realigning the guides proved more of a problem. Their construction was intimately bound up with the truss, which would mean that it was the truss which would effectively have to be straightened. The general experience is

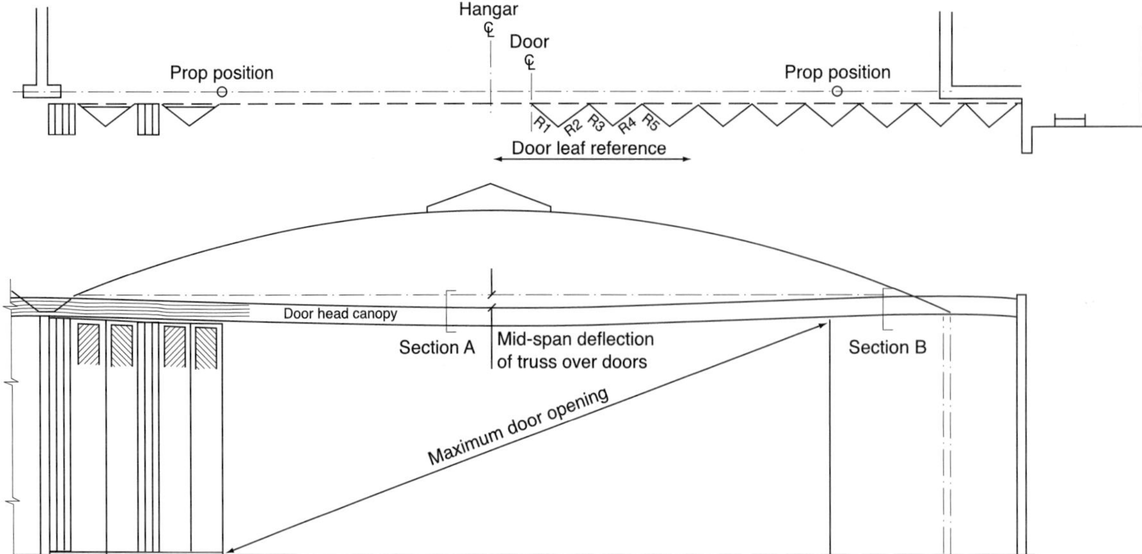

Fig. 18.1.5(a) Door details

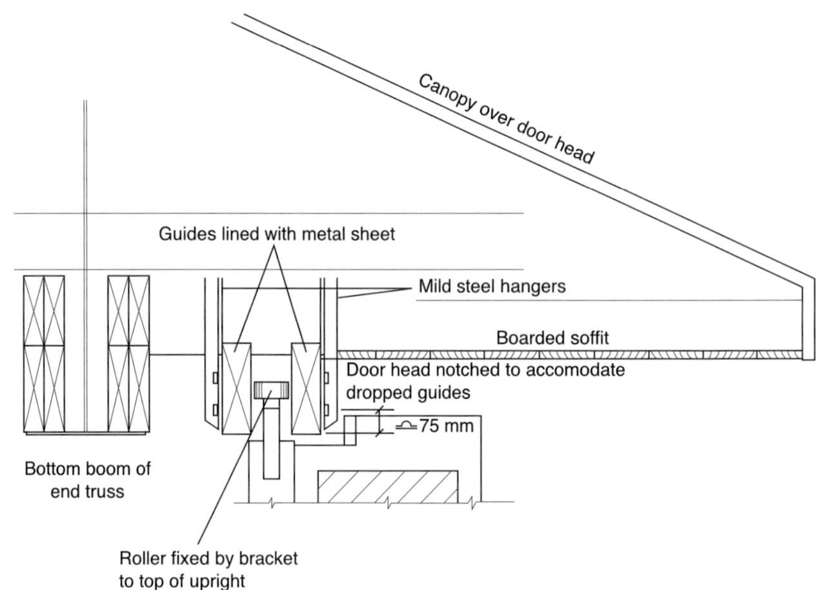

Fig. 18.1.5(b) Centre section A

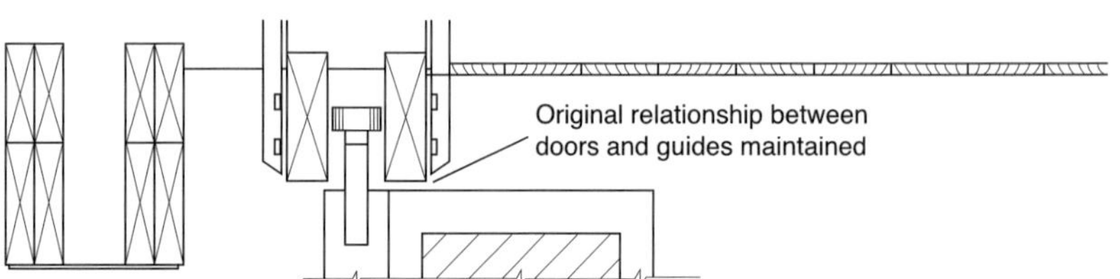

Fig. 18.1.5(c) Support section B

Fig. 18.1.6 Door head notched by 80 mm to accommodate the deflecting guide rails

that creep deflection results in a permanent set of timber members. It was decided therefore to design the two props with screw jack heads (adapted from concrete falsework props) in order to test the potential for lifting the trusses (Fig. 18.1.7). This could not be done 'blind', however, because the jacks might simply lift the truss off its bearings. Thus a Fressinnet flat-jack with a pressure gauge was placed on each jack to indicate the load in the prop, and an estimate was made of the truss dead weight.

This arrangement indicated that the truss could be lifted about 30 mm while still bearing on its supports. In other words, around half the creep deflection could be removed.

The remaining amount could be trimmed off the guides, enabling the notches in the doors to be repaired, and a soffit board built over the leaves to close the airway.

18.2. 26–28 Charlotte Square, Edinburgh

The 'New Town' of Edinburgh was built during the latter half of the eighteenth century, and consists of large elegant town houses set around landscaped squares and linking streets. Most are still in existence today, although many have been converted to other uses. Numbers 26–28, Charlotte Square, have for some time been interconnected as offices, and in 1990 were purchased by a company whose aim was to comprehensively refurbish the properties, and be able to confirm to lessees that all the floors were capable of carrying a superimposed load of 2·5 kN/m^2. Although the building had previously been used as an office, there was no way of determining what load it had actually carried in the past, although it would have been very unlikely to have been as high as 2·5 kN/m^2. The floors would have to be assessed in detail.

Fig. 18.1.7(a) View of prop

Fig. 18.1.7(b) Detail of jack head

The first stage was to lift some boards (which fortunately lie parallel to the principal beams) and survey the construction (Figs 18.2.1 and 18.2.2). The houses are typical of the area, with solid masonry walls, and timber floors of large principal beams with common joists notched into them. A 'deafening'

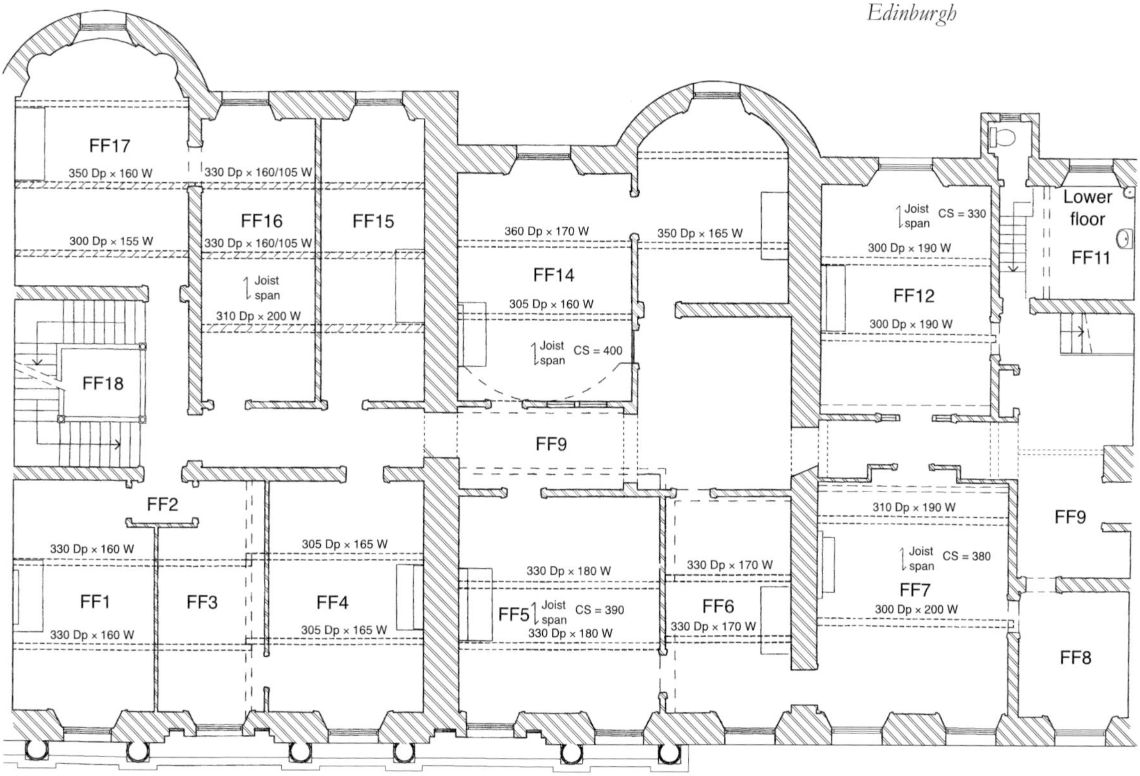

Fig. 18.2.1 First floor plan of 26–28 Charlotte Square, Edinburgh

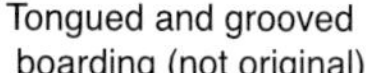

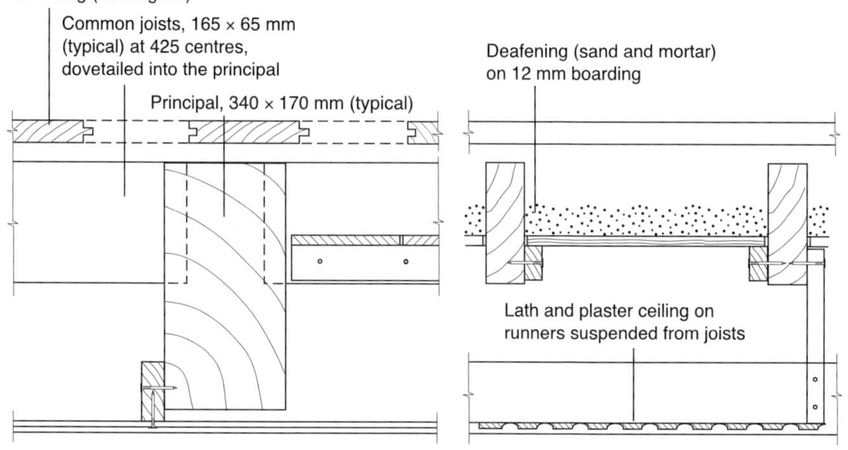

Fig. 18.2.2 Details of the floor construction

layer of boards and mortar is fitted between the joists, and the plaster ceiling below has elaborate covings. At some time in the past, the original boards (which would have been plain butt-edged) had been lifted, and replaced with tongued and grooved boarding laid on tapered firrings to correct an average mid-span creep deflection of around 50 mm. In addition to the joist notches, the top flanges of the principal beams have been randomly grooved for electrical conduits, locally up to 40 mm deep.

From the survey information a first evaluation of applied stress levels can be made under an estimated permanent load of 1·39 kN/m^2 and the required imposed load of 2·5 kN/m^2 (see Fig. 18.2.7). The common joist stresses are around 2 N/mm^2 (Fig. 18.2.7). The stresses in the principal beams vary, but are often in the region of 10 to 15 N/mm^2 based on the gross cross-section. Additionally, there will be local stress concentrations at the points of reduced section between the notches and below the grooves, which would give peak stresses of 20 N/mm^2.

The timber seen was of good quality, and so even a conservative assumption of strength would indicate that the common joists are adequately strong. Stress levels in the principal beams, however, are much higher, and in some cases are out of the grading range altogether. This does not necessarily mean that the beams are under strength, for the reasons given in appendix 2.

There would thus be three options for authorising a permissible superimposed load of 2·5 kN/m^2

- strengthen the beams generally
- visually grade the beams, and strengthen those where the applied stress is in excess of the grade stress
- visually grade the beams, and load test a representative number of the beams where the applied stress is in excess of the grade stress.

Fig. 18.2.3 Floorboards removed locally, exposing a principal beam with the common joists dovetailed into it

A cultural audit of the floor construction showed the floorboards were recent, and of low significance on the basis of replaceability. The floor structure below was largely original, with a high standard of workmanship. Dovetail ends to the common joists were well fitted, and the timber was generally in sound condition, the only damage being the notches and holes cut later for services. The ceilings below were in many cases original lath and plaster, and much of the elaborate decorative coving has survived. Overall, the ceilings and, more particularly, the covings had the highest significance, with the floor structure also significant. From a conservation viewpoint the ideal solution would be one which left the ceilings and floor framing unaltered, and if necessary disturbed only the boarding and deafening.

The options for strengthening the beams are shown in Fig. 13.4. The location and spacing of the joists mean that any steel added from the top would have to be in the form of a flitch plate let into a central groove cut into the member. This could either be fixed with an epoxy resin, or bolted into position, and would need cutting to a curved profile based on a survey, to allow for the creep deflection. Where the floors had been firred up to level over all the span, a fabricated T-member could be used. The beams could more easily be spliced from below with, e.g., channels, but this would involve cutting into the ceilings and, more importantly, the covings. A broad estimate of the cost of strengthening most of the beams by one or other of these methods was around £50 000. Against this, a budget price for grading the beams and load testing 20 of them (25% of the total) was in the order of £13 000. The test proportion was provisional, but based upon the proportion of beams which had critical applied stresses.

The arguments put forward in appendix 2 show that there was a reasonable chance of many of these beams passing a load test. Bearing in mind the large difference in cost between strengthening and testing (a factor of almost four), it is clear that testing could well be the economic option even if a proportion of beams failed the test, as well as the preferred option from a conservation viewpoint. This approach would be evaluated in a first phase of work and, if successful, extended to all the beams. Floorboards were removed to expose around half of the beams (all floors in No. 26, and all first floor beams), and two beams were tested (Fig. 18.2.4).

The beams were of a single species (redwood) and could well have been from a consistent source. The timber was slow-grown, often with 20 or more growth rings in 25 mm, and relatively dense. Many of the beams received high grades (75/65), a few had low grades (50/40) and very few fell below grade 40.

The load tests were carried out in accordance with the procedure in appendix 2, using cast iron weights (Fig. 18.2.4), and measuring deflection on dial gauges installed at low level below weights suspended on piano wires (Fig. 18.2.6). Deflections were also measured on beams adjacent to the beam under test, to assess the degree of load sharing.

The test load would be held for 24 hours (a medium-term loading) to represent the design load case of self-weight plus full superimposed load (the latter

Fig. 18.2.4 Load testing

regarded by the Code as a long-term loading). As explained in appendix 2, the test load was therefore increased by 25%.

The density of the timber was assumed to be 5 kN/m^3, and all the critical beams (i.e. those which were subject to design stresses appreciably above their grade stresses) were tested. Thus no further increases were applied to the test load.

Fig. 18.2.5 Safety framework in place during test. The screw heads are adjusted to give a minimal clearance

Fig. 18.2.6 Dial gauges measuring the deflection of a weight attached by a piano wire to the floor above

The first phase of testing gave good results, and so the procedure of grading and load testing was applied to all the critical principal beams. In every case, the load/deflection graph remained linear and recovery after loading was virtually complete. For a typical beam, of the order of 6 m span, deflection under test loading was only of the order of 16 mm. (L/375) and load sharing (estimated from the deflection of adjacent beams) was generally not more than 5–10%. From this information the E value of the beam could be calculated as 12,900 N/mm^2 (Fig. 18.2.7). The values of applied stress and E could now be entered in the graph in appendix 2 (Fig. A2.3(B)) which showed that the beam still had a large reserve of strength. This result was typical of the test results generally.

It was decided that for one beam this reserve of strength would be explored more fully. A test load was applied which produced a bending stress of 26 N/mm^2. The corresponding deflection over a span of 4·6 m was 27 mm (L/170). Despite this, the load/deflection graph was linear, and all but 1·5 mm of this deflection was recovered. Entering the graph again (C) it can be seen that the reserve of strength indicated by the general tests did indeed exist for this beam, although here the safe upper limit was being approached.

This approach of grading and load testing resulted in all beams being accepted for the required superimposed load without the need for any strengthening work. Only one beam needed an end repair, due to damage by wet rot.

Calculations for the floors at Charlotte Square, Edinburgh

1. Loading (see figure 18.2.2)

   Assume timber density 5 kN/m^3

T + G floors	30 mm thick	$5 \times 0{\cdot}03$	0·15 kN/m^2
Deafening	50 mm ash/sand	$12 \times 0{\cdot}05$	0·60 kN/m^2
Boarding	12 mm thick	$5 \times 0{\cdot}015$	0·08 kN/m^2
Joists	$0{\cdot}165 \times 0{\cdot}065 \times 5 \div 0{\cdot}425$		0·12 kN/m^2
Main beams	$0{\cdot}340 \times 0{\cdot}170 \times 5 \div 2$		0·14 kN/m^2
Ceiling	battens/plaster. Allow		0·30 kN/m^2
			1·39 kN/m^2
Required superimposed load			2·50 kN/m^2
		Total applied load	3·89 kN/m^2

2. Applied stresses

   Principal beams @ 2 m centres, 5·5–6·5 m span
   Check 6·0 m span for bending

   Load $W = 6 \times 2 \times 3{\cdot}89 = 46{\cdot}7$ kN

   $M = WL/8 = 46{\cdot}7 \times 6/8 = 35$ kN m

   $\delta_{m,a} = M/Z$

   $= 35 \times 10^6/3{\cdot}28 \times 10^6 = 10{\cdot}7$ N/mm^2

   (Acceptable if beam is 75 grade or better)

   Check shear: $\dfrac{46{\cdot}7 \times 10^3}{2} \times \dfrac{1{\cdot}5}{340 \times 170} = 0{\cdot}6$ N/mm^2

   (Acceptable for any grade)

   Beam: 340 mm × 170 mm

   $Z = bd^2/6$

   $= \dfrac{170 \times 340^2}{6}$

   $= 3{\cdot}28 \times 10^6$ mm^3

   $I = bd^3/12$

   $= \dfrac{170 \times 340^3}{12}$

   $= 5{\cdot}5 \times 10^8$ mm^4

3. Calculation of test load

   (See appendix 2)

   Duration of test load: 24 hours
   i.e., medium-term loading (see figure A2.2)

   Design load: combination of superimposed load and self-weight,
   i.e., long-term loading.

   ∴ test load must be increased by a factor of (K_3) 1·25

   i.e. $3{\cdot}89 \times 1{\cdot}25$ = 4·86 kN/m^2
   deduct dead load already present 1·39 kN/m^2
   3·47 kN/m^2

   Say 3·5 kN/m^2, applied in seven equal steps of 0·5 kN/m^2

4. Calculation of E from early test readings

   After four increments, test loading is 2 kN/m^2
   Maximum deflection = 9·5 mm (adjacent beams <1 mm)

   Load $W = 6 \times 2 \times 2 = 24$ kN

   $$\therefore \quad E = \frac{5}{384}\frac{W}{\Delta}\frac{L^3}{I}$$

   $$= \frac{5}{384}\frac{24{,}000}{9{\cdot}5} \times \frac{6000^3}{5{\cdot}5 \times 10^8} = 12{,}900 \text{ N/mm}^2$$

   Applied stress at this stage (from 2 above) $= 10{\cdot}7 \times 3{\cdot}39/3{\cdot}89 = 9{\cdot}3$ N/mm^2

Fig. 18.2.7 Calculations for the floors at Charlotte Square, Edinburgh

18.3. The Royal Festival Hall: strength assessment of the acoustic canopy

The Festival Hall, as its name implies, was built in 1951 as part of the South Bank Festival of Britain exhibition in London. In one sense it could be said to be our 'first' modern building, since nothing that went before on this scale so consciously followed the tenets of Modernism.

The building was designed within the then London City Council's Architects department, by a team led by Leslie Martin. It was, and remains, an outstanding achievement, admired both by the profession and the general public. Why the story of modern architecture from this point on is not one of unalloyed joy is an interesting question, but one which is outside the scope of the present text.

The main auditorium was originally designed for concert performances only, with an acoustic canopy suspended above the platform (Fig. 18.3.1). After some years the London Festival Ballet came into being, and gave regular performances in the Hall, using a scenery frame at the rear of the stage. This latter arrangement was rather restrictive, since it was directly under the lowest point of the canopy.

In 1991 the lighting consultants Techplan were asked to co-ordinate a study to determine whether a new scenery grid could be designed for temporary installation, to a height which would on occasion necessitate lifting the rear of the canopy by some 2·0 m. They, in turn, commissioned Arups to make a structural appraisal of the canopy, and to determine the feasibility of a lifting arrangement.

The canopy

The canopy acts as an acoustic reflector, and consists of a lower profiled surface of blockboard faced with beech plywood, supported by six plyweb

Fig. 18.3.1 The acoustic canopy over the stage

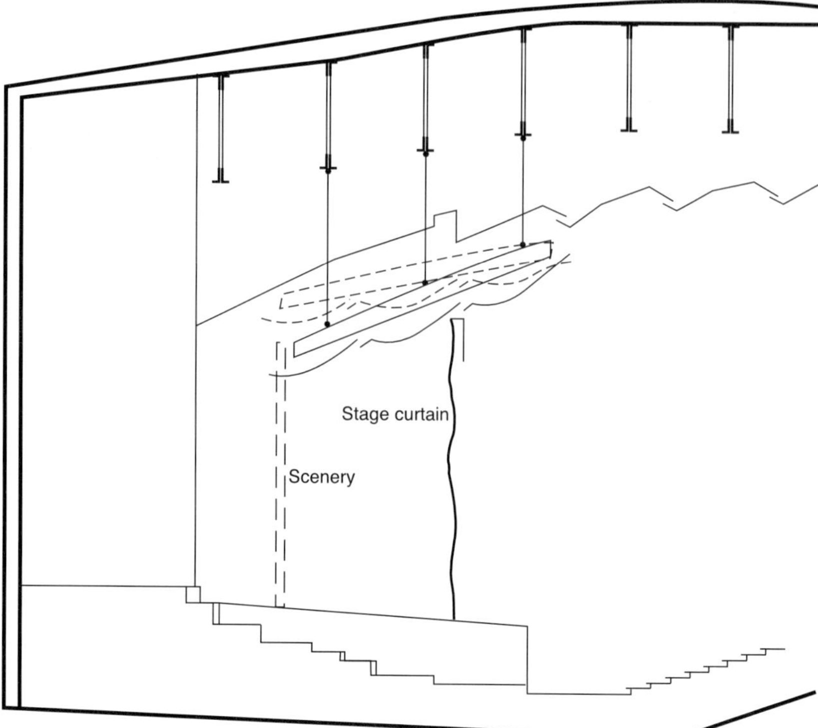

Fig. 18.3.2 Section of the Royal Festival Hall, showing the position of a stage curtain, and the potential for lifting the acoustic canopy

beams, each in turn suspended by three steel drop-rods from the roof trusses above the auditorium ceiling (Fig. 18.3.2). If each beam was structurally dependent upon the three points of support, it would be difficult to avoid a temporary overstress when they were lifted. A possible method would be to introduce a spreader beam to pick up the front two hangers, but this would be relatively expensive to install. If it could be shown that the beams were able to span between the outer rods only, the canopy could simply be raised by lifting the rear rods.

The canopy, in common with all the other elements of the Hall, is beautifully detailed. The reflectors are suspended by metal rods from the grillage formed by the plyweb beams and trimmer joists which span between them, and catwalks in clear beech allow access to the recessed spotlights and control points.

The beams themselves are plyweb boxes, with top and bottom flanges of four laminates in redwood, set vertically with staggered butt joints. Only the top face of each laminate can be seen, and so it is not possible to grade them. However, all the faces are clear, which makes it probable that the pieces themselves are of clear timber. The webs are cut from sheets of 7-ply mahogany plywood, 19 mm thick, with butt joints covered by glued lapping pieces.

Strength assessment of the beams

Calculation of mid-span bending moments for the three beam types under self-weight, lighting and personnel loads, assuming the centre rod to be

Fig. 18.3.3 Canopy suspension

removed, is relatively straightforward. Analysis of the cross-section shows that the applied bending stresses are not particularly high, but the unknowns, in terms of the timber grading and the butt joints (as opposed to finger joints) make it difficult to decide if the beams are adequate. The structure is convincing enough, however, to propose a load test, although we would have to compare the cost of a test to the costs of strengthening the beams. The latter is quite difficult to do—the only practical method would be to attach steel members in some way to the bottom flange, which, in view of the difficulties of access, would be very expensive.

At first sight the load test also looks expensive. The canopy is not designed to have weights distributed across it, and there would be the possibility of accidental damage. In addition, a safety scaffold from the platform below would be a substantial undertaking. However, a hydraulic jack could be used to apply a central point load to each beam, acting against a strut from the roof truss above (Fig. 18.3.4).

Hydraulic jacks are a much better way of applying load than kentledge (if an anchor point can be arranged) since the amount of stored energy is small. Moreover, the beams could be tested one at a time, as the trimmer joists are virtually a pinned connection and provide no form of load sharing. Load tests would clearly be cheaper than strengthening.

The tests

The tests were carried out during a rare period of Hall closure for maintenance. The test load factor was determined in accordance with the procedure described in Appendix 2. A duration-of-load factor of 1·5 was used, together with a dead load factor of 1·2, giving an overall load factor of 1·8. The point load necessary to increase the central bending moment by this factor is approximately 1 tonne. This load was applied to each beam in 0·25 tonne increments, and held for one hour. The operation was carried out safely,

Fig. 18.3.4 Load test arrangement. A scaffold tube from the roof truss above sits on a load cell, which in turn sits on a hydraulic jack, which can be activated by the pump in the foreground

because the middle hangar remained in place, with the turnbuckle simply adjusted to the position of slackness. Deflection was very simply measured from the relative movement of the rod ends in the turnbuckle, using vernier callipers—just occasionally one has this sort of luck. All the beams took the load satisfactorily, with deflections of only 3–6 mm. Residual deflection (around 1 mm) probably relates to a slight embedment of the supporting bolts.

18.4. The church of St. Mary the Virgin, Sandwich, Kent; the repair of the seventeenth century roof

Sandwich is today a small town, close to the East coast of Kent and one of the Cinque Ports. During Edward III's reign (1327–1377) the Cinque Ports, (which actually number more than five), were obliged to provide ships and men for the King's service because he had no standing naval force. In return, the King granted the towns certain privileges.

Sandwich had been built at what was originally the mouth of the River Stour, but a steady silting-up of the estuary has left it effectively two miles inland. As trade declined the town lost importance, and today it remains one of the best time capsules in England, with timber frames end to end in Sadler Street.

In medieval times there were three churches in Sandwich; St. Mary's, St. Peter's and St. Clement's. Only St. Clement's is still in regular use as the parish church; St. Peter's and St. Mary's are both in the care of the Redundant Churches Fund.

The church

St. Mary's church stands on the oldest site of Christian worship in the town close to the bank of the River Stour, and dates from the twelfth century. A few fragments of stonework, such as the responds of the nave arcades, indicate its earlier form, which was a conventional narrow nave with North and South aisles, a chancel and a central tower (Fig. 18.4.1(a) and (b)). In 1579 the town was badly damaged by an earthquake, and in 1668 the central tower fell down demolishing most of the church interior.

The form of the rebuild is something of a surprise. The new nave included what was originally the North aisle, with a roof spanning 14·5 m—almost the width of the nave of York Minster, and far in excess of any country church of the time. The rebuild took place at a time of emerging classicism, when exposed timber structures were no longer the fashion. King-post trusses support the roof, originally concealed by a panelled ceiling which, regrettably, was removed in the 1950s (c).

The ceiling had to be splayed, partly to include the east windows in the nave, and also to give a much needed height to this substantial width. In order to accommodate the splay, the principal rafters of the trusses had been extended. Clearly they would be inadequate on their own, and so they were strengthened with raking ties. The line of the ties was dictated by the ceiling and therefore they were connected not to truss nodes, but to the mid-bay points of the bottom tie (d). Thus, although the structure appears to be triangulated, the bottom tie is actually put into significant bending.

The inspection

In 1984 Purcell Miller Tritton and Partners were asked to inspect the church and provide the Redundant Churches Fund with a report on its condition. While the tiles were in good condition, repairs were needed to the valley gutter over the arcade, together with some minor work to the masonry. However, it was clear that the trusses had spread considerably, and so Arup's were commissioned to make a structural appraisal, together with recommendations for remedial work. The initial inspection was carried out from a mobile platform, pushed around the floor of the church.

Most of the timber is redwood, probably from the Baltic, with occasional pieces of oak. The basic sections are approximately 200 mm square, although the lowest bay of the rafters is increased in width.

The joints are also typical of seventeenth century work, with an increasing reliance on metal. Wrought iron straps and forelock bolts (tightened by driving an iron wedge into a slot in the shank) are used at tension joints, with the occasional later threaded bolt. Compression joints are connected by mortices and pegged tenons.

There was much beetle attack of the sapwood, but the residual sections were basically sound. The principal defect was the bending deflection of the bottom ties (Fig. 18.4.2), which varied from 50–200 mm. This member had already been replaced in one truss, another was fractured, and a third braced with steel straps (Fig. 18.4.3). This has lead to a pronounced spread of the rafter feet at A, and bending of the tie at C in Fig. 18.4.2.

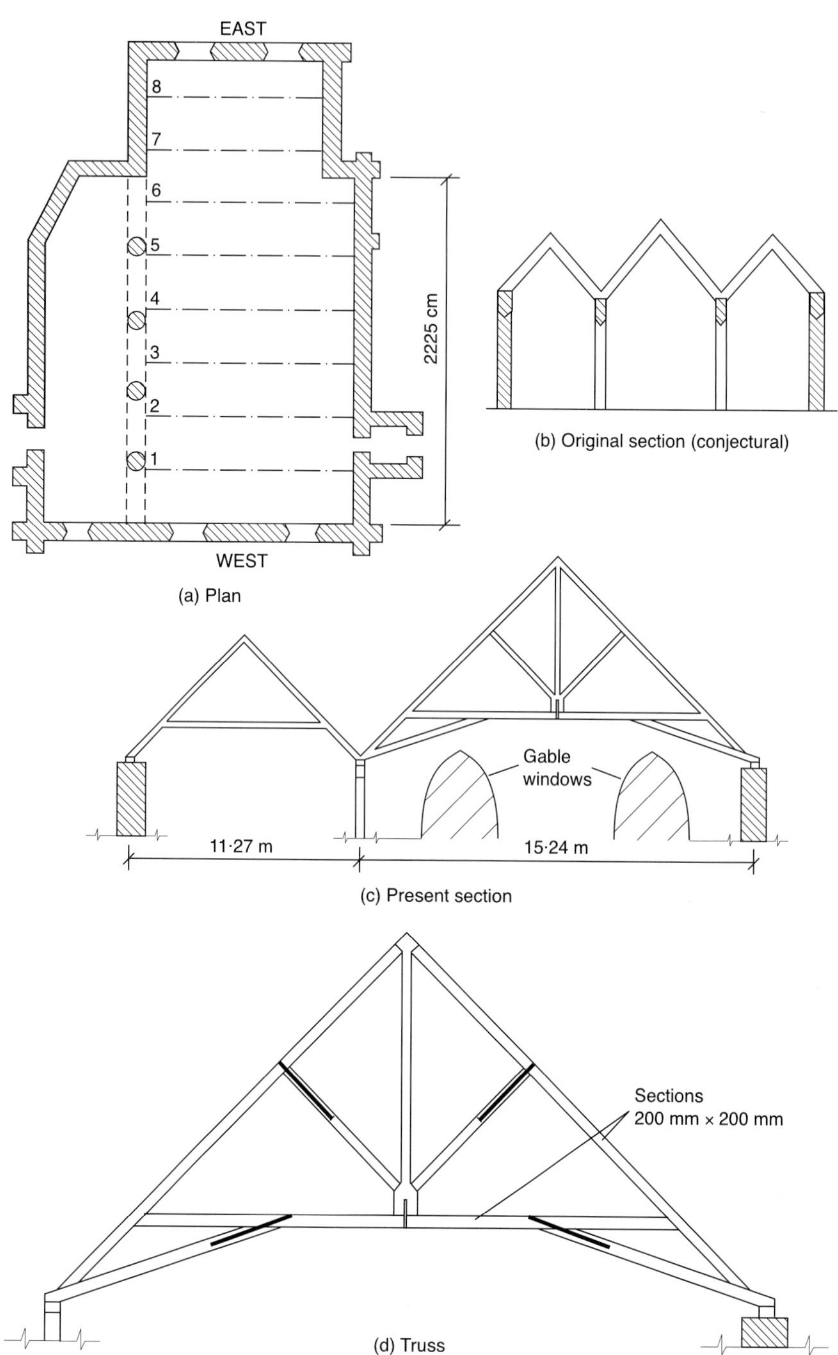

Fig. 18.4.1 Plan and sections of the church of St Mary the Virgin at Sandwich

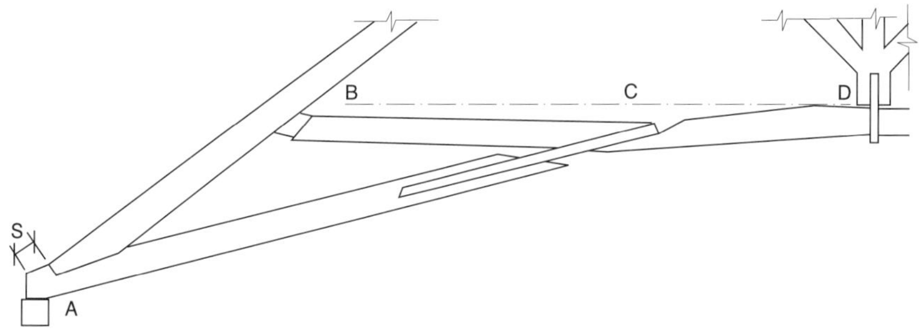

Fig. 18.4.2 Bending deflection of the bottom tie

Truss analysis

An elastic analysis was made of the critical condition which, as is usual for roofs, is dead load (self-weight and tiles) and snow load, and the member stresses compared with the permissible stresses in BS 5268. The results showed high, but not unacceptable, stresses in the timber, and an outward deflection of only 20 mm using a 'dry' modulus of elasticity (E_{dry}) of 10 000 N/mm^2 (Fig. 18.4.4, condition 1). The assumption of dry timber was obviously not correct, and it is more likely that the truss had been fabricated 'green', as large members such as these take many years to dry out. The effect of creep can reduce the apparent E value by a factor of three or even more. The deflection of member BD would thus increase considerably if it were erected and loaded at an unseasoned moisture content of around 60%, which then dropped to a cold roof equilibrium moisture content of 16–18%. It was also evident that the two-bolt connection of the strap at C was overloaded and the trusses showed varying degrees of slip at B of up to 100 mm.

Both these factors increase the spread of rafter feet, and increased the bending moment in the rafter at C. Some of the timber joints at B, originally in compression, were now subject to tension, pulling the pegs out of the

Fig. 18.4.3 Bending and part fracture of the bottom tie

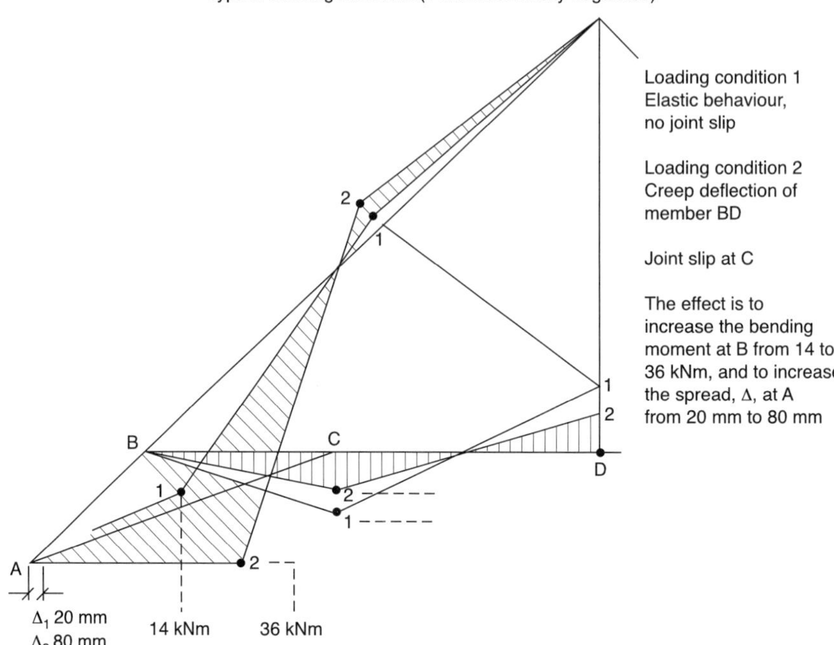

Fig. 18.4.4 Load conditions 1 and 2

tenon, and needing the later addition of steel straps and bolts. A second analysis, using an equivalent E value of $3\,000\,\mathrm{N/mm^2}$, and introducing joint slip at C, gave results which were close to the observed distortions, and showed almost a three-fold rise in the bending moment at B (Fig. 18.4.4, condition 2).

The analysis now modelled the observed form of the trusses, and indicated areas where the timber or the joints were substantially over-stressed. While it could be understood that the trusses had not collapsed, the factor of safety against failure was unacceptably low.

In addition, there was a concern for the end shear distance on the raking tie, restraining the rafter (Fig. 18.4.2, S), which on some trusses was very small.

Remedial strategy

The aims were to make the church safe to use, and to retain as much of the original fabric as possible. To achieve this the strengthening would have to be added discreetly, but it should be apparent that the work was of the twentieth century. The span of the trusses for their date made it important that the original form was maintained and could be clearly seen. In addition, since the tiles were in a satisfactory condition, all work would have to be done from below.

A first option, a parallel structure of steel trusses between the timber trusses, was rejected on grounds both of cost and visual intrusion. Repairs

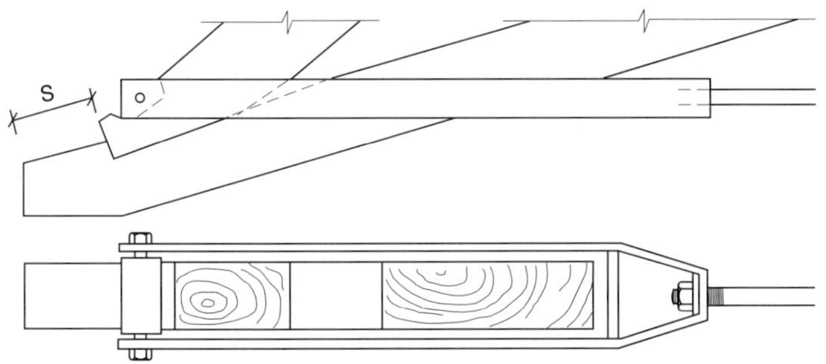

Fig. 18.4.5 The introduction of a steel tie

in a general sense would not be possible, since to replace members on a large scale, and reinforce joints until the frame had an acceptable factor of safety would be both prohibitively expensive and, ultimately, false.

The basic problem was the inadequacy of the tension connection between the feet of the rafters, both in strength and stiffness. Since the trusses were still standing, it would only be necessary to relieve a proportion of the load, and prevent further spread, as this would be the mechanism of collapse.

The ideal solution would be to buttress the supports. In our medieval churches generally, the ability of the arcade walls to resist lateral thrust has often contributed significantly to the life of the roof. In the context of St. Mary's, however, the timber arcade and the aisle roof precluded this. The most straightforward solution was the introduction of a steel tie (Fig. 18.4.5), which would reduce the stresses in the lower part of the truss, and provide a passive restraint to the increase in out-thrust under snow load.

Repair work

The initial survey had been carried out from a moveable tower scaffold, using a portable floodlight, and recording details with photographs (Fig. 18.4.6). It is important at this time to obtain enough information to establish the general condition, so that the scope of the remedial works is reasonably well defined. A further detailed survey could only be done when full access had been provided by the contractor.

With the contract awarded, the nave was completely scaffolded and boarded out just below the eaves. A tower could then be moved around on this level for inspection and remedial work within the pitch of the roof. The timbers were first 'de-frassed', that is, scraped clean of any wood denatured by beetle attack, and then systematically examined. After this inspection it was found necessary to replace only five members—two halves of bottom tie members, one king post and two braces.

Although the original trusses were made of redwood, the only commercially available species of the required size is Douglas fir. There was a problem in fitting a new member into the position occupied by the previous, distorted member. Here, a template was made, and a curved member 200 mm square was cut from a section 300 × 200 mm. Even so, a small make-up piece was needed to extend the raking tie.

The scaffolding was arranged with slots in it, so that the new pieces could be lifted into position after removing temporary ties. The layout was also

Fig. 18.4.6 Roof illuminated by a portable floodlight for initial inspection

Fig. 18.4.7 Work complete, with the tie rods just discernible

related to the module of the trusses, so that a pair of scaffold frames could be used to prop the truss while a member was replaced.

When jointing the new section to the existing, no attempt was made to imitate original joints. A straightforward vertical half lap was used, with 30 mm connecting bolts. The heads were recessed and plugged to avoid an undue reduction in fire resistance.

The repairs complete (Fig. 18.4.7), all the timbers were given two coats of a gel preservative insecticide.

Acknowledgments

Client: The Redundant Churches Fund
Architects: Purcell Miller Tritton & Partners
Contractor: W W Martin (Thanet) Ltd.

18.5. The dismantling and re-erection of Alderham Farmhouse

Alderham Farmhouse, three miles from Warwick, stood with a few outbuildings at the end of a gravel lane—and 35 m from the Warwick bypass, built in

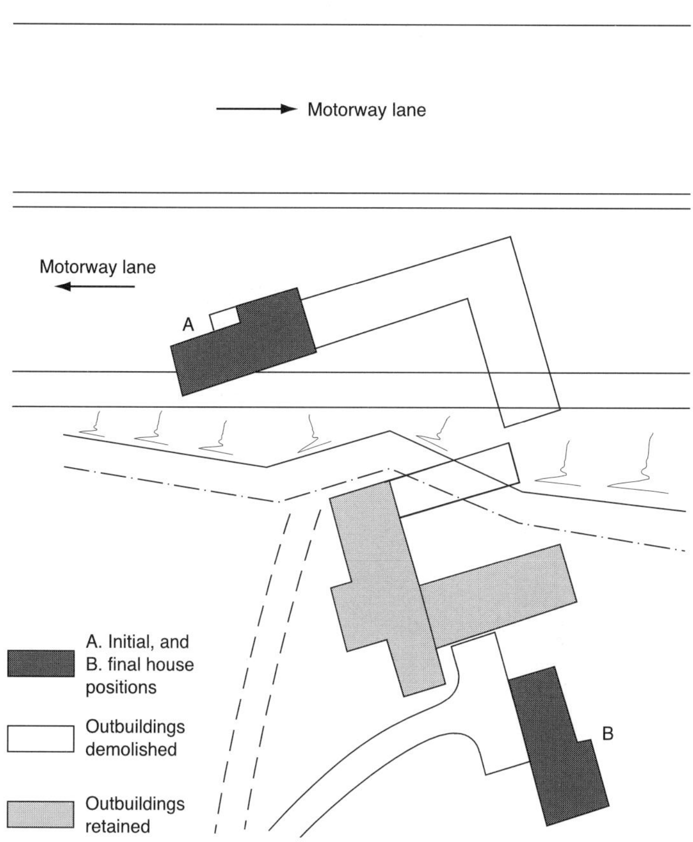

Fig. 18.5.1 Position of Alderham Farmhouse

1967. When in 1980 the Department of Transport decided to upgrade the road to full motorway standard, Arups became responsible for this, the Gaydon section of the new M40—with the farmhouse now roughly in the middle of the northbound carriageway (Fig. 18.5.1).

As the property has a Grade II listing, the Department agreed to a feasibility study for moving it. Originally two houses, the building is a composite structure—part timber frame, part brick (Fig. 18.5.2). A lift-and-slide move did not look feasible, due in part to the length of the building but, more significantly, to the general slope of the land. This left dismantling and re-erection as, in conservation terms, a last option.

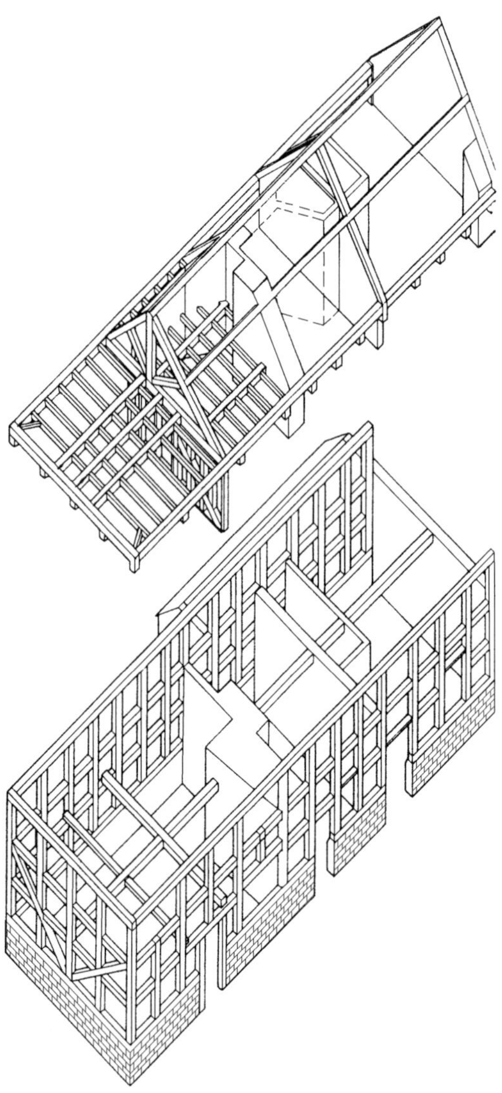

Fig. 18.5.2 Axonometric of the frame

The survey

The frame itself is of oak, probably seventeenth century, and a typically northern pattern with double-pegged mortise and tenon joints. It is now infilled with brick, obviously a later replacement for wattle and daub, and dating probably from the eighteenth century. There was, in fact, evidence of the original infill, since some of the frame members showed a shallow groove into which the hazel twigs would have been set to form the wattle, before daubing with a render—some of the members, that is, but not all—and it was clear that with tenoned joints throughout, individual members could not be replaced without dismantling the whole assembly. It seemed that the frame, like so many others, had already been dismantled and re-erected, and our proposal was nothing new. The bricks date variously from the eighteenth and nineteenth centuries, but the external joinery, much repaired, as well as most of the internal finishes, are clearly twentieth-century work (Fig. 18.5.3).

The appraisal

The conclusion was reached, with consulting architect Rodney Melville & Associates, that the principal materials of historic significance—the frame, the bricks, the tiles and some of the joinery—could all be reused, and that the items which would be lost, mainly the internal plaster and decorations, were of relatively recent date. The farmhouse would still retain enough of its historic significance for the move to be a valid option in conservation terms. There remained the question of the form of the necessary twentieth century construction. Engineers take a simple view on these matters—contemporary work should be expressed frankly as such. It had become obvious, after all, that this was the approach favoured by the previous rebuilders of the house.

Fig. 18.5.3 View of Alderham Farmhouse

The contract

With a contractor appointed, the dismantling began in November 1988 (Fig. 18.5.4). The individual frame members were identified with a code stamped onto metal tags, since so many of them were almost identical. Apart from the cill, which was to be renewed totally, the frame members were in good condition for their age (Fig. 18.5.5). Only one member was replaced, and

Fig. 18.5.4 Dismantling of Alderham Farmhouse

Fig. 18.5.5 Frame members with identification tags

Fig. 18.5.6 The few members which needed repair

three others received new ends. These were joined by simple half-laps, fixed with stainless steel bolts. Bituminous paint had been applied to the external timber, creating the black-and-white image of the frame which was first popularised by the Victorians. This was removed by careful sand-blasting, using very fine material.

An adequate number of bricks was recovered, due to the relatively weak mortar, and the additional stock obtained from out-buildings which were not to be rebuilt. And so by Christmas the farmhouse lay in kit form, ready for reassembly.

The base plinth of the external wall was originally a solid nine inch leaf. The contemporary equivalent is the cavity wall, which would give better thermal and moisture performance. These improvements would be useful, since Warwick District Council, after some hesitation, had decided to regard the rebuild as a 'new' building, which would be required to comply with the Regulations. The existence of the cavity is honestly expressed, as the outer leaf appears as plain stretcher bond.

The timber frame is a very robust box, and there were no problems in justifying the members for strength. Small patch repairs were made, mainly to improve the weather resistance of the surface and eliminate any pockets where water could lie (Fig. 18.5.8).

The most difficult decision related to the way in which the frame panel infill (originally a single brick leaf) was to be rebuilt. Apart from a very poor thermal performance, which could perhaps be supplemented by an inner

Fig. 18.5.7 The frame during reassembly

Fig. 18.5.8 A corner post with small patch repairs, and the frame infilled with woodwool panels

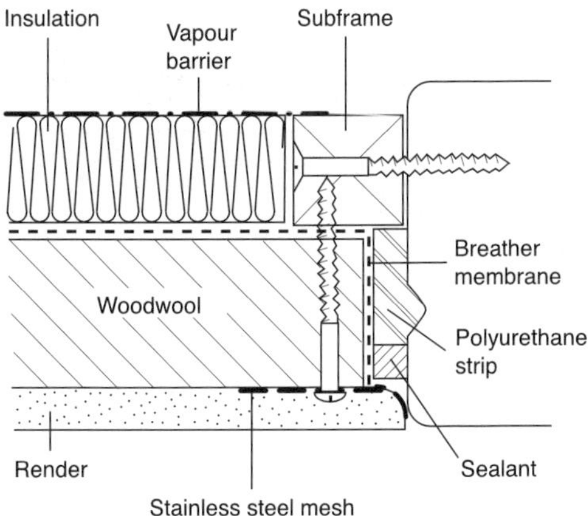

Fig. 18.5.9 New external wall construction

lining, it would be difficult to stop the brick holding water against the frame—a point which had become evident during the initial survey. Eventually it was decided to revert to the 'original' solution of a render infill. The base for the render is a panel of woodwool fixed to a sub-frame (Fig. 18.5.9). The panel is enveloped by a breather membrane, and the perimeter gap is filled by a bitumen-impregnated polyurethane strip. The aim of this detail is to minimise the depth to which water can penetrate along the side of the frame.

The render itself is a 1:1:6 mix, finished off with a weaker coat of 1:2:9. Stainless steel mesh supports the render at the perimeter of the panel (Fig. 18.5.10). The original intention had been to coat the panels with a lime wash, but the final appearance of the render was pleasing enough for them

Fig. 18.5.10 Panel sealant

Fig. 18.5.11 Internal view of the frame, infilled with foil-backed plasterboard

to be left plain. Indeed the work on site generally bears testimony to the skill and experience of the contractor.

The external frame and finishes were completed by the end of June 1989 (Fig. 18.5.12), although the internal finishes and services, have, by agreement, been left for completion by the owner. The farmhouse is now starting out on its third life. Not a bad performance for a frame which is already 300 years old.

Fig. 18.5.12 The completed building

Acknowledgements
Client: Sir Charles Smith-Ryland
Consulting Engineers: Ove Arup and Partners
Consulting Architects: Rodney Melville & Associates
Contractor: Linford-Bridgman Ltd.

18.6. The Tyne Theatre

The Tyne Theatre, designed by William B Parnell and built in 1867, is a building which is at the same time both typical and unique. It is typical of its time, when theatres were conceived as two brick boxes (Fig. 18.6.1); the dividing wall both marking the proscenium and, in conjunction with the newly-developed fire curtain, providing fire compartmentation for a high-risk area.

The roof is supported by a series of queen post trusses which span 20 m. Those over the auditorium support the wooden framed 'oyster shell' ceiling, while those over the fly tower form a part of the stage machinery which, with a gradually increasing complexity, was installed in theatres from the late eighteenth century onwards. It is this stage machinery, stripped or subject to major modification in practically every other Victorian theatre in England, which now makes the Tyne Theatre unique. Used latterly as a cinema, a screen had been erected in front of the proscenium, leaving the stage tower and its contents untouched until 1976, when the director of a local amateur operatic company discovered it while looking for a production base.

In December, 1985, a fire broke out in an electrical switchroom below the stage. The original stage curtain performed well, and the auditorium suffered little damage. Unfortunately, at that time the roof was in the process of being reslated, allowing the fire to spread at high level to some of the auditorium trusses.

The first task was to survey the damage (Fig. 18.6.2). Normally, a fire-damaged roof would be propped before any survey work began, but the ceiling below was the original, and virtually undamaged, and so there was a reluctance to create large openings in it. A cautious inspection showed that the truss member sections were generally not reduced by more than 25%, and the absence of the slates meant that no roof dead or superimposed snow load could be built up. There was thus an adequate margin of safety to carry out a general inspection. One node had suffered extensive charring due to the effect of a broken ventilation duct, which had acted like a blowtorch. This was strengthened with shaped splice plates and tie rods (Fig. 18.6.3). An analysis of the trusses, allowing for the general charring reductions, showed that there was still an adequate residual strength, and the replacement of the purlins, rafters and slates would then be relatively straightforward. An outline scheme for the repair of the roof was prepared, and the loss assessors approved the work in a series of contract packages.

In the meantime, the auditorium roof was temporarily sheeted over (Fig. 18.6.4) to avoid rain and snow doing further damage to a predominantly timber interior.

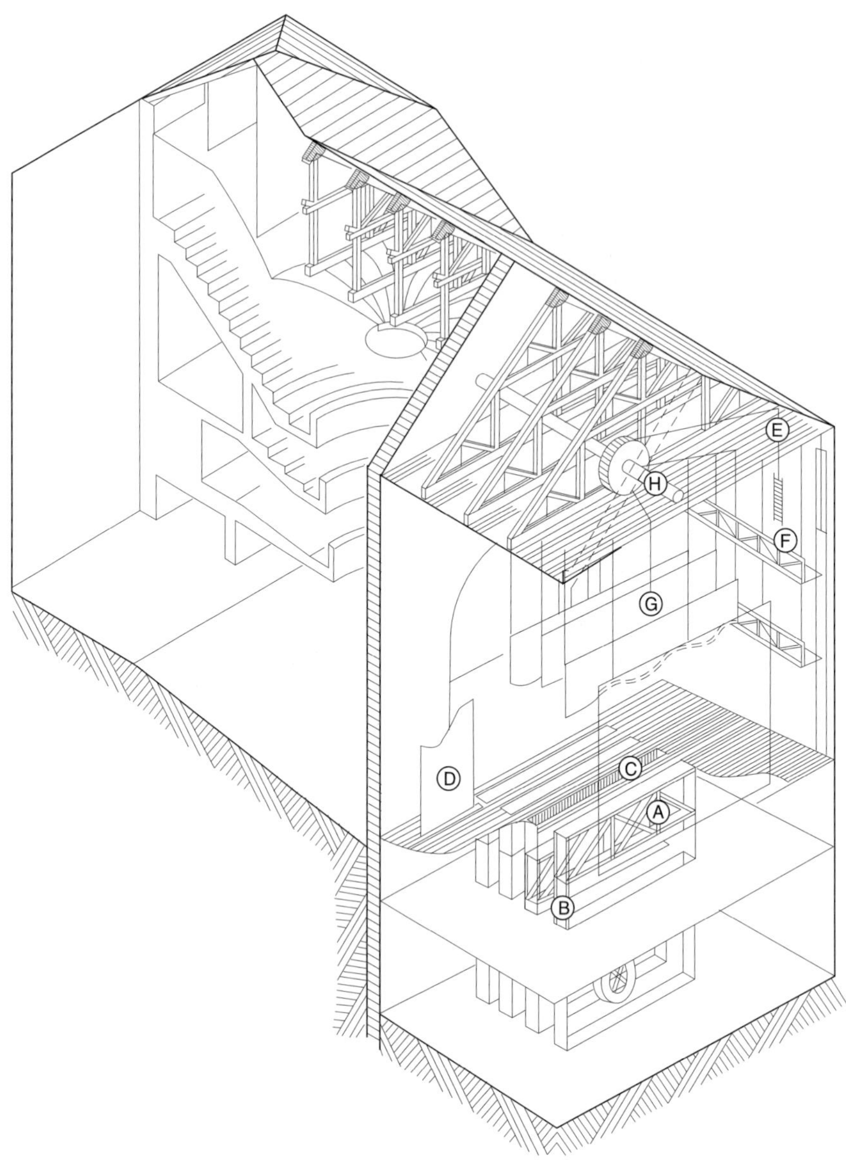

Fig. 18.6.1 Plan of Tyne Theatre

Of the four trusses over the stage, two had already collapsed, leaving two which were obviously past repair, and which were demolished (Fig. 18.6.3). With the roof removed, the rear gable wall was now potentially unstable, and was reduced to a safe level.

In order to decide on the replacement form of the trusses, it is necessary to consider their supporting role as part of the stage machinery. The development of English stage design has been described more fully elsewhere but, by the middle of the nineteenth century, mechanisms had been provided to bring scenery onto the stage from above, the wings and even from below

Fig. 18.6.2 Charred trusses over the auditorium, with the theatre ceiling suspended below

Fig. 18.6.3 The two remaining trusses over the stage, subsequently demolished

Fig. 18.6.4 Temporary sheeting over the auditorium

(Fig. 18.6.1), since the stage is set over a ten metre deep pit. Bridges (A), running between guides (B) and fitted with counter-balances, could be lowered from stage level through cuts (C). Large sets (D) could be slid side-ways into the wings, between floor runners and head guides.

Fig. 18.6.5 Truss strengthening with shaped splice plates and tie rods

Scenes, painted on canvas sheets, could be 'flown' out of sight into the void above the stage, thus known as the fly tower. This was done by means of ropes, passing over pulleys fixed to the grid (E), a series of slats supported by the truss ties, and then tied off to cleats on the bridge rail (F). Borders (G) could be raised a relatively short distance by ropes wound around a central shaft (H), also supported on the trusses. If another border was wound the opposite way, it could be lowered at the same time and 'the sky' replaced by 'the forest'. All these effects (given a sufficiency of 'hands') could be made to happen simultaneously as, for instance, in the transformation scene of a pantomime.

Some of the machinery at the Tyne had been damaged in the fire (Fig. 18.6.6), but much below stage was recoverable. Since the staff had an intimate knowledge of the construction and most of the elements were straightforward items of carpentry, it was feasible to replace the damaged parts with replicas, thus allowing the machinery to be understood and appreciated once more (Fig. 18.6.7).

From this decision, it followed that the trusses, as part of the machinery, should also be rebuilt as replicas. It was not difficult to produce detailed drawings, as the trusses were virtually identical to those over the auditorium.

The main truss members were around 300 mm × 150 mm. The originals were redwood, slow grown (around 20 growth rings per 25 mm) and probably from the Baltic region. The only economic commercial supply available

Fig. 18.6.6 Fire damage below the stage, which is the top level in the figure

Fig. 18.6.7 Below-stage machinery after repair

to match this was Douglas fir in 300 mm square sections, which could be halved. Much of the original metalwork was recovered from the pit, checked, and reused.

The contractor's workshop was large enough to allow the trusses to be laid out and assembled on the floor (Fig. 18.6.8). Transporting an assembled truss

Fig. 18.6.8 Truss assembly. The joint between a principal rafter (to the left) and the mid-height collar (to the right)

Fig. 18.6.9 Erection of truss

Fig. 18.6.10 Scaffolding and 'toast-rack' supporting the truss as the slings are slackened off

Fig. 18.6.11 Roof complete with sarking felt above and the fly tower grid rebuilt on the bottom members of the trusses

to site, however, would have been difficult (due to the height, rather than the length), and so the trusses were dismantled and reassembled in a street beside the theatre.

Although it had been easy to put a temporary cover over the auditorium, the stage tower, with the four trusses demolished, was a gaping hole. A temporary cover would be expensive, and would in any case have to be removed to place the new trusses. On balance it was decided to leave the tower uncovered, and to negotiate a short fabrication time for the trusses, which were in fact on site for erection within ten weeks of the fire (Fig. 18.6.9).

Lifting and placing a complete truss was feasible, although a large crane would be needed. In addition, there would have to be some way of stabilising the trusses, which each weighed about 2·5 tonnes, once they were in position. Thus a perimeter scaffold was built inside the tower, needed in any case for the rebuilding of the rear wall and general cleaning, and bridged over at high level (Fig. 18.6.10). On this, in turn, was built a 'toast-rack', from which the trusses could quickly be propped once they had been correctly aligned. By this means the four trusses were lifted in one day.

Two weeks after placing the trusses, the roof was complete to sarking felt (Fig. 18.6.11), and work could begin in the pit. The theatre reopened for business in November 1986, 11 months after the fire.

18.7. York Minster: the south transept fire

York Minster is the largest of the English medieval cathedrals and dates originally from Norman times, although no part of that fabric exists above ground today. The long rebuilding programme began in the mid-thirteenth century with the two transepts (Fig. 18.7.1), which would originally have

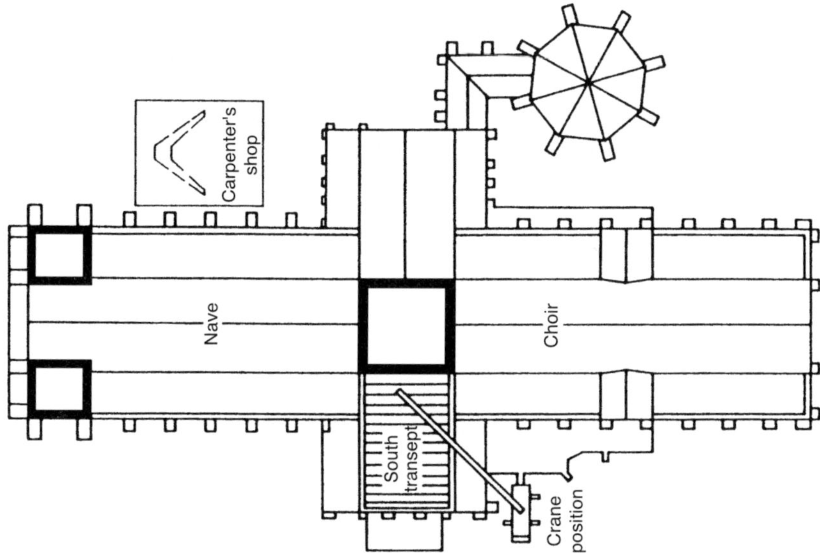

Fig. 18.7.1 Plan of York Minster

had open timber roofs, supported by the arcade walls with their small clerestory windows (Fig. 18.7.2(a)). The nave and the choir were demolished and rebuilt in the fourteenth and fifteenth centuries respectively. The nave cross-section (b) shows the development of the gothic style, with the larger clerestory windows and ribbed vaulting.

Standing at the West end today, both the nave and the choir appear to be vaulted in stone. In fact, all the high vaults at York are built of timber. The reason can only be guessed at—but it is a fact that the masons in the fourteenth century elected to reuse the Norman foundations to the original (aisleless) nave. While these were undeniably sound, they generated a nave width of 14·5 m. If the masons had succeeded in vaulting this, they would have created the greatest English span of the time, rivalling those of France. When the moment came, it is possible that they decided that the buttresses were inadequately prepared to receive such a massive out-thrust, and arranged for the carpenters to provide lightweight substitutes in timber.

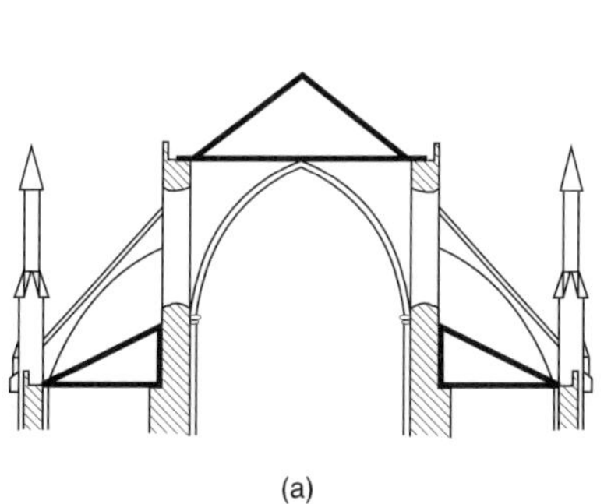

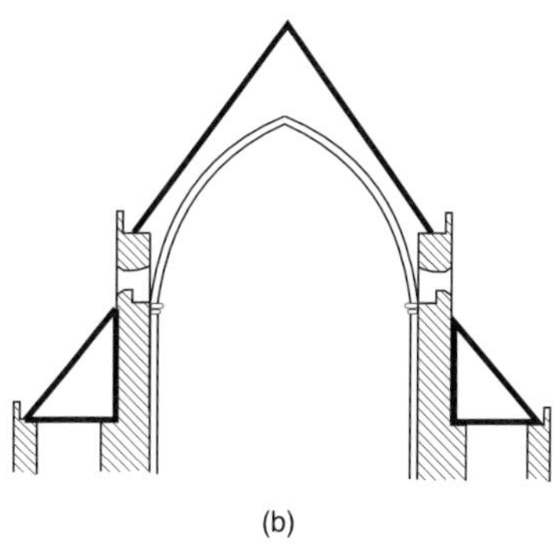

Fig. 18.7.2 (a) Nave cross-section, showing the triangular trusses, clerestory windows and vault in the 'correct' relationship. (b) South transept cross-section, showing the original thirteenth century steep roof and small clerestory windows. The fifteenth century vault could only be built by an incursion into the roof space

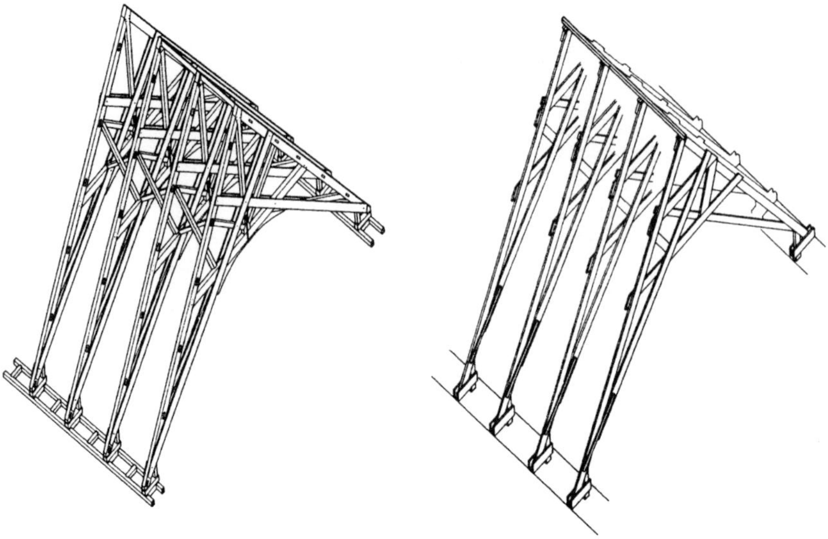

(a)

(b)

Fig. 18.7.3 A comparison of the two roof structures: (a) the eighteenth century trusses overlain with scissor bracing in the nineteenth century (b) the post-fire scheme, shown in more detail in Fig. 18.7.7

At the end of the fifteenth century, with all this magnificent new work, the transepts were looking somewhat old-fashioned, and so the Dean and Chapter commissioned what would be regarded now as a refurbishment, instructing their Superintendent to vault the transepts to match the rest of the Minster. Strictly speaking, this would not have been possible without a major rebuild, but a compromise was reached by building the vault up into the roof space (Fig. 18.7.2(b)). This meant that the new roof trusses were not simple triangles, like the nave, but A-frames, and that the vault would again have to be built of timber, as the structure would have been incapable of restraining the out-thrust of a stone vault.

Some of the original vault timbers were still preserved in the 1970s, but much repair work had been done. Indeed, the original roof had suffered a fire, and the existing trusses dated from the middle of the eighteenth century. They had been strengthened with scissor braces by the architect, George Street, during the restoration of the 1870s (Fig. 18.7.3(a)). Thus, although the roof was of archaeological interest in terms of the record which it gave of the work of various periods, it had been much altered and strengthened with time.

The fire

On the night of 9 July 1984 a storm passed over the city of York. There was heavy rain for a while, and some lightning was seen. In the small hours of the next morning, the alarm was raised at the Minster—a fire had started in the roof of the South transept. Worse than that, it had taken a good hold by the time it was discovered, and the Fire Brigade, although arriving promptly, were faced with a fire which was well alight and blazing. The height of the roof, and the difficulty of access, meant that fighting the fire at roof level was a losing battle, and there was a risk of it spreading to other parts of

Fig. 18.7.4 The central tower, after the fire, showing the outlines of the roof and the vault

the Minster. The Brigade concentrated their efforts on demolishing the roof by deliberately knocking out the purlins which held the trusses in place, and soon the whole structure was on the Minster floor. Once this was achieved, the fire was quickly extinguished, but daylight found the smoking transept open to the sky, its roof removed with an almost surgical precision (Fig. 18.7.4). The destruction was virtually complete. All that could be salvaged from the wreckage were six of the minor bosses.

The options for restoration

Ideas were offered in abundance for the rebuilding. Why not leave the transept roofless, or provide a glazed roof? Or build new vaults in concrete or glass fibre? Against these proposals of the modernists, the traditionalists demanded an exact replica of what was there before the fire—or even a 'day-one' approach, rebuilding a vaultless thirteenth century roof, although the details were totally unknown.

On the practical front, it was clear that an exact replica would give the same performance in a future fire, and there were arguments for increasing the fire resistance of the vault, and the survival time of the structure.

In the event, sanity prevailed. The symmetry of the cathedral more or less demanded that the vault, with its pattern of ribs, be replaced in something like its original form, as could still be seen in the North transept (Fig. 18.7.5), and the new vault would, of course, need a roof structure to support both it and a replacement covering of lead.

Fig. 18.7.5 The undamaged North Transept vault

The vaults

The original vault ribs were single curved pieces of oak, approximately 300 × 300 mm in cross-section, and up to 6 m long. To find equivalent pieces for all the various conditions of curvature would have been almost impossible, and so they were fabricated as vertical glulams, using four laminates for the major ribs, fitting in neatly with the original profile (Fig. 18.7.6). The individual planks were kiln-dried and then glued with a urea–formaldehyde adhesive. In addition, occasional through-bolts were used, with recessed and plugged heads. Thus, the new ribs to all intents and purposes replicated the originals, although the bosses, traditionally regarded as an opportunity for contemporary craft, were newly designed by the carvers themselves.

The original webs, however, were made up of thin boards, and were very much at risk in a future fire. They could not, therefore, be regarded as a model for the new construction. While it was not possible to achieve the absolute barrier of a masonry vault, webs of plaster were built, based on a stainless steel mesh, which were incombustible and which would have a fire resistance in excess of one hour.

The new roof structure

The options for the new roof structure were, in practical terms, limited to lightweight framing, that is timber or steel, by the height and cranage reach. Both these options were considered in detail, but the Dean and Chapter eventually chose oak as the most direct replacement for the

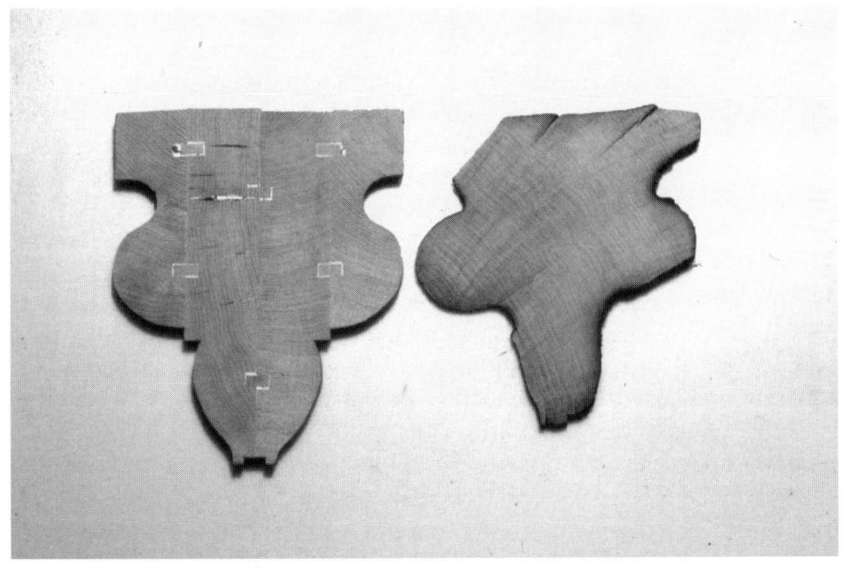

Fig. 18.7.6 Vault rib sections. To the right, the charred original timber. To the left, the new section of four laminates glued and jointed

original—the work was, after all, being funded by their insurers. Moreover, oak had a known durability, and was a more familiar material to the Minster workforce in terms of maintenance.

In view of the size of the principal members which would be needed, enquiries were made with major suppliers, and it became clear that suitable timbers could be obtained, but not from existing stock. Thus in order to build to any practical timescale, the trusses would have to be fabricated from timber that was not just green, but freshly cut. This restriction to unseasoned timber became the most significant factor in the design of the structure.

The truss outline is determined by the profiles of the roof and vault (Fig. 18.7.7(a) and (b)). A truss of this form, with no eaves tie, produces an out-thrust at its feet. In addition, there was some evidence that the original

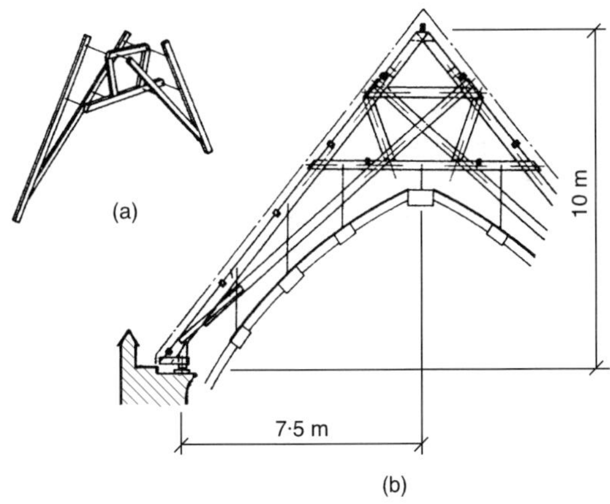

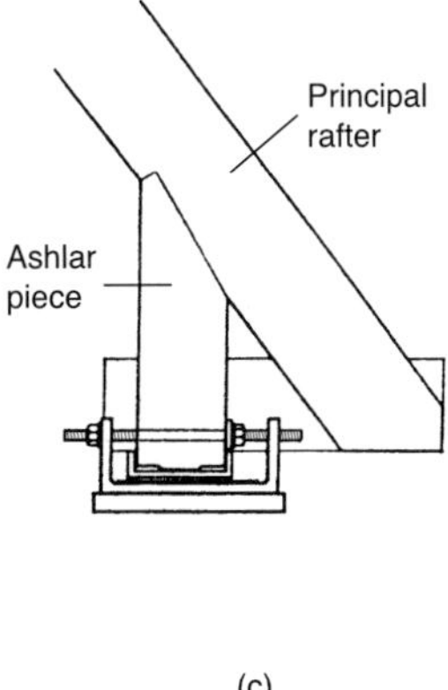

Fig. 18.7.7 The roof trusses (a) concept: two 'scissors' on each side of the collars (b) overall dimensions (c) sliding foot detail

roof had caused small outward movements of the clerestory walls, and so it would be necessary to limit the horizontal reaction of the new truss.

The desirability of an increased period of fire resistance has already been mentioned. If the trusses were also designed for a specific period of resistance, and the vault suspended from them by protected hangers, then the damage caused by a future fire would be greatly reduced.

The design of the trusses

In view of the repaired form of the original trusses, it would not have been appropriate to replicate them. The original truss positions and general form were reused, in order that support could be given to the vault bosses, but the truss itself is a twentieth century design which is a direct response to the brief. While this was a unanimous team decision, it also follows the approach to major roof repairs which has been taken for the last two centuries. When the nave roof was destroyed in the fire of 1840, the new roof trusses were contemporary queen posts. When later in the nineteenth century the North transept roof was replaced, an incredible structure, of single length principal rafters joined to giant cast iron brackets, totally Victorian in concept, was erected. Each one of these roofs contributes to the layers of history which are contained within the cathedral, and at the same time have an integrity which comes from using the technology of the time.

A typical truss consists of an upper and lower collar, with scissors legs applied to each side (Fig. 18.7.7(a)). This arrangement minimises the length of the principal members, but 12·5 m long pieces are still required (b). These needed to be 300 mm × 150 mm in cross-section for a one hour fire-surviving design. There are 13 trusses in all, which places each truss over a line of vault bosses.

A check of the clerestory masonry indicated that the outward component of reaction of a fixed-foot truss which supported both the roof and vault would give an unacceptably low factor of safety against overturning. It was decided to reduce the outward reaction by allowing one foot of each truss to slide after completion of the roof, and then fixing it for the addition of the vault loading (Fig. 18.7.7(c)).

The timber was obtained from estates throughout Britain. The programme of construction meant that the timber had sometimes only been cut two months before fabrication, with moisture contents in the range 70–90%. Significant shrinkage would obviously occur at a later date across the grain, and for this reason almost all the joints, with the exception of the small notch for the ashlar piece, are simple laps, with no halving or housing of one member into another.

Since most of the members are only in face contact with each other, the obvious method of connecting them is to use bolts. However, most of the joints are near the ends of the members, and so there would be an unacceptably high risk of splits developing through the bolt holes. Therefore, connectors were used, as they are much more tolerant of splits in the timber, with the overlap of two timbers allowing the use of four 102 mm

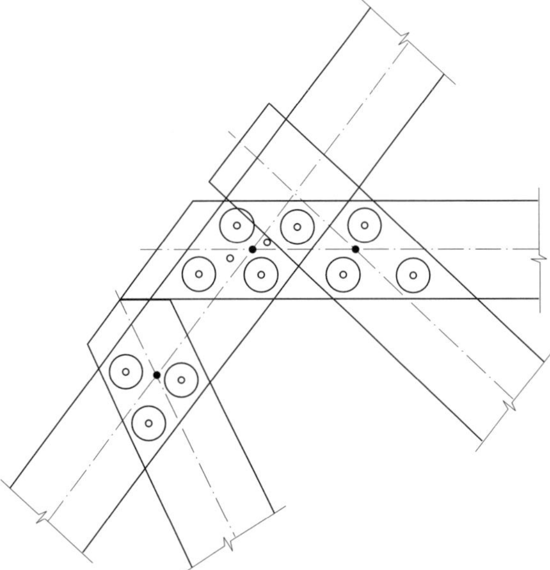

Fig. 18.7.8 Top frame joint, showing the layout of the bolts and connectors, and the offsets in the centreline intersections

connectors (Fig. 18.7.8). The split ring connector is the more efficient, but if on drying twisting of the timber should occur which could not be restrained by the bolts, then the purchase of the ring in the timber would be reduced. For this reason double shear plate connectors were used on each bolt. All metal components are made from Grade 316 stainless steel, including the shear connector castings and bolts, which are in fact rods threaded at each end.

The frame is basically triangulated, but a strict application of the principle of intersecting centre lines would make it necessary to connect three members together at most joints. This would involve drilling through a total thickness of 450 mm of timber, with each bolt taking four connectors. Small offsets of the members allowed joints to be made between two pieces of timber only, which considerably reduced the problem of fabrication. The eccentricity is limited so that the resulting moments and shears will lie within the capacity of the member.

In order to prevent the bolts from becoming the Achilles' heel of a fire-surviving structure, all the heads are recessed and covered with 40 mm timber plates. Periodic tightening of the bolts was, of course, necessary for some years.

The roof covering

The trusses are linked together by oak purlins, which support the decking. The fire-surviving properties of the trusses would be of little use unless they were held in position for the required period, and so the purlins are also sized for fire, and notched down between the trusses, strutting them from the masonry at each end of the transept. The purlin restraint of the trusses serves a double purpose, for it also keeps them firmly in line during the drying-out period.

Fig. 18.7.9 The first temporary roof cover, with the second in process of assembly over it

Temporary covers

A cover for the transept was obviously required, to protect the remaining masonry structure from the weather, and to allow repair work to proceed without interruption. The first temporary cover (Fig. 18.7.9) consisted of aluminium framed arches covered with PVC sheeting. Successive frames were built at the gable end, and 'launched' out over the transept on alloy rails set in each gutter line on the head of the wall, as the void below was not yet scaffolded out. The transept was covered within three weeks of the fire.

The first cover was high enough to accommodate the work on the vault, but would not contain the roof. A higher cover was needed, set on rails cantilevered out from the clerestory walls, and in three separate, moveable sections. This would enable the trusses to be placed by crane and allow all the lead sheet to be fixed under cover. The second cover was erected over the first, which was then dismantled and reused as a workshop.

Fabrication and erection

The trusses were fabricated in the temporary workshop erected on the North side of the nave (Fig. 18.7.10). The profile of the truss was drawn on the floor, and the large timbers were manhandled over it using simple shear legs—assembly techniques which almost certainly had medieval antecedents.

The high moisture content of the timber meant that if, after fabrication, the truss was taken apart for any length of time, reassembly might prove difficult. The problem was solved by avoiding it; the trusses, once made, were left assembled until a group of four were complete. With a Sunday road closure, the trusses were taken around the West end of the Minster by mobile crane and stacked against a side chapel, ready for lifting into position the following day by a larger mobile crane (Fig. 18.7.11).

Fig. 18.7.10 The first temporary cover, re-used as the workshop. Two trusses have been fabricated and moved clear of the fabrication outline drawn on the floor

The trusses weigh around 3·4 tonnes, and require a crane capable of lifting them to a maximum radius of 34 m—not, of course, a medieval technique, but an economic alternative to small-piece lifting and reassembly.

The first four trusses were lifted in December 1985, followed by the second group of four in February 1986 (Fig. 18.7.12). The work of fabrication

Fig. 18.7.11 Craning the trusses into position

Fig. 18.7.12 The first four trusses erected over the ribs of the vault, with minimal clearance

followed closely on the delivery of the cut timber, and the last group of five trusses was lifted in June 1986. They were all similar in form except for truss 13 (nearest the South gable), which has a higher collar level. This modification is necessary in order to clear the ridge of the vault, which rises steeply in the last bay to meet the top of the rose window.

As soon as the first trusses were in position, the work of fitting the purlins and rafters began. The profile of the roof is not constant for the length of the transept, as the span reduces by 200 mm, and ridge line rises by 250 mm, from the central tower to the South gable. Rather than attempt to make 13 trusses with different dimensions, a mean size was used for each group. The resulting steps in profile were 'sweetened' by adjusting the depth to which the purlins were notched over the trusses (Fig. 18.7.13).

During the autumn the roof was completed by fixing the oak rafters and the preservative-treated softwood boarding, and then covering the whole structure with lead sheet, double-welted at the seams. Now the roof was watertight, the temporary cover could be dismantled.

With the full load of the roof in place, it was now possible to relax the truss feet, using the threaded rods built into each bearing on the East side (Fig. 18.7.7(c)). In order to monitor the outward thrusts, three of the rods were fitted with small flatjacks connected to pressure gauges, which acted as load cells. The centre trusses (6 and 7) were relaxed to give a residual 10% thrust, obtained with an outward movement of 30 mm. The relaxation of the other trusses was tapered down to zero at trusses 1 and 13, as the purlins were fixed to the masonry at each end of the transept.

Fig. 18.7.13 The dripstone on the central tower generates the basic roof line. Small variations along the length can be sweetened by varying the depth of the truss notches to receive the purlins

The roof was now complete, but much work remained to be done on the vault (Fig. 18.7.14). The curved ribs, of glued laminated oak, were painstakingly fitted together, and each web was infilled with plaster on a base of expanded metal lath. When all was dry, the decoration and gliding could begin. The roof trusses had been drying out all this while, and the resulting shrinkage across the grain had produced the inevitable longitudinal splits. These are all well within acceptable limits, however, and the trusses have remained true to line. Checks in the summer of 1988, with the timber some three years cut, showed that the heart timber was down to a moisture

Fig. 18.7.14 Finishing work to the crown of the vault

content of about 28%. The old carpenter's rule of an inch a year doesn't look far out. If green timber had not been accepted as a parameter of design, the work could scarcely have begun by the time that it was, in fact, completed ready for the official ceremony of reconsecration in November 1988.

Fig. 18.7.15 The central tower, with the new Transept roof, and (to the right) the nave roof

Appendix 1: Codes and Standards

This book is not a manual of design, but since I have been looking at the engineering aspects of repair, it is necessary to make reference to the timber Code and its supporting Standards. A Code for timber design was first issued as a British Standard in the post-war years, and has been revised at intervals since then. The various revisions are identified below, as they may be relevant to appraisals of recent structures, and because the original grading rules can still be used for survey work. The current edition, of course, would be used for the design of any new timber introduced as part of a repair.

A1.1. The UK Design Codes and Standards

The Code of Practice for the Structural Use of Timber was first issued in 1952, and revised as follows

- *CP 112: 1952* (Imperial units): design information for solid timber, plywood and metal fasteners. Grading rules and stresses for various species with percentage references (i.e., stresses expressed as a numerical percentage of the strength of clear, or defect-free timber, e.g., 60 grade). The rules are given in Appendix 3 of this book.
- *CP 112: 1967* (Imperial units)
- *CP 112: 1971* (metric units): the metric version introduced stresses for softwoods graded in accordance with the newly-written BS 4978. This Standard described two visual grades (General Structural, GS, and Special Structures, SS) together with other machine grades, which were established by passing the timber through a machine that graded it by first measuring the modulus of elasticity and then using the correlation between modulus of elasticity and modulus of rupture referred to in section 3.5 to allocate each piece to a strength class. Most timber used in structural work from this time onward is marked with its grade, and typical stamps will be found in the Code.
- *BS 5268: 1984*. A major revision, in several parts
    - Part 1: reserved for a limit state version which has not been written to date.

- Part 2: design information for solid timber, glulam and plywood. Softwood grades were based on the rules in BS 4978, and tropical hardwood grades on the rules in the new BS 5756. Oak was no longer included, since no new grading rules for temperate hardwoods had been written, and so no grade stresses could be allocated. For routine construction work, where strength requirements predominated, Strength Classes were introduced, (SC1–SC9), to allow suppliers a wider choice of species.
- Part 3: trussed rafter roofs. Revised in 1979 and 1996.
- Part 4: fire resistance of timber structures. Revised in 1990. Outlines a method of calculating the fire resistance of unprotected timber members, and protected stud walls and joist floors.
- Part 5: preservation treatments. This part also covers the option of species durability, and level of perceived risk. Revised 1989.
- Part 6: timber frame wall design (modern, not medieval!)
- Part 7: the calculation basis for the span tables in the Regulations.

Part 2, the central part of the Code, was revised in 1988, 1991 and 1996. The revisions have largely broadened the scope of the document, with no radical changes in design method or overall factor of safety. Deflection criteria have also remained unaltered.

In the 1996 revision, the strength classes were changed to accord with the new EN 338 (BSI, 1995b). These are prefixed C (for softwoods) and D (for hardwoods), followed by a number which is the characteristic bending strength in N/mm^2 (e.g., C30). The strength values tabulated in BS 5268: 1996 are, of course, the permissible stress equivalents. In addition to the softwoods, grade stresses are given for tropical hardwoods. BS 5756 was also revised in 1996, and now includes visual grading rules for both tropical and temperate hardwoods. Thus, it is once more possible to design in oak using the current Code.

Table A1.1 gives a selection of the strength classes in the current Code and the previous approximate equivalents, and Table A1.2 illustrates the system of notation.

Table A1.1. Strength class systems and species grades

Bending strength N/mm^2 (‖ to grain)	*4*	*6*	*8*	*10*	*12*	*14*	*16*	*18*	*20*	*22*	*24*	*26*	*28*	*30*
CP 112: 1971	Redwood:	40 grade		75 grade		Greenheart:	40 grade							75 grade
BS 5268 strength classes: –1984			SC4	SC5	SC6									
–1996	C14	16 18	22 24	27	30 35	40								
				D30	35 40		50	60		70				

Table A1.2. System of notation used in the current Code

Symbols	*Subscripts*		
	Types of force	*Significance*	*Direction*
σ Stress τ Shear stress i Radius of gyration	c Compression m Bending t Tension	a Applied adm Permissible	$\|\|$ Parallel $\perp$ Perpendicular α Angle to the grain
e.g., $\sigma_{c,adm\|\|}$	compressive stress	(permissible)	parallel to the grain

Of the supporting standards, the grading rules (BS 4978 and BS 5756) have already been mentioned. Adhesives for structural work are covered by BS 1203 (BSI, 1991) and BS 1204 (BSI, 1993). The manufacture of glued laminated members is covered in BS 4169 (BSI, 1988), (issued in 1988). It should be remembered that much of the glulam installed in the UK originates from abroad, and would have been fabricated to the equivalent standard in the country of origin. A full list of relevant standards is given in the back of the Code.

A1.2. Design procedures

BS 5268 remains the only British material code which is still in permissible stress format. Since most engineers are now more familiar with limit state codes, it may be worth restating that all permissible stress design is done under working loads, with no partial factors. The total factor of safety is contained within the permissible stresses.

The procedure is as follows

1. Analyse the structural model under relevant load combinations (i.e., load patterns related to each load duration). Determine APPLIED stresses $\sigma_{*,a}$
2. Estimate the timber strength (e.g., C18)
3. Determine GRADE stresses $\sigma_{*,grade}$ relevant to applied stress conditions
4. Modify GRADE stresses by relevant factors ($K_{(n)}$) to obtain PERMISSIBLE stresses $\sigma_{*,adm}$
5. Check that $\sigma_{*,a} \leq \sigma_{*,adm}$ (design OK).

The principal modification factors ($K_{(m)}$) for solid timber are as follows

- K_2 moisture content (reduction of strength of wet timber)
- K_3 duration of load (Appendix 3)
- K_7 depth, related to 300 mm
- K_{12} slenderness (for compression in a strut).

A1.3. European Codes and Standards

During the post-war period most European countries developed their own range of Codes and Standards. As part of a European initiative to remove barriers to trade, a unified series of codes, with associated product standards, are in the process of being prepared. The timber Eurocode (No. 5) has been completed as a draft, and together with its UK National Application

Document (NAD) is available under the formal title DD ENV 1995-1-1: 1994. Under this ENV status, (Euronorm Voluntaire) it has been accepted by the DETR as an alternative to BS 5268, but has not replaced it.

When a product standard is adopted as an EN, the equivalent National standard should then be withdrawn. Mention has already been made of EN 338, which defines European Strength Classes.

The decision to replace the national code BS 5268 with Eurocode 5, however, will finally be a decision for the UK, because it sets national levels of safety. Following national comments, a revised text has been prepared and will be published in 2003. The hope is that all Europe will eventually be working to a common set of Codes and Standards, but whether this plan comes to fruition remains to be seen.

Appendix 2: Analysis and load testing procedures

Section 11.1 outlined three approaches to the assessment of strength; the 100-year rule, analysis and load tests. If the 100-year rule is not being relied on, then some form of analysis will have to be done to establish the applied stresses. Converting the different load cases into equivalent long-term stresses, the possible options for e.g. applied bending stresses of slower grown softwoods and temperate hardwoods

- *less than 5 N/mm*^{2}: unless the members contain obvious and gross defects, they would be deemed satisfactory without any formal grading
- *between 5–10 N/mm*^{2}: if these members are visually graded to CP 112 rules (appendix 3) they may well be shown to be adequate
- *between 10–20 N/mm*^{2}: if the allocated grade strength is not sufficient, or if the applied stress is above the highest visual grade stress, then it is still possible that the members might pass a load test. For applied stresses below 20 N/mm^2, and for older timber, the chances of success are high. Above this level the chances gradually reduce.

Thus, analysis and the calculation of applied stresses should precede a load test, since they may justify the member without any further work, and they would also establish the chance of a load test giving a positive result.

A load test should not be carried out unless there is a reasonable expectation of positive results. Apart from the risk of damaging the structure, the cost of the test, which is often considerable, might exceed the cost of strengthening work. In this latter case, there has to be a very strong justification for a test, such as the retention of the fabric of a historic structure.

Method of application

The load test is most often used for floors. A typical test arrangement is shown in Fig. A2.1. The most reliable and practical form of test load is a set of scale weights; generally 56 lb, or 25·5 kilos. Bags of sand may be acceptable, if they have been properly checked for weight. Barrels filled

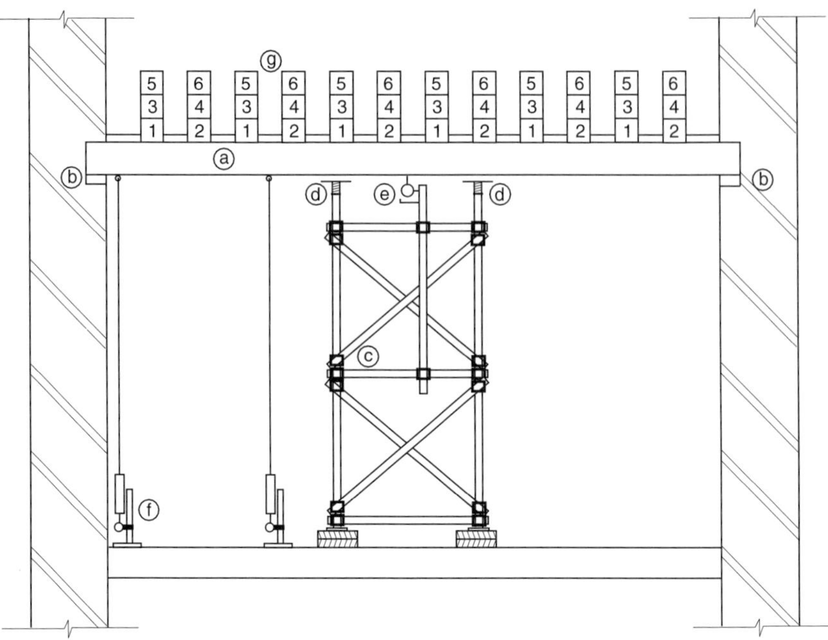

(a) Element to be tested
(b) Check adequacy of element bearings
(c) Safety scaffold, designed to take at least twice the applied load (e.g., by lateral spread if the floor below is of identical construction)
(d) Screw heads to scaffold, set to minimal clearance and further adjusted if necessary during test
(e) Dial gauge firmly mounted on the scaffold, or
(f) firmly fixed to the floor, reading the deflection of a weight suspended on a piano wire
(g) Test weights, applied in, e.g., six steps in the order noted

Notes:
Weight dispersed for storage when 'unloaded'
Deflection readings may be necessary to adjacent beams to assess degree of load sharing

Fig. A2.1 Typical test arrangement

with water sound cheap, but are awkward to move if several tests are involved. Hydraulic rams are a much safer way of applying the load, because the stored energy is very small, but it is often difficult to provide a bearing point without significant temporary works (but see section 18.3).

Load sharing

The test load must be applied in a way which represents the service conditions. For common joists under boards, for instance, or other members which have a load-sharing mechanism that cannot be temporarily 'disconnected', the whole assembly must be loaded. Principal beams can be loaded individually, if the load-sharing capability of the secondary members can be shown to be less than, say, 10%. If there is doubt, the movement of adjacent beams should be monitored, and the distributed load (calculated, perhaps, from the beam deflection) deducted from the gross test load to give the true net load on the test beam.

Safety

Introducing large loads into a building is potentially a hazardous procedure. Although the number of men on site, or the period of testing, may mean that the work falls outside the scope of the CDM Regulations, it should be treated as if it did, and a sequence of work outlined and agreed, including, for instance, the positions of the weights when unloaded. A temporary scaffold should be in place below the floor to be tested, capable of carrying the load plus a dynamic factor, and with adjustable supports only a few millimetres below the beam or ceiling.

Test load values

In general, there may be a need to modify the value of the test load to represent the design load under three headings: the duration of the test itself, uncertainty regarding the maximum value of the design load, and for tests which are only applied to a proportion of the total population.

- **The test duration:** reference has already been made (sections 3.5, 11.1) to the time-dependent nature of the strength of timber, in that the maximum load which could be carried indefinitely by a member would only be just over half the load which it could carry in the short term. Tests to investigate this strength/duration of load relationship were first carried out in the 1940s at the Forest Products Laboratory in Madison, Wisconsin, which produced the so-called Madison Curve. Although the Curve was based on testing small clear specimens in bending and might not necessarily apply to full-size members that contained grade defects, much subsequent work around the world has confirmed the original conclusions as being generally valid. Most design codes, therefore, include a duration-of-load factor based on the Curve. It is shown Fig. A2.2 with the values of K_3 the BS 5268 factor, superimposed.

  Most load tests are, of necessity, brief, and so it is necessary to increase the test load by some factor to compensate for the shorter load duration. To take the example of the Royal Festival Hall canopy (18.3), the test load was held only for an hour i.e., a short-term load duration, but represented predominantly the canopy self-weight, or permanent load. But using the graph it can be seen that the test load has to be increased by a factor $K_{3\,test}/K_{3\,design}$, i.e., 1·5. At Charlotte Square (18.2) the test load was held for 24 hours (a medium-term load) representing predominantly superimposed load (classified by BS 5268 as long-term load). Thus the design load was increased by a factor of 1·25 to give the test load.
- **Uncertainty of loading:** it may be difficult to calculate the self-weight of the structure accurately, because it is complex or some elements are concealed. In this case it would be prudent to add, say, 10% or 20% to the estimated weight. If the density of the timber is not known, reference

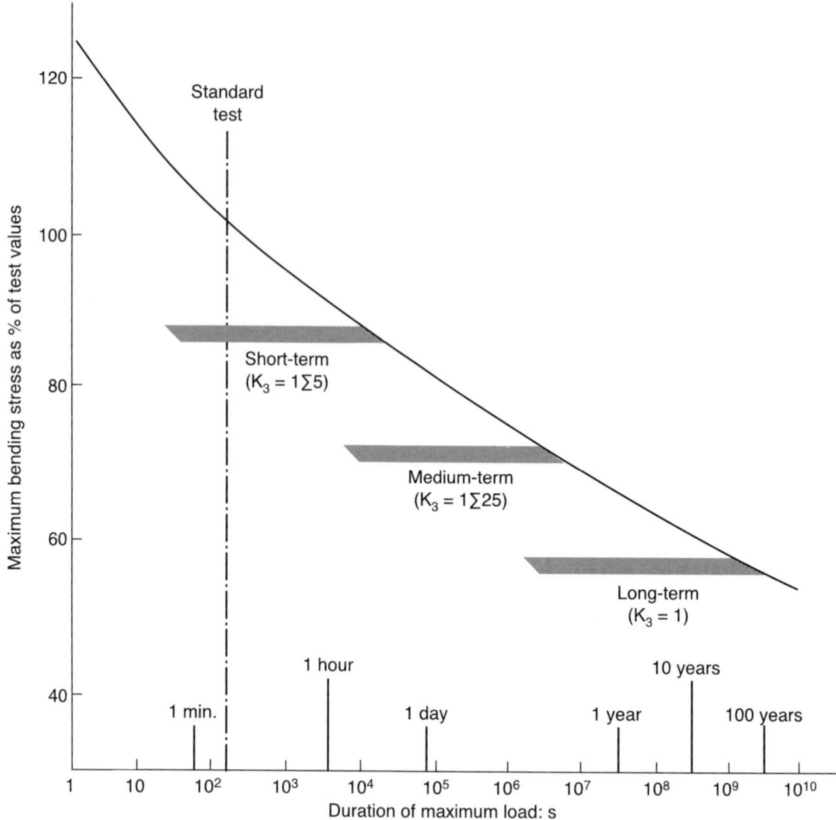

Fig. A2.2 The relation between maximum bending stress and duration of load (Fig. 3.9) with the values of K_3, the duration-of-load factor from BS5268, superimposed upon it

could be made to the species densities given in BS 5268. If the species is not known, it may be acceptable to take one or two cores and measure their density.

Failing this, maximum densities could be assumed of, say, 5 kN/m^3 for softwood and 8 kN/m^3 for hardwood.

- **Testing a sample of the population:** If it is not possible or practical to test every element in a particular population, then the most obvious course is to test those which have the lowest grading (as was done at Charlotte Square). If the elements are assemblies, such as trusses, then it is not so easy to decide on the relative strengths, and the test subset may effectively be based on a random choice. Although it is difficult to generalise, it may be appropriate in this case to make a further increase in the test load to reflect the fact that only a proportion of the population are being tested. Do not ask a statistician—make a robust engineering judgement.

In carrying out the test, it is important to remember that the stress/strain curve for timber shows relatively little plasticity before failure. For this reason an accurate plot should be made of the load/deflection relationship as the test load is increased; a departure from a linear relationship would indicate that the member is close to maximum load. If there is doubt, unload, and check for complete recovery.

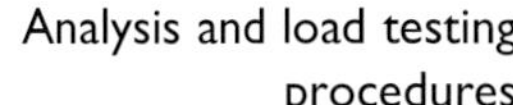

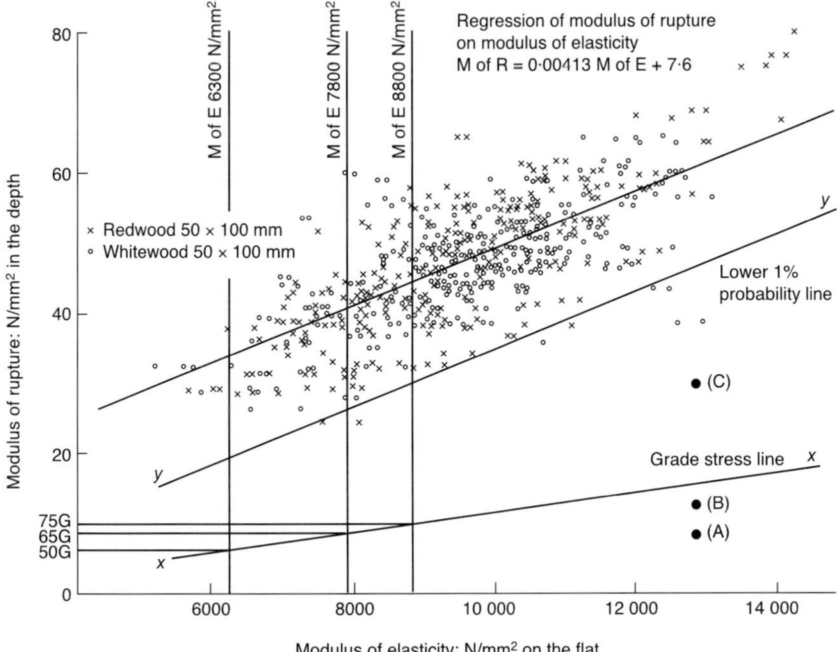

Fig. A2.3. The relationship between modulus of rupture and modulus of elasticity for redwood and whitewood (Crown copyright)

For simple beams of softwood an additional check may be made, using the broad relationship which exists for timber between stiffness and strength. Figure A2.3 shows the relation between the modulus of rupture and the modulus of elasticity, based on tests of sample planks of redwood and whitewood. Line x–x represents the grade stress, and line y–y the lower 1% probability failure line of the test population. The margin between the two is the factor of safety.

In the early stages of a load test, when say only half the test load is in place, the deflection of the member, together with the loading, span and section properties, will allow a back analysis to be made of the modulus of elasticity (E). This was done at Charlotte Square (Fig. 18.2.7), where the calculated value was 12,900 N/mm^2. This result is plotted onto Fig. A2.3 as point A, and shows the likelihood of a considerable reserve of strength. Thus it would be reasonable to continue the test programme. Under full test load, the applied stress has risen to 13·3 N/mm^2, and this result is entered as point B, still indicating a probable reserve of strength.

The single test which produced an applied stress of 26 N/mm^2 is plotted as point C. This result suggests that there is probably still a reserve of strength, but it would be unwise to load the beam further.

Measurements

Since deflections under test are relatively small the method of measurement should be correspondingly sensitive. Dial gauges will normally read to 0·01 mm, and can either be fixed to the safety scaffold (Fig. A2.1) or, more conveniently, located at ground level under weights supported on piano wires, as long as variations in temperature are not sufficient to affect the wire length. Readings should always be taken at, or near, the supports, and should act as a datum in this respect.

Loading regime

The test load would normally be applied in five or six steps. Observation of the early deflection readings is important, to see that they are of an order which could be expected, and to check that the load/deflection graph is linear as noted above. The test load should ideally be held for a period of 24 hours, and at least for one hour. Deflection should not significantly increase over this period and recovery should be virtually complete. Small residual deflections at the supports often result from a small amount of indentation of the bearing surface (hence the need for deflection measurements here) and may be accepted. All these conditions are directed toward demonstrating that the member has remained within the elastic limit, and is not unacceptably close to failure.

Appendix 3: The CP 112 grading rules

As noted in appendix 1, the CP 112 rules made up the first grading system for timber which specifically defined its strength. They also defined the structural function of the piece (beam, column or tie), and this led to inefficient marketing, since the merchant had to decide whether the piece was to be used as a beam or a column, and the rules were replaced by those in BS 4978, which were independent of function. The functions of members in existing structures are, of course, already defined, and so the CP 112 rules can be used without disadvantage. In addition,

- the rules apply to both softwoods and temperate hardwoods
- there is a wide range of grade strengths within the system
- they are simple prescriptive rules and can, with some practice, be used by a non-specialist.

They are to be preferred to the rules in BS 4978, because these require a visualisation of the knot profiles within the piece, which is not practical for in situ timber.

The CP 112 rules essentially set grade limits for the defects noted in section 3.5. When using them to grade existing structures, the applied stress pattern should also be taken into account in order to maximise the grade applicable to the critical sections of the member. For a simply supported beam, for instance, lower grades may be acceptable near the ends, or near the point of contraflexure of continuous beams. In addition, if one defect is responsible for a significant reduction in grade, it is sometimes possible to re-analyse a modified section, as noted below.

The extracts from CP 112 have been grouped together, allowing copies to be made for use at site. The grade defects are

- *Knots* Although the knot rules look complex they, in fact, reduce to a few sizes for each face width. Larger knots than the grade allowance may be accepted at positions of low shear. In this case, check by analysing the section, with the knot considered as a hole.
- *Wane* The rules are written for modern timber, and the limits are often exceeded in older material. In this case measured profile may be used for analysis, and wane may be omitted from the grade criteria.

Table 4. Dry stresses

Standard name	Bending and tension parallel to the grain					Compression parallel to the grain				
	Basic	75 Grade	65 Grade	50 Grade	40 Grade	Basic	75 Grade	65 Grade	50 Grade	40 Grade
	N/mm^2	N/mm^2	N/mm^2	N/mm^2	N/mm^2	N/mm^2	N/mm^2	N/mm^2	N/mm^2	N/mm^2
SOFTWOODS										
a. Imported										
Douglas fir	18·6	13·1	11·0	8·6	6·6	14·5	10·3	8·6	6·6	5·2
Western hemlock (unmixed)	15·9	11·4	9·3	7·6	5·9	12·4	9·3	7·9	6·2	4·8
Western hemlock (commercial)	14·5	10·0	8·6	6·6	5·2	11·0	8·3	6·9	5·2	4·1
Parana pine	14·5	10·0	8·6	6·6	5·2	12·4	9·3	7·9	6·2	4·8
Pitch pine	18·6	13·1	11·0	8·6	6·6	14·5	10·3	8·6	6·6	5·2
Redwood	14·5	10·0	8·6	6·6	5·2	11·0	7·9	6·6	4·8	3·8
Whitewood	14·5	10·0	8·6	6·6	5·2	11·0	7·9	6·6	4·8	3·8
Canadian spruce	13·8	9·7	7·9	6·2	5·2	11·0	7·9	6·6	4.8	3·8
Western red cedar	11·0	7·6	6·6	5·2	3·8	9·0	5·9	4·8	3·4	2·8
b. Home-grown										
Douglas fir	14·5	10·0	8·6	6·6	5·2	11·0	7·9	6·6	4·8	3·8
Larch	14·5	10·0	8·6	6·6	5·2	11·0	7·9	6·6	4·8	3·8
Scots pine	14·5	10·0	8·6	6·6	5·2	11·0	7·9	6·6	4·8	3·8
European spruce	11·0	7·2	5·9	4·8	3·4	9·0	5·9	4·8	3·4	2·8
Sitka spruce	10·3	6·6	5·5	4·5	3·4	8·3	5·2	4·1	3·1	2·4
HARDWOODS										
a. Imported										
Abura	16·5	12·1	10·3	7·9	6·2	13·8	10·0	8·3	6·2	4·8
African mahogany	15·2	10·7	9·0	7·2	5·5	13·1	9·3	7·6	5·5	4·5
Afrormosia	26·2	19·3	15·9	12·4	9·7	22·1	15·2	12·4	9·3	7·6
Greenheart	41·4	31·0	28·9	20·7	16·5	30·3	22·8	19·7	15·2	12·1
Gurjun/keruing	22·8	14·8	12·4	9·7	7·9	19·3	13·1	11·0	8·3	6·6
Iroko	23·4	17·6	15·2	11·7	9·3	19·3	14·5	12·1	9·0	7·2
Jarrah	23·4	16·9	14·1	11·0	8·6	20·7	15·2	12·4	9·3	7·6
Karri	26·2	19·3	15·9	12·4	9·7	22·1	15·9	13·1	9·7	7·9
Opepe	29·0	22·4	18·6	14·5	11·7	24·8	18·6	15·9	12·4	9·7
Red meranti/red seraya	15·2	10·7	9·0	7·2	5·5	13·1	9·3	7·6	5·5	4·5
Sapele	23·4	16·9	14·1	11·0	8·6	20·7	15·2	12·4	9·3	7·6
Teak	26·2	19·3	15·9	12·4	9·7	22·1	15·9	13·1	9·1	7·9
b. Home-grown										
European ash	22·8	14·8	12·4	9·7	7·9	15·2	10·3	8·6	6·6	5·2
European beech	22·8	14·8	12·4	9·7	7·9	15·2	10·3	8·6	6·6	5·2
European oak	20·7	13·8	11·7	9·0	7·2	15·2	10·3	5·6	6·6	5·2

NOTE. These stresses apply to timber having

Fig. A3.1. Extracted from CP 112: Part 2: 1971, Appendix A. Sizes and grading of hardwoods and softwoods

and moduli of elasticity

Compression perpendicular to the grain			Shear parallel to the grain					Modulus of elasticity for all grades	
Basic	75/65 Grades	50/40 Grades	Basic	75 Grade	65 Grade	50 Grade	40 Grade	Mean	Minimum
N/mm^2	N/mm^2	N/mm^2	N/mm^2	N/mm^2	N/mm^2	N/mm^2	N/mm^2	N/mm^2	N/mm^2
2·62	2·34	1·93	1·93	1·34	1·21	0·90	0·76	11 700	6 600
2·07	1·72	1·52	1·65	1·21	1·07	0·83	0·66	10 000	5 900
2·07	1·72	1·52	1·52	1·14	0·97	0·76	0·62	9 300	5 500
2·21	1·93	1·65	1·65	1·21	1·07	0·83	0·60	9 000	4 800
2·62	2·34	1·93	1·93	1·34	1·21	0·90	0·76	11 700	6 600
2·21	1·93	1·65	1·52	1·14	0·97	0·76	0·62	8 300	4 500
2·07	1·72	1·52	1·52	1·14	0·97	0·76	0·62	8 300	4 500
2·07	1·72	1·52	1·52	1·14	0·97	0·76	0·62	9 000	5 500
1·52	1·31	1·10	1·38	0·97	0·83	0·69	0·55	6 900	4 100
2·21	1·93	1·65	1·82	1·12	0·97	0·76	0·62	8 300	4 500
2·21	1·93	1·65	1·82	1·12	0·97	0·76	0·62	8 300	4 500
2·21	1·93	1·65	1·82	1·12	0·97	0·76	0·62	8 300	4 500
1·65	1·38	1·24	1·24	0·90	0·76	0·62	0·45	6 900	3 800
1·65	1·38	1·24	1·24	0·90	0·76	0·62	0·45	7 200	3 800
3·45	3·10	2·48	2·41	1·65	1·45	1·14	0·90	9 300	4 800
3·10	2·62	2·21	1·93	1·34	1·21	0·90	0·76	8 600	4 500
6·21	5·17	4·48	2·76	2·07	1·79	1·38	1·10	12 100	7 900
9·31	7·93	6·90	5·52	3·93	3·38	2·62	2·14	18 600	13 400
4·48	3·79	3·45	2·62	1·86	1·65	1·28	0·97	13 800	9 300
6·21	5·17	4·48	2·62	1·86	1·65	1·28	0·97	10 300	6 900
6·21	5·17	4·48	2·62	1·86	1·65	1·28	0·97	12 100	7 900
7·24	6·21	5·17	2·76	2·07	1·72	1·34	1·10	15 500	9 700
8·27	7·24	6·21	3·72	2·48	2·21	1·65	1·34	13 800	9 300
2·62	2·34	1·93	1·72	1·21	1·07	0·83	0·66	8 300	4 500
6·21	5·17	4·48	2·76	1·86	1·65	1·28	0·97	11 000	6 900
6·21	5·17	4·48	2·62	1·86	1·65	1·28	0·97	12 400	7 900
4·48	3·79	3·45	3·10	2·28	2·00	1·52	1·24	11 400	7 200
4·48	3·79	3·45	3·10	2·28	2·00	1·52	1·24	11 400	7 200
4·48	3·79	3·45	3·10	2·07	1·72	1·34	1·10	9 700	5 200

moisture content not exceeding 18%.

Table 58. Minimum number of growth rings per 25 mm for softwood grades

Softwood grade	Minimum number of growth rings per 25 mm
75	8
65	6
50	4
40	4

There are no limits for hardwood grades or for laminating grades.

A.8 Fissures

A.8.1 Measurement. The size of fissures at the end of the member should be taken as the distance between lines enclosing the fissures and parallel to a pair of opposite surfaces (see Fig. 12). The sum of all fissures measured at either end of the member should be taken for the purpose of assessing the magnitude of the defect.

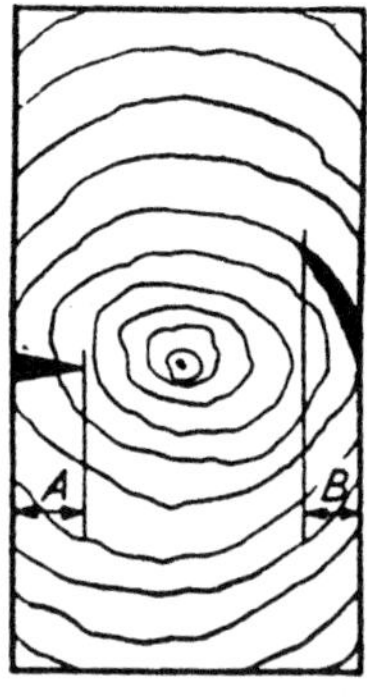

Size of fissure is *A* + *B*

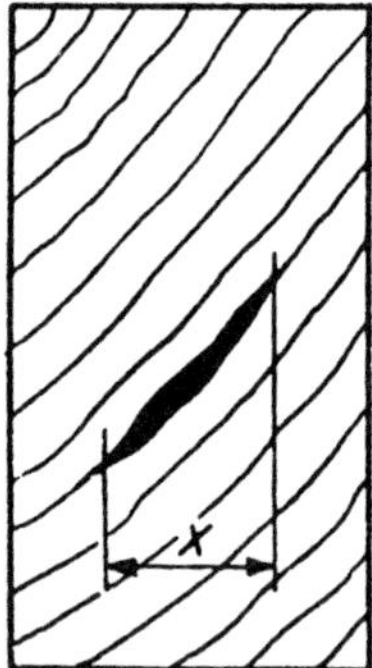

Size of fissure is *X*

Fig. 12. Fissures

The size of fissures occurring on the surface of the member should be measured by means of a feeler gauge, not exceeding 0·15 mm thick, and the maximum depth of fissures occurring at any cross section should be taken for assessing the magnitude of the defect.

A.8.2 Grading limits. To qualify for a particular grade, a hardwood or softwood member should not have fissures whose size, expressed as a fraction of the thickness of the member, exceeds the maximum value given in Table 59.

Table 59. Maximum size of fissures

Grade (hardwoods and softwoods)	Maximum size of fissure expressed as a fraction of the thickness of the member
75	0·3
65	0·4
50	0·5
40	0·6

Outside the middle half of the depth of the end cross section, and at a distance from the end equal to three times the depth of the piece, and on compression members, the depth of fissures may be $1\frac{1}{2}$ times the amount permitted in Table 59.

For laminating grades there is no limit to the depth of fissures, but any having an angle of less than 45° with the wide face are not permissible.

Fig. A3.1. Continued

A.9 Slope of grain

A.9.1 Measurement. The slope of grain should be measured over a distance sufficiently great to determine the general slope, disregarding slight local deviations.

The method by which slope of grain is measured should be either:

(1) by taking a line parallel to the surface checks; or
(2) by the use of a grain detector (see A.17).

A.9.2 Grading limits. To qualify for a particular grade, a hardwood, softwood or laminated member should not have a slope of grain steeper than the value given in Table 60.

Table 60. Maximum slope of grain

Grade (hardwood, softwood and laminated members)	Maximum slope of grain
75	1 in 14
65	1 in 11
50	1 in 8
40	1 in 6
LA	1 in 18
LB	1 in 14
LC	1 in 8

A.10 Spiral grain. Where spiral grain occurs, the slope of grain should be determined by measuring the worst slopes of grain on the faces and on the edges and taking the square root of the sum of the squares of the slopes. For example, if these slopes are 1 in 18 and 1 in 12, the combined slope is

$$\sqrt{\left(\frac{1}{18}\right)^2 + \left(\frac{1}{12}\right)^2} = \frac{1}{10} \text{ or a slope of 1 in 10.}$$

NOTE. This procedure is intended to apply where it is deemed necessary to measure the slope of grain: in most cases, it will be sufficient for the grader to use his judgment in selecting timber containing spiral grain to an undesirable extent.

A.11 Wane

A.11.1 Measurement. The amount of wane on any surface should be the sum of the wane at the two arrises, and should be expressed as a fraction of the width of the surface on which it occurs (see Fig. 13).

A.11.2 Grading limits. To qualify for a particular grade, a hardwood or softwood member should not have wane whose total width, expressed as a fraction of the width of the surface on which it occurs, exceeds the amount given in Table 61.

For laminating grades, no wane should be permitted.

Table 61. Maximum amount of wane

Grade (hardwood or softwood)	Maximum amount of wane, expressed as a fraction of the width of the surface on which it occurs
75	0·1
65	0·1
50	0·2
40	0·2

Fig. A3.1. Continued

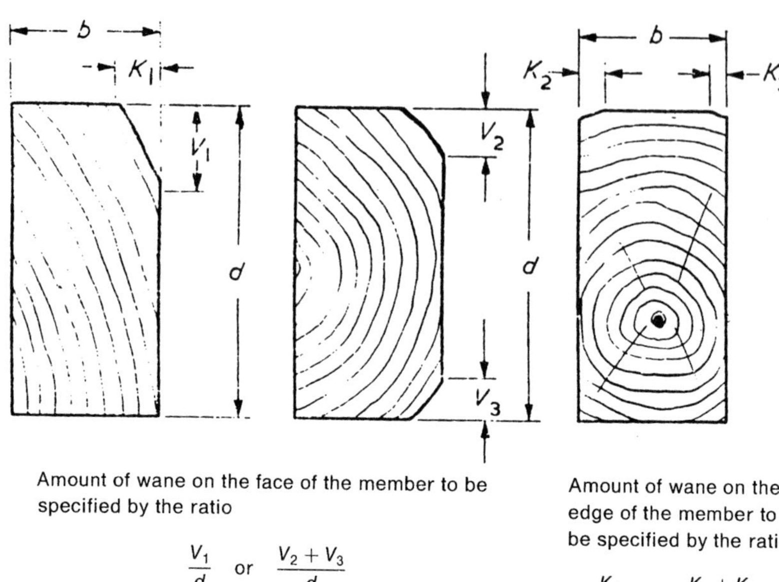

Amount of wane on the face of the member to be specified by the ratio

$$\frac{V_1}{d} \quad \text{or} \quad \frac{V_2 + V_3}{d}$$

Amount of wane on the edge of the member to be specified by the ratio

$$\frac{K_1}{b} \quad \text{or} \quad \frac{K_2 + K_3}{b}$$

Fig. 13. Extent of wane

A.12 Wormholes. Scattered pin boles and small occasional wormholes are permissible in all grades. All pieces, however, showing active infestation should be rejected or subjected to preservative treatment in accordance with CP 98*.

A.13 Resin. Resin pockets should be measured and accepted on the same basis as fissures. Substantial exudations of pitch or resin should be excluded from the faces of Grades LA, LB and LC.

A.14 Sap wood. Sap wood, whether bright or blue-stained, is not a structural defect and is acceptable.

A.15 Other defects. All pieces showing fungal decay. brittleheart or other abnormal defects affecting strength should be excluded from all grades.

A.16 Knots

A.16.1 Measurement

A.16.1.1 *Splay knots.* A splay knot should be measured only on the edge of the piece and its size taken as the width between the arris on which it occurs and a line touching the knot parallel with the arris (see Fig. 7).

A.16.1.2 *Arris knots.* The size of an arris knot depends on whether the knot is on the heart side of the piece or on the side furthest from the pith.

Where it emerges on the heart side of the piece, the knot should be measured as a splay knot.

Where it emerges on the side further from the pith, the size should be taken as the width of the knot on the edge between the arris on which it occurs and a line touching the knot parallel with the arris, plus one third of its depth on the face (see Fig. 8).

* CP 98, 'Preservative treatment for constructional timber'.

Fig. A3.1. Continued

A.16.1.3 *Edge knots.* The size of an edge knot should be taken as the width between lines containing and touching the knot and parallel with the arrises of the piece (see Fig. 9). Splay and arris knots should be assessed as edge knots.

A.16.1.4 *Margin knots.* Where a margin knot breaks through and shows on an edge, its size should be taken on the face of the material as the width between the arris and a line parallel with the arris touching the far side of the knot. Where the knot does not break through the arris, the measurement should be taken in the same way as for edge knots (see A.16.1.3 and Fig. 9).

A.16.1.5 *Face knots.* The size of a face knot should be taken as the average of its largest and smallest diameters (see Fig. 9).

A.16.1.6 *General.* Knots should be measured between lines enclosing the knot and parallel to the edges of the wide faces. If two or more knots are in line, i.e. partially or completely enclosed by the same parallel lines and separated length-wise by less than 200 mm, the effective width of the knots should be the distance between two parallel lines which enclose the knots.

Where two or more knots occur in the same cross section, the sum of their maximum sizes, determined as in the previous paragraph, should be taken when determining the grade.

Two or more knots of maximum size should be permitted if they are separated in a lengthwise direction, by a distance, measured centre to centre of the knots, of at least 300 mm.

In the assessment of knots, pin knots, i.e. knots with a diameter not exceeding 3 mm, may be disregarded.

A.16.2 Grading limits. To qualify for a particular grade, a hardwood or softwood member should not have knots whose sizes exceed the maximum values given in Table 62.

To qualify for a particular grade, a laminated member should not have knots whose sizes exceed the maximum values given in Table 63.

A.17 Guide to the determination of slope of grain. To ascertain the slope of the grain in timber it is necessary to study both the quartered and the flat-sawn faces of the member.

If seasoning checks are present, these will indicate the slope at the grain.

Slope of grain can be more accurately determined by means of a scribe, as shown in Fig. 14, comprising a cranked rod with a swivel handle and a needle, similar to a gramophone needle, at the tip, set to a slight trailing angle. The

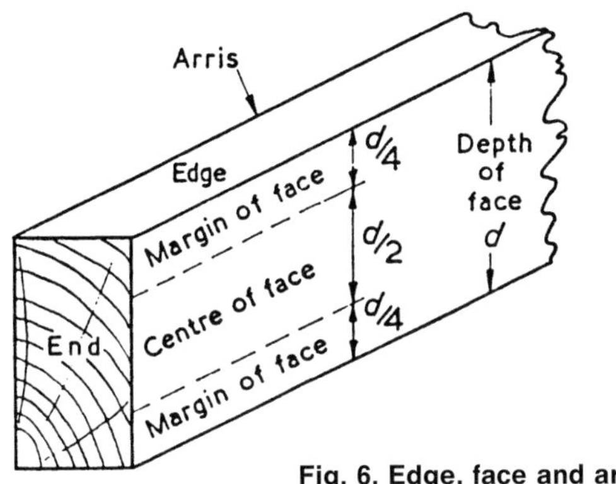

Fig. 6. Edge, face and arris

Fig. A3.1. Continued

needle is pressed into the wood and the scribe is drawn along with a steady action in the apparent direction of the grain, which is indicated more precisely as the needle forms a groove. If the pressure on the needle is insufficient it may be dragged across the grain; on the other hand, a steady action is impossible if the pressure is excessive and the needle penetrates too far into the wood. In Douglas fir the summerwood is relatively dense and the needle meeting it tends to be diverted, resulting in a step in the groove, the avoidance of which requires a particularly slow and steady action as each springwood stripe is met.

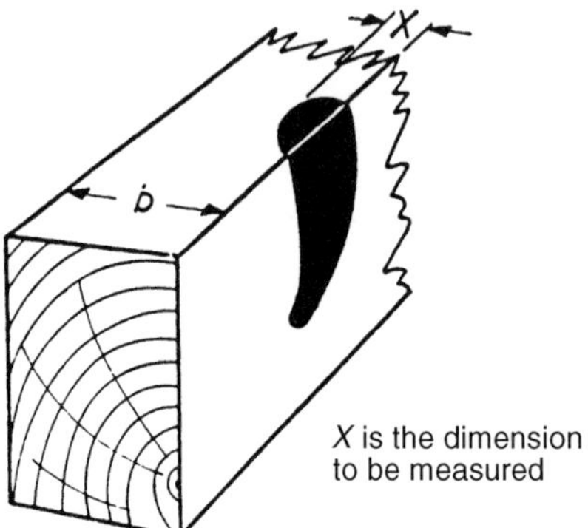

Fig. 7. Splay knot

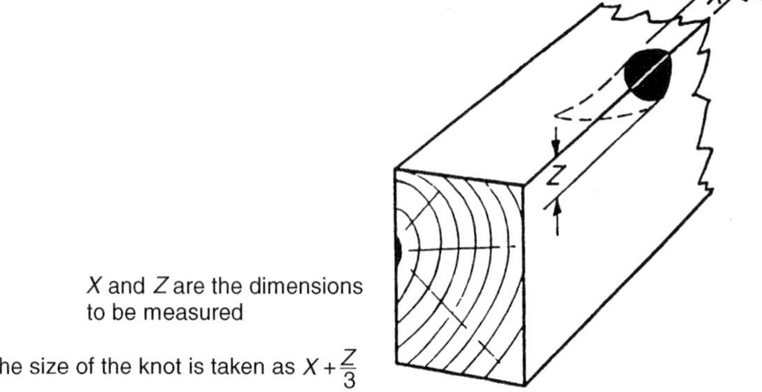

Fig. 8. Arris knot

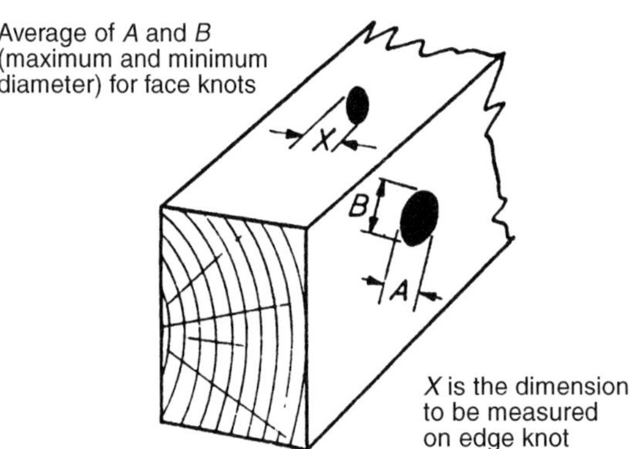

Fig. 9. Edge and face knot

Fig. A3.1. Continued

Table 62. Maximum permissible size for knots in sawn and precision timber

Width of surface	Beams: Edge, arris and splay knots				Beams: Margin knots				Beams: Face knots, in centre half of depth				Knots on any surface of compression member				Knots on any surface of tension member			
	75 Grade	65 Grade	50 Grade	40 Grade	75 Grade	65 Grade	50 Grade	40 Grade	75 Grade	65 Grade	50 Grade	40 Grade	75 Grade	65 Grade	50 Grade	40 Grade	75 Grade	65 Grade	50 Grade	40 Grade
mm	mm	mm	mm	mm	mm	mm	mm	mm	mm	mm	mm	mm	mm	mm	mm	mm	mm	mm	mm	mm
16	4	6	8	11				6	4	7	9	10	4	7	9	10				6
19	5	7	9	13			4	7	5	8	10	11	5	8	10	11			4	4
22	6	8	11	14			5	8	6	9	11	13	6	9	11	13			5	8
25	7	9	13	16			6	9	6	10	13	15	6	10	13	15			6	9
32	8	12	16	20		4	8	11	8	12	16	18	8	12	16	18		4	8	11
36	9	13	18	22		5	9	12	9	13	17	20	9	13	17	20		5	9	12
38	10	14	19	23		6	10	13	10	14	18	21	10	14	18	21		6	10	13
40	10	15	20	24		6	10	14	10	15	19	22	10	15	19	22		6	10	14
44	11	16	22	26	4	8	12	15	11	16	21	24	11	16	21	24	4	8	12	15
50	13	18	25	29	5	9	14	17	13	19	23	27	13	19	23	27	5	9	14	17
63	16	23	31	37	7	12	18	21	16	23	29	33	16	23	29	33	7	12	18	21
75	19	28	37	43	9	16	21	25	19	27	34	39	19	27	34	39	9	16	21	25
100	25	37	50	56	13	20	29	33	25	35	45	51	25	35	45	51	13	20	29	33
125	31	47	63	69	17	25	37	41	32	43	56	64	32	43	56	64	17	25	37	41
150	37	56	75	83	20	30	44	48	38	51	66	74	38	51	66	74	20	30	44	48
175	41	61	82	88	24	34	52	56	44	59	75	84	44	59	75	84	24	34	52	56
200	44	66	87	93	28	39	59	64	50	66	85	94	50	66	85	94	28	39	59	64
225	47	70	92	97	32	44	67	72	55	72	92	101	55	72	92	101	32	44	67	72
250	51	75	97	102	35	48	75	79	60	78	99	108	60	78	99	108	35	48	75	79
300	54	79	107	112	40	59	88	92	69	91	114	122	69	91	114	122	40	59	88	92

Note 1. Two or more knots of maximum size are not permitted in the same 300 mm length.

Note 2. For members subjected to simple bending on a single span, e.g. floor joists, the knot size quoted may be increased outside the middle third of the span. These may increase proportionally towards the ends to sizes 25% greater than the quoted values.

Note 3. For widths of surface other than these listed, e.g. for processed timber, the maximum size of permissible knots may be obtained by interpolation, rounding up to the nearest millimetre.

Fig. A3.1. Continued

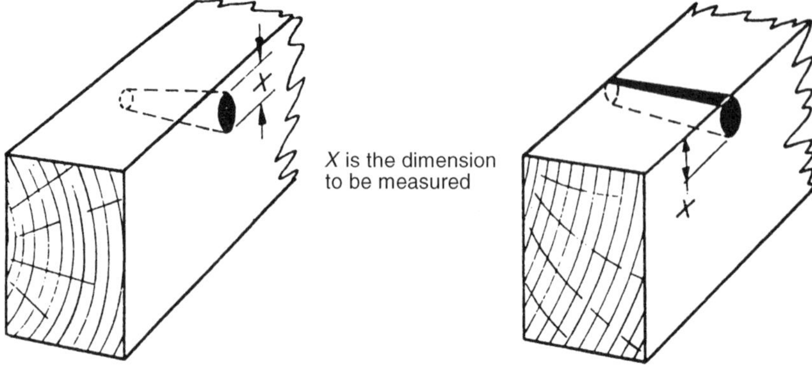

Fig. A3.1. Continued

Fig. 10. Margin knots

- *Fissures* Measured with a 0·1 mm feeler guage. However, larger fissures than the grade allowance may be acceptable by checking the shear stress on the residual section, against the allowable 'clear' stress.
- *Slope of grain* Do not confuse slope of the grain with figure. Fissures indicate the true slope of grain but, in their absence, the slope can be determined with a scribe (Fig. A3.2) which consists of a cranked rod with a swivel handle and a needle at the tip. When drawn across the timber, the needle will follow the grain line. When spiral grain occurs, the slope of grain should be determined by measuring the worst slopes of grain on the faces and edges, and taking the square root of the sum of the squares and slopes.
- *Distortion* The grading rules in the original Code for distortion may be put aside when estimating strength, since the in-service deflection will be assessed separately.

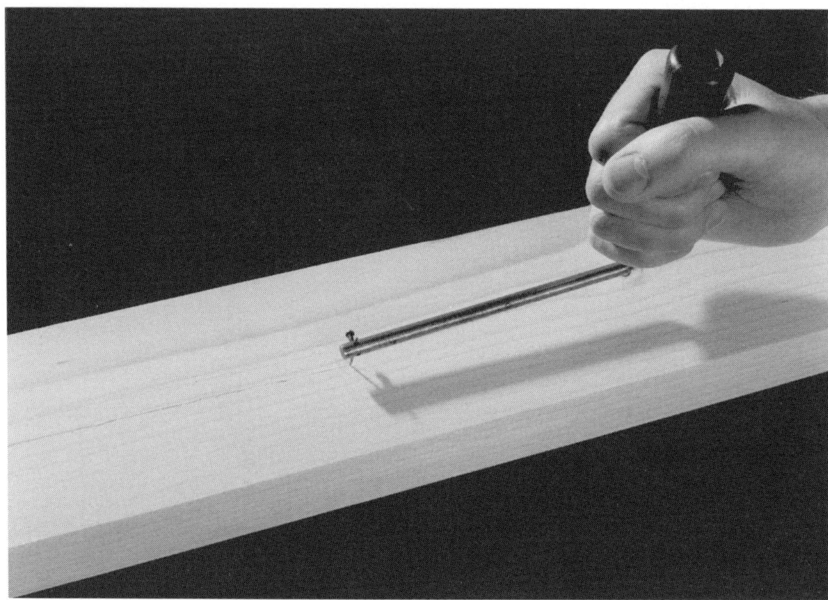

Fig. A3.2 Use of a scribe to determine the slope of grain

- *Rate of growth* Unfortunately the rings cannot usually be reliably measured on the face, so a view of the end, or a small core sample, is necessary. The aim for softwood is to exclude very fast grown, i.e., less dense (and less strong) timber. For older timber grade allowances are very generous, and the growth ring spacing, particularly in older timber, is almost always less than the maximum permitted.

Strictly, the rules apply to all four sides of a member, but it is often the case that only the top and two sides can be seen. In general these faces will still give a reliable result, but a grade result from only two faces would have to be used with some caution.

Cuts into the section may also have to be taken into account. Small notches may be counted either as knots or wane. Larger rebates can be dealt with, conservatively, by analysing the reduced section, using clear stresses if there are no defects in that area.

Since all the grade criteria seem precise, it may be thought that the prediction of strength which results is precise. This is, of course, not so, because the rules are simplistic and one important parameter, density, is not included. The rules are useful because they allow us to make some estimate of the strength of a member, but like all simple rules they are conservative, and we should not rush to condemn or to attempt to strengthen a member which appears to be 'below grade'; the more so when it has been performing adequately for some time.

The actual grade of a member, or selected part of a member, is the lowest grade which has been found under the five headings.

The design stresses for each grade which should be used for the purpose of strength assessment are given in table 4 of CP 112 (and **not** those given in the current BS 5268). It will be seen that bending and tension stresses have the same value, unlike the BS 5268 stresses. The reason for this is that the CP 112 knot grading rules are more stringent for tension than bending. However, it is generally agreed that a conservative view should be taken of the design stresses which are given for members in tension.

BSI codes

BSI (1952). *Code of practice for the structural use of timber*. CP 112 (withdrawn). BSI, London.

BSI (1957). *Methods of testing small clear specimens of timber*. BS 373: 1957 (1986). BSI, London.

BSI (1967). *Dead and imposed loads*. CP 3: Chapter V: Part 1: 1967. BSI, London.

BSI (1987). *Specification for sizes of sawn and processed softwood*. BS 4471: 1987. BSI, London.

BSI (1988). *Specification for manufacture of glued-laminated timber structural members*. BS 4169: 1988. BSI, London.

BSI (1988). *Code of practice for imposed roof loads*. BS 6399: Part 3; 1988. BSI, London.

BSI (1989). *Code of practice for preservation of timber*. BS 5589: 1989 (1997). BSI, London.

BSI (1991). *Specification for synthetic resin adhesives (phenolic and aminoplastic) for plywood*. BS 1203: 1979 (1991). BSI, London.

BSI (1992). *Classification of hazard classes*. BS EN 335-1: 1992. BSI, London.

BSI (1992). *Guide to evaluation of human exposure to vibration in buildings (1 Hz to 80 Hz)*. BS 6742: 1992. BSI, London.

BSI (1993). *Specification for type MR phenolic and aminoplastic synthetic resin adhesives for wood*. BS 1204: 1993. BSI, London.

BSI (1994). *Design of timber structures. Part 1.1. General rules and rules for buildings*. DD ENV 1995-1-1, Eurocode 5. BSI, London.

BSI (1995a). *Structural timber. Coniferous and poplar*. BS EN 336: 1995. BSI, London.

BSI (1995b). *Structural timber. Strength classes*. BS EN 338: 1995. BSI, London.

BSI (1996). *Specification for visual strength grading of softwood*. BS 4978: 1996. BSI, London.

BSI (1996). *Code of practice for dead and imposed loads*. BS 6399: Part 1: 1996. BSI, London.

BSI (1997). *Specification for visual strength grading of hardwood*. BS 5756: 1997. BSI, London.

BSI (1997). *Code of practice for wind loads*. BS 6399: Part 2: 1997. BSI, London.

BSI (1997). *Method of test to determine the classification of the surface spread of flame of products*. BS 476: Part 7: 1997. BSI, London.

Bibliography

Alcock N. W. *et al.* (1996). Recording timber-framed buildings: an illustrated glossary. *Practical Handbook in Archeology 5*. Council for British Archeology.

Arthur E. and Witney D. (1972). *The barn. A vanishing landmark in North America*. Arrowwood Press, New York.

Association of Consulting Engineers; Conditions of Engagement. (1998). *Agreement D: Report and Advisory Services*. Second edn. ACE, London.

Baird J. (1990). *Timber Specifiers Guide*. BSP Professional Books, Oxford.

Barnswell P. S. and Adams A. T. (1994). *The house within. Interpreting medieval houses in Kent*. RCHM, Swindon.

Beadell S. (1972). *Windmills*. Bracken Books, London.

Beckmann, P. (1995). *Structural aspects of building conservation*. McGraw-Hill International.

Benny R. W. (1994). *Remedial treatment of wood rot and insect attack in buildings*. BRE, Watford.

Bravery A. F. *et al.* (1992). *Recognising wood rot and insect damage in buildings*. BRE, Watford.

Brown R. J. (1986). *Timber-framed buildings of England*. Robin Hale, London.

Brunskill R. W. (1971). *Illustrated handbook of vernacular architecture*. Faber and Faber, London.

Charles F. W. B. with Mary Charles. (1984). *Conservation of timber buildings*. Stanley Thomas (Publishers) Ltd., Cheltenham.

Clifton-Taylor A. (1972). *The pattern of English building*. Faber and Faber, London.

Cocke T. *et al.* (1996). Recording a church: an illustrated glossary. *Practical Handbook in Archeology 7*. Council for British Archeology.

Cooper B. M. (1964). *Writing technical reports*. Penguin Books, Middlesex.

Corkhill T. (1979). *A glossary of wood*. Stobart Davis, London.

Department of the Environment, Transport and the Regions (2000). *Building Regulations 2000: Approved documents*. HMSO, London.

Desch H. E. (revised Dinwoodie J. M.) (1981). *Timber, its structure, properties and utilisation*. Sixth edn, Macmillan Education, Hampshire/London.

Desch H. E. and Dinwoodie J. M. (1996). *Timber: structure, properties, conversion and use*. Seventh edn, Macmillan Education.

Everett A. (1970). *Mitchell's building series: materials*. Fifth edn, Longman Scientific and Technical, Harlow.

Fielden B. (1982). *Conservation of historic buildings*. Butterworth Scientific, London.

Fishlock M. (1993). *The great fire at Hampton Court*. The Herbert Press Ltd., London.

Forman W. (1983). *Oxfordshire mills*. Phillimore, Sussex.

Foster R. (1981). *Discovering English churches*. British Broadcasting Corporation, London.

Giles C. and Goodall I. H. (1992). *Yorkshire textile mills*. HMSO, London.

Gordon J. E. (1976). *The new science of strong materials, or why you don't fall through the floor*. 2nd edn, Penguin Books, Middlesex.

Gordon J. E. (1978). *Structures, or why things don't fall down.* Penguin Books, Middlesex.

Gower Sir E. (1973). *The complete plain words.* Revised edn by Sir Bruce Fraser. HMSO, London.

Harris R. (1978). *Discovering timber-framed buildings.* Shire Publications Ltd. (Buckinghamshire).

Harrison H. W. (1996). *Roofs and roofing—performance, diagnosis maintenance, repair and the avoidance of defects.* BRE Watford.

Haslam J. M. (1988). *Writing engineering specifications.* Spon, London

Hewett C. A. (1980). *English historic carpentry.* Phillimore, London.

Hewett C. A. (1982). *Church carpentry. A study based on Essex examples.* Phillimore, London.

Hewett C. A. (1985). *English cathedral and monastic carpentry.* Phillimore, London.

Hoadley R. B. (1980). *Understanding wood. A craftsman's guide to wood technology.* The Taunton Press.

Howard F. E. and Crossley F. H. (1917). *English church woodwork. A study in craftsmanship during the medieval period, AD 1250–1550.* Batsford, London.

Hume I. (1994). *Office floor loading in historic buildings.* English Heritage.

Kerr J. S. (1996). *The Conservation Plan.* Fourth edn, National Trust of Australia, Sydney.

Kidson P., Murray P. and Thompson P. (1965). *A history of English architecture.* Penguin Books, Middlesex.

Laidlaw W. B. R. (1960). *Guide to British hardwoods.* Leanard Hill (Books) Limited, London.

Lancaster O. (1938, reprinted 1963). *Pillar to post* and *Home sweet homes.* John Murray, London.

Lavers G. (1983). *The strength properties of timber*, Third edn, rev. by G. L. Moore. Also 1997 supplement. BRE, London.

Leacroft R. (1973). *The development of the English playhouse.* Eyre Methuen Ltd, London.

Libby E. F. (1955). *Radiocarbon dating.* Second edn, University of Chicago Press, Chicago.

Marquis-Kyle P. and Meridith Walker. (1992). *The illustrated Burra charter: making good decisions about the care of important places.* Australia ICOMOS 1992 (available through ICOMOS UK).

McKay W. B. (1944 and later editions). *Building construction.* Longmans, London.

Melville I. A. and Gordon I. A. (1973). *The repair and maintenance of houses.* Estates Gazette, London.

Bromwell M. (ed.) (1976). *The international book of wood.* Mitchell's Building Series. Longman Scientific and Technical.

National Building Specification (1973 and later). RIBA Publication, London.

Newlands J. (1857). *The carpenter and joiners assistant.* Blackie, Glasgow. Reprinted 1990, Studio Editions, London.

Nicolson A. (1997). *Restoration—The rebuilding of Windsor Castle.* Michael Joseph, London.

Pearce D. (1989). *Conservation today.* Routledge, London.

Peters J. E. C. (1981). *Discovering traditional farm buildings.* Shire Publications Ltd.

Pevsner N. (1943). *An outline of European architecture.* Penguin Books, Middlesex.

Phillips R. (1978). *Trees in Britain, Europe and North America.* Pan Books Ltd., London.

Powell-Smith V. and Billington M. J. (1995). *The Building Regulations explained and illustrated.* Tenth edn, Blackwall Science.

Quiney A. (1995). The *traditional buildings of England.* Thames and Hudson.

Rackham O. (1976). *Trees and woodland in the British landscape.* J. M. Dent & Sons Ltd., London.

Rackham O. (1986). *The history of the countryside.* J. M. Dent & Sons Ltd., London.

Richardson B. (1995). *Remedial treatment of buildings.* Second edn, Construction Press.

Ridout B. (1999). *Timber decay in buildings—the conservation approach to treatment.* E. & F. N. Spon, London and New York.

Salzman L. F. (1952, reissued 1997). *Building in England down to 1540—a documentary history.* OUP Oxford.

Stanhope Properties (1992). *An assessment of the imposed loading needs for current commercial office buildings in Great Britain.* OAP and Stanhope Properties PLC.

Suddards R. W. (1988). *Listed buildings.* Second edn, Sweet & Maxwell, London.

Sunley J. and Bedding B. (1985). *Timber in construction.* Batsford Ltd., London.

TRADA Technology Ltd. (2001). *Timber frame construction.* Third edn, TRADA Technology.

TRADA Technology Ltd. (1994). *Timber frame construction.* Second edn, TRADA Technology.

Tredgold T. (1840). *Elementary principles of carpentry.* Third edn, Barlow P. (ed.), John Weale, London.

Wainwright R. B. and Keyworth B. (1988). *Timber frame construction.* Timber Research and Development Association, High Wycombe.

Watkin D. (1992). *A history of western architecture.* Laurence King.

Watt D. and Swallow P. (1996). *Surveying historic buildings.* Donhead Publishing.

Wheatcroft A. (general ed.) (1983). *The making of Britain: The Norman Heritage; The High Middle Ages; The Age of Exuberance; The Georgian Triumph; The Transformation of Britain.* Paladin Books, London.

Wood M. (1981). *The English medieval house.* Ferndale Editions, London.

Yeomans D. (1992). *The trussed roof: its history and development.* Scolar Press.

Index

N.B. Page numbers in italics refer to figures and plates.

accelerometers 85
access and contract specifications 146
accidental damage 69, 85–87, 104–106
acoustic canopy 173–176
adhesives 26, 83–84, 119–124, 213
Alderham Farmhouse case history 129, 183–191
alignment 102–103
All Saints Church, Lyndhurst *23*
alterations
  causing damage 86
  cultural significance 127–129
  listed buildings 66
  proposed 68–69
analytical models, strength 99–100
appearance of deflection 102
applied stresses 215–220
appraisals 72–73, 98–106
arch action 11, *12*
Arkwrights Mill, Derbyshire *97*
arris knots 226, 227, *228*
audits, cultural significance 127
auger drilling 91, *92*, 104
Avoncroft cruck barn *8*

balloon frames 25
barns *5*, *8*
beetle attack *see* wood-boring insects attack
Belfast truss 22, 23, 160–165, 166
Bell Inn, Gloucester 131, *132*
bending
  deflection case history 177–178, *179*
  moments 179–180
  scarfs 110, *111*, 112, 114–116
  strength 40–42
  stresses
    /duration of load *43*, 217, *218*
    grading 222, 231
  tests *39*, *40*
Bessie Surtee's House, Newcastle-upon-Tyne *89*
bolts 22
boroscopes 90, *91*
boundaries 146
boxed heart 151
bracing 82–83, *200*
bricks 14
briefs 69, 138
brown rots 80–81
BSI codes 232
building environment 52–57
building legislation 60–66
Building Regulations 60–62
Burrell Musesum, Glasgow *137*

calculations in reports 140
capacitance instruments 90
case histories
  26–28 Charlotte Square, Edinburgh 165, 167–172
  Alderham Farmhouse 183–191
  Duxford airfield hangars 160–165, 166

case histories *cont.*
Royal Festival Hall 173–176
St Mary the Virgin, Sandwich 176–183
Tyne Theatre 191–198
York Minster 198–210
cast iron 19–20
cathedrals *see* churches and cathedrals
Center Parcs, Sherwood Forest *27*
change of use
Building Regulations 60–61
commissions 68–69
characteristics of timber
behaviour in fire 46–47
commercial supply 47–49
durability 37, 38–39
grades 45–46
moisture content and movement 35–38
strength 39–45
26–28 Charlotte Square, Edinburgh case history 165, 167–172, 217
charring 47, 87, 105
rate 65
Tyne Theatre 191, *193*
Chatham Dockyard 20, *21*
churches and cathedrals
All Saints Church, Lyndhurst *23*
Cranbrook Church, Kent *116*
Kenton Church, Devon *7*
medieval 6–8
Saffron Walden Church *7*
St Andrew, Greensted-juxta-Ongar, Essex *1*
St Andrew's Church, Cullompton, Devon *79*
St John the Baptist's Church, Bere Regis *75*
St Mary and St James' Church, Wymondham, Norfolk *67*
St Mary the Virgin, Sandwich 176–183
Victorian 22
Walderslade, Kent *25*
York Minster *143*, *147*, 198–210
cill plates 108, *109*, 110
clarity of reports 142
classification of trees 33–34
clients, concerns and briefs 68–69
coatings, protective 57, 150
codes
BSI 232
European Codes and Standards 213–214
UK Design Codes and Standards 211–213
commercial supply 47–49
commissions 68–70
common building timbers 37
compression
joints 112, *113*, 117
strength 40, *41–42*
stresses/grading 222–223
concealed areas 78
conditions of engagement 69–70
consequential losses 105, 106
conservation requirements 105
contracts
documentation 145
repair 144–146
time period 146
costs in reports 139
CP 112 grading rules 45–46, 211, 221–231
Cranbrook Church, Kent *116*
creep deflection 101–102, 161–165
Cromford Mill, Derbyshire *16*, *97*
crown-post roofs 11, *12*
cruck frames 8, 11, *12*
cultural significance audits 126–129, 169

damage, accidental 69, 85–87, 104–106
dating timbers 94–95
datum points 101
de-frassing 181
defects
patent 68, *139*
range of 80–87
strength reducing 43, *44*, 45
deflection
creep 101–102, 161–165
limits 102–103
deformation 84, 101–103
demolition of listed buildings 66

dendrochronology 94
density 40
design procedures 213
deterioration of joints 83–84
diagnostic sequence 72–74
diaphragm action 82
dismantling and re-erection 155, 183–191
distortion *36*, 45, 150, 230
documentation, contracts 145
doors, sliding-folding 160–165, 166
dovetail joints *13*, 14
drawings 76, 140–141
dry interiors 52–53
dry rot 81
drying effects *36*, 37–38, 150
durability 37, 38–39
  appraisal 103–104
  hazard classes 57
  natural 56
  softwood specifications 149–150
duration of loads 41, *43*, 217, *218*, 220
Duxford airfield hangars *23*, 126, 160–162, *163*, 164–165, *166*

edge knots 227, *228*
eighteenth century building form 14–18
elasticity modulus 35, 179, *219*, 223
Eltham Palace, London *51*
EMC *See* equilibrium moisture content
engagement conditions 69–70
environmental conditions and timber performance 57
epoxy resins 122–124
epoxy-bonded steel 122, *123*, 124
equilibrium moisture content (EMC) *35*
erection of trusses *197*, 198, 206–208
European Codes and Standards 213–214
explosion damage 86
exposed members repair 108–117
extensions *see* alterations
external wall construction *189*
extinguishing water damage 87, 106

fabrication of trusses 206
face knots 227, *228*
fastener deterioration 83
fees 69–70, 139
fibre saturation point (FSP) 35
finish of softwoods 149
fire
  behaviour in timber 46–47
  Building Regulations 64–65
  damage 86–87, 105, 106
  flame spread 64
  resistance additions 133, *134*, 135
  resistance periods 64–65
  Tyne Theatre 191–198
  York Minster 198–210
fissures *36*, 37–38, 44–45
  grading *224*, 230
flame spread 64
flitch plates 117, *118*, 119
floor joints 11, *13*, 14
floors
  26–28 Charlotte Square, Edinburgh 165, *167–168*, 169–172
  Building Regulations 63
  nineteenth century 22, *24*
  seventeenth and eighteenth centuries 15–16, *17*, 18
  strengthening 130, *131–132*
  vibrations 84–85
fly towers 191, 195, *198*
formaldehyde adhesives 120–122
foundations *109*, 110
frames
  infill 9, 11, 187–189
  medieval 9, 11, *12*
  moving 154–157, 183–191
  nineteenth century 22, *24*
  reinforcement 119, *120*
  twentieth century 25–27, *28*
Frensham Heights School, Farnham, Surrey *153*
fresh water exposure 54
Fressinnet flat-jack 165
FSP *See* fibre saturation point
fungal attack 38–39, 53, 80–81

Gloucester Docks warehouse *19*

glued joints deterioration 83–84
glued laminated construction 26, *27–28*
glues *see* adhesives
grading
  26–28 Charlotte Square, Edinburgh 168–172
  codes and standards 211, *212*, 213
  grade defects 221, 230–231
  rules 45–46, 100, 211, 221–231
grain
  formaldehyde adhesives 120
  spiral 225, 230
  strength 41–42, 44
grain slope
  determination 227–228
  grading 225, 230
  strength reduction *44*
Grant of Listed Building Consent 66
Great Coxwell Barn, Oxfordshire *5*
green timber 150, 203, 210
greenheart 40
ground contact 54, 57
ground movement 62
growth rate 44
growth rings 33, *34*, 94
  grading 224, 231
The Guildhall, Faversham *71*
The Guildhall, Thaxted, Essex *59*

halls, medieval 9
hammer beam roofs 11, *12*
hammer probes 91
Hampton Court 14, *15*
hardwoods
  characteristics 33–34, 37
  supply 48–49
  temperate 150–151
hazard classes 52–54, *55*, 57
heartwood 32, 35
highland style timber frames 9
historic buildings
  cultural significance 126–129, 185
  remedial work 129–130
  upgrading 130–135
history
  medieval period 6–14
  nineteenth century 18–25
  seventeenth and eighteenth centuries 14–18
  twentieth century 25–28
humidity 53
100-year rule
  stability 101
  strength appraisal 98–99

identification tags 186
illumination 181, *182*
impact damage 86
Imperial War Museum 160
impermeability 37, 53, 56
Industrial Revolution 18, 22
infill 9, 11, 187–189
insect attack *see* wood-boring insects attack
inspections, initial visual 76–78
instability defects 82–83
insulation 26, 132, *133*
insurance 105, 106
internal linings 64
investigative techniques 90–95
iron straps 15
iron technology 19–20

jacking *see* propping and jacking
jetties 9
jetty beams 11, *12*
joints
  compression 112, *113*, 117
  deterioration 83–84
  dovetail *13*, 14
  floor 11, *13*, 14
  medieval 11, *13*, 14
  metal reinforcements *118*
  mortice and tenon 11, *13*
  notched lap 11, *13*
  posthead and tie beam joints 14
  scarf 110, *111*, 112, *113*, 114, *115*, *116*, 117
  shear *113*, 117
  tension *113*, 114, 117

Kenton Church, Devon *7*
king post trusses 14–15, *17*, 18
knots 43, *44*

grading rules 221, 226–227, *228*, 229, *230*

later additions *see* alterations
layout of reports 138, *139–140*
leaks 53
legislation, buildings 60–66
level of inspections 76–77, 78
lift and slide method 155, *156–157*
listed buildings 65–66
litigation reports 69
Littledown Sports Centre, Bournemouth *125*
load-bearing partitions *17*, 18
load/deflection relationship 218, 220
load duration 41, *43*, 217, *218*, 220
load sharing 216–217
load shedding 103
load testing
  26-28 Charlotte Square, Edinburgh 168–169, *170–172*
  procedures 215, *216*, 217, *218–219*, 220
  Royal Festival Hall 175, *176*
  strength appraisal 100
loading
  100-year rule 99
  Building Regulations 62, 63–64
  case history 165, 167–172
  overload damage 86
  St Mary the Virgin, Sandwich 179, *180*
  uncertainty 217–218
lowland style timber frames 9

margin knots 227, *230*
material change of use 60–61
MC *see* moisture content
mechanical strength grading 92–94
medieval building form 6–14
members
  repairs 108–117
  replacement 108–110, 181, 183
    Tyne Theatre 195–198
    York Minster 202–205
  steel 119, *120*
metal reinforcements 117–119
mills *16*, 19–20, *97*
modernism 26
modifications to historic buildings *see* alterations
modulus of elasticity 35, 179, *219*, 223
modulus of rupture 37, *219*
moisture, durability effects 103–104
moisture content (MC) 40
  creep deflection 101–102
  formaldehyde adhesives 121
  measuring instruments 90–91
  timber movement 35–38
  timber specifications 149, 150–151
monitoring stability 101
mortice and tenon joints 11, *13*
movement 35–38, 101
moving timber frames 154–157, 183–191

nails 22, 25
National Building Specification 145–146
natural durability 56
nineteenth century building form 18–25
noise transmission 84–85
non-destructive testing 92–94
notation, codes of practice *213*
notched lap joints 11, *13*

opening-up 78, 144–145
order of reports 141
original structures 127
overload damage 86

panel sealant *189*
patent defects 68, *139*
Paycocke's house, Essex *9–10*
Penhurst Place, Kent *31*
performance 57, 98–99
permeability 37, 53, 56
permissible stresses 100, 213
phasing
  appraisals 105
  contracts 144
photographs 78, 140–141
platform frame 25
plywood 26
population sampling 218

portals 11, *12*
Portcullis House, London 159
posthead and tie beam joints 14
potential instability 82–83
precision of reports 141–142
precontract work 144–145
preservative treatments 56, 57, 226
propping and jacking 108, *109*
  Duxford airfield hangars 163–164, 165, *166*
protective coatings 57, 150
Protimeter 90–91
pugging 18
purlins 205, 208

queen post truss *17*, 18

radial shrinkage *36*
radiocarbon dating 94–95
railway sheds, Temple Meads, Bristol *20*
Railway Station, Copenhagen *107*
raking struts 18
re-erection 155, 183–191
recording techniques 77–78
redwood 40
regulations
  building 60–62
    see also codes
reinforcements 117–119, *120*
relative humidity (RH) 35–37
remedial work 73
  cultural significance 129–130
  durability appraisal 104
  reports layout 139, 140
render infill 189
repairs
  adhesives 119–124
  Building Regulations 61–62
  contracts 73, 144–146
  member replacement 108–110, 181, 183, 195–198, 202–205
  metal reinforcements 117–119
replacement of members 108–110, 181, 183, 195–198, 202–205
reports
  drawings and photographs 140–141
  layout 138, *139–140*
  style 141–142
residual risks 104
resin 226
resistance, fire 64–65, 133, *134*, 135
retardants 150
reversible remedial work 129–130
RH *see* relative humidity
roof trusses
  Duxford airfield hangars *161*, *162*
  York Minster *203*, 204–205
roofs
  covering 205
  erection and fabrication 206–210
  medieval 6, 8
  nineteenth century 22, *24*
  St Mary the Virgin, Sandwich 176–183
  seventeenth/eighteenth centuries 16
  twentieth century 25
rots 80–81, 104
Royal Festival Hall case history *173*, 174–176, 217
rupture modulus 37, *219*

safety issues
  accidental damage 87, 105
  load testing 217
Saffron Walden Church *7*
St Andrew, Greensted-juxta-Ongar, Essex *1*
St Andrew's Church, Cullompton, Devon *79*
St John the Baptist's Church, Bere Regis *75*
St Mary and St James' Church, Wymondham, Norfolk *67*
St Mary the Virgin, Sandwich, case history 176–183
salt water exposure 54
sapwood 32, 35, 151, 226
scarf joints 11, *13*, 14, 110, *111*, 112, *113*, 114, *115*, *116*, 117
scarf repairs
  all timber 110–114
  with metal fasteners 114–117
scissor bracing *200*
scissor scarfs 112, *113*

scribes 227–228, *230*
seasoning timber 150–151
Serpula lacrymans see dry rot
service classes 98
service life 98
seventeenth century building form 14–18
shear joints *113*, 117
shear plate connectors *205*
shear strength 41
shear stresses 223
shrinkage 35–38
Sibert drill 92, *93*, 104
sliding-folding doors 160–165
slip tenons *109*, 110
smoke damage 87
snow loading 63
softwoods
  characteristics 33–34, 37
  specifications 148–150
  supply 47–48
sound transmission 84–85
soundness assurance 68
species
  grades *212*
  specifications 148, 150
specific gravity 37, *41*
specifications
  in contracts 145–146
  hardwoods 150–151
  softwoods 148–150
Speke Hall, Liverpool 9, *10*
spiral grains 225, 230
splay knots 226, *228*
splice plates 117, *118*
  Tyne Theatre 191, *193*
splits *see* fissures
Square Chapel, Halifax *15*
stabilisation 82–83
stability
  100-year rule 99
  appraisal 100–101
stage machinery 191, 192, 194–195, *196*
standards 211–214
steel
  epoxy-bonded 122, *123*, 124
  members 119, *120*
  ties *181*, *182*
stiffness *see* modulus of elasticity
Stratford House, Birmingham 127, *128*
strength
  100-year rule 99
  -reducing alterations 86
  /duration of load relationship 217, *218*
  acoustic canopy 173–176
  appraisal 98–100
  characteristics 39–45
  classes *212*
  formaldehyde adhesives 120–121
  grading 92–94
  moisture content 35
  prediction 231
  reducing defects 43–45
  scarf joints 112
  timber specifications 149, 151
strengthening floors 130, *131–132*, 168–169
stresses
  applied 215–220
  grading 222–223
superimposed loads
  Building Regulations 63
  case history 165, 167–172
supply 47–49
surface preparation, formaldehyde adhesives 121
surface treatments 57, 150
surveys 72
  moving timber frames 154–155, 185
  phasing 73–74

tangential shrinkage *36*
temperate hardwoods
  specifications 150–151
  supply 48–49
temperatures, formaldehyde adhesives 121
Temple Meads, Bristol *20*
temporary works
  contract specifications 146
  roof covers *206*
tendering 145

tension
joints *113*, 114, 117
stress grading 222, 231
test load values 217–220
test weights 215, *216*
thermosetting of formaldehyde adhesives 121
tie rods 191, *193*
timber
behaviour in fire 46–47
characteristics 32–49
durability 37, 38–39
grades 45–46
medieval period 11
moisture content and movement 35–38
repairs 108–124
seventeenth/eighteenth centuries 16, 18
specifications 148–151
strength 39–45
timber frames, moving 154–157, 183–191
timber-to-timber joints deterioration 83
toast-rack *197*, 198
treatments
preservative 56, 57
softwood specifications 150
trees
classification 33–34
structure and function 32–33
triangulation 8, 11, 82–83
tropical hardwoods supply 48
truss analysis 179–180
twentieth century building form 25–28
26–28 Charlotte Square, Edinburgh, case history 165, 167–172
Tyne Theatre case history 129, 191–198

UK Design Codes and Standards 211–213
Unicorn (frigate) Dundee *127*
upgrading historic structures 130–135

vaulting, York Minster 199–200, 202, *203*
veneers 26
ventilation, lack of 53
vibration of floors 84–85
visual inspections, initial 76–78

walls, seventeenth/eighteenth centuries 16
wane 43, *44*
grading 221, 225, *226*
timber specifications 151
warehouses 20
water damage from fire-fighting 87, 106
water exposure 54
wattle and daub 9
weathering 54
wet rots 80–81
wetting 54
white rots 81
wind loading 64
wood-boring insects attack 39, 81–82, 104, 181, 226
woodwool *188–189*
wormholes 226

York Minster *143*, *147*
case history 198–210
cultural significance 129